The Retreat from Race

The Retreat from Race

Asian-American Admissions and Racial Politics

DANA Y. TAKAGI

Rutgers University Press
New Brunswick, New Jersey

Library of Congress Cataloging-in-Publication Data

Takagi, Dana Y., 1954–
    The retreat from race : Asian-American admissions and racial politics /
Dana Y. Takagi.
        p. cm.
    Includes bibliographical references and index.
    ISBN 0-8135-1913-6 (cloth) — ISBN 0-8135-1914-4 (pbk.)
    1. Discrimination in higher education—United States—Case
studies. 2. Universities and colleges—United States—Admission—
Case studies. 3. Asian American college students—Case studies.
I. Title.
LC212.42.T35 1993
370.19′342—dc20   92-1337
                                                                        CIP

British Cataloging-in-Publication information available

For my father and in memory of my mother

Contents

Tables

Preface

On June 23, 1973, my father, a criminology professor at the University of California, Berkeley, testified before the California Advisory Committee to the Civil Rights Commission on the status of Asian American students. Relying on statistical information provided by the university, he explained to the commission that of the 9,269 graduate students at Berkeley in 1972–1973, there were more foreign students (1,805) than minority students (1,137) and more blacks (456) than Asian Americans (421). According to my father, there were only 22 Asian American graduate students spread across fourteen fields of social science at Berkeley. He rejected as "stereotypic myth" the notion that Asians were "overrepresented" in the biological and physical sciences and further suggested that there was no shortage of Asian American applicants to various graduate programs at Berkeley. The problem, he testified, was that "Asian Americans were viewed as competitive but not qualified" and that "Asian American students have historically done poorly on administration tests measuring verbal skills, such as the Graduate Record Examination, the LSAT for the law schools, and the MCAT for medical schools." He concluded his testimony by saying, "It is usually difficult to document the practice of institutional racism. However, the data I have presented for the Berkeley campus strongly suggests the existence of systematic discrimination toward Asian students, particularly at the graduate level" (Civil Rights Commission 1973).

His words were a harbinger of the political struggle over Asian American admissions that would unfold a decade later. In the early 1980s, Asian American charges of admissions quotas at the elite universities in the United States provoked a controversy about discrimination, diversity, and affirmative action that lasted through the end of the decade. In the course of that debate university officials characterized Asian American applicants as "overrepresented" and "competitive but not qualified." Apparently my father's testimony about graduate admissions at Berkeley in 1973 was an accurate forecast of discourse in the 1980s.

At the time my father appeared before the commission I was a sophomore at Berkeley. Though I saw my parents regularly, I do not remember any mention of his testimony. As one of only two tenured Asian American professors at Berkeley, he was frequently asked to speak or report on matters relating to Asian Americans. His activities were often the subject of conversation at the family dinner table, but I confess that my overall memory of Dad's numerous speaking engagements for this or that group, agency, or commission remains blurry. Although I know that he traveled often and gave speeches, I cannot recall the specifics.

I don't feel too bad that I don't remember my father's testimony, however, because, as I recently found out, he didn't remember it either. While I was in the finishing stages of research for this book, my father retired from Berkeley. Retirement energized him to reorganize his study, a large room downstairs overrun with books, files, and papers. Six months into the "reorganization," my father discovered a copy of his 1973 testimony in his files. With an embarrassed chuckle, he handed me the dusty two-volume report of the Civil Rights Commission, saying, "You may find this interesting for your own work."

When he spoke before the commission in 1973, I think my father little suspected the extent to which charges of discrimination against Asian students would rumble through the most prestigious universities in the United States in the next decade, exploding into the most important debate about race and equity in higher education since the *Bakke* decision. In a happy coincidence, this book documents and analyzes the development of that debate over Asian admissions, demonstrating how specific and localized complaints of discrimination, like the one outlined by my father in 1973, evolved into an urgent and demanding social problem of national scope.

This book would not have been written had it not been for two extraordinary individuals. My colleague John I. Kitsuse encouraged me to undertake this project during one of our regular afternoon exchanges about contemporary social issues and then oriented me toward social problems theory as a means of understanding Asian admissions. Social problems theory, in turn, opened an exciting set of post-structuralist doors through which I have come to appreciate the meaning, importance, and consequence(s) of racial politics via an analysis of discursive practices. L. Ling-chi Wang, a mentor since my graduate days at Berkeley and one of the major figures in the admissions controversy, has done more to democratize the university than anyone else I know. He helped me begin my research by sharing his personal files with me and then, over the next several years, in addition to commenting on the manuscript at every stage, indulged my frequent requests for information about, and explanations of, the latest developments in Berkeley admissions.

I also thank the many people who agreed to be interviewed for this study. They explained to me how admissions worked at their universities, how the federal bureacracy investigated Title VI complaints, and how they situated themselves in this important controversy. Their patience and candor helped make this study possible. In addition to granting interviews, many individuals shared with me private papers, letters, and official documents that helped me to understand better the intricacies of university policy and the politics of admissions.

Numerous colleagues and friends helped me keep up to date on the latest developments in the admissions controversy by supplying me with newsclips, articles, and relevant data. I am especially indebted to Gary Curran, Arthur Hu, John Liu, Pam Roby, Gerald Shimada, and L. Ling-chi Wang.

This project has occasioned spirited discussion with colleagues, interviewees, and friends. For their encouragement, stimulating conversation, and reading of part, or all, of the manuscript, my special thanks go to Wendy Brown, John Bunzel, John Brown Childs, Peter Dougherty, Toby D'Oench, Patrick Hayashi, Mary James, David Karen, Madhulika Khandelwal, Rebecca Klatch, Dorinne Kondo, Sandra Meucci, Marcia Millman, Don Nakanishi, Michael Omi, Keith Osajima, Brian Powers, Pam Roby, Roger Sanjek, Joseph Schneider, Judy Stacey, Jack Tchen, Norma Wikler, and Howard Winant.

My research assistants, Eric Engles, Leslie Jue, Dennis Loo, Sandra Meucci, and Libby Wheatley, cheerfully undertook many tasks that I did not have the time, presence of mind, or spirit to face. In addition, Joni Tannheimer and Judy Burton of the UC Santa Cruz Word Processing Center did an accurate and timely job of transcribing the tape-recorded interviews.

Research funds for this project were provided by the Academic Senate and the Division of Social Sciences of the University of California, Santa Cruz. The Board of Studies in Sociology at Santa Cruz graciously extended me leave from teaching duties so that I might devote my full attention to this project. In 1990–1991, a Rockefeller Humanities Fellowship at the Asian American Center, Queens College, New York, provided financial support and the right amount of seclusion to draft most of the manuscript. In the following year, a fellowship at the Institute of American Cultures, Asian American Studies, at the University of California, Los Angeles, allowed me to finish it.

Parts of this book were first presented at seminars and meetings. Exchanges with students and faculty at other campuses offered me important opportunities to refine and develop my understanding of racial politics in higher education. Thanks are due to those who invited me and to those in the audience at Colgate, Yale, the University of Wisconsin–Madison, UCLA, Cornell, and Queens.

I began correspondence with Marlie Wasserman of Rutgers University Press in the early stages of writing this book. Her queries, comments, and suggestions challenged me to write a book that would transcend traditional disciplinary boundaries in the academy. I thank her for the support, enthusiasm, and encouragement she brought to this project. Also, a special thanks is due to Elizabeth Gretz for her meticulous editing of the manuscript.

My family has been supportive in ways that have been particularly significant for me, offering the riches of love, moral support, encouragement, intellectual passion, and dinner—not necessarily in that order. My father has by example urged me toward a critical analysis of contemporary issues. In New York City, my sister and her family, Tani, Toby, and Robin, tended to my needs, always mindful that try as I did, I never fully acclimated to the unforgiving, but always exciting, environs of Manhattan. Their subway directions were always perfect. Finally, a special thanks to Cherie Barkey, who has warmed my life, enlivened me with her wit, and read every page of the manuscript, offering wonderful suggestions along the way.

February 1992

The Retreat from Race

CHAPTER 1

Asian Americans and Racial Politics

*R*ace has become a ubiquitous social fact of American life. Issues of race—racial identity, race relations, and racism—permeate politics, culture, and even the language with which we speak, read, and write. Traditionally, race relations has been governed by a language of "us" and "them."[1] But three developments during the 1980s and early 1990s have contributed to a realignment of the ways in which racism and racial identity are now articulated.

First, racial minorities have become racial majorities, thus shifting or tipping the balance of power between "us" and "them." Demographic shifts in the racial composition of cities, for example, have spawned redistricting battles for political power in local and state governments. Second, increasing interethnic tensions—for example, Asian-black and Asian-Latino conflicts—have altered our notion of who is defined by the categories of "us" and "them." The world of racial politics is no longer black and white; contemporary racial politics are dictated by changing coalitions among many different interest groups—including Asians, Latinos/Hispanics, and Native Americans as well as blacks and whites. And, finally, the very language of "us" and "them" has been reconstituted by "them" in ways that "us" no longer recognizes. Current demands for affirmative action by whites and criticisms of affirmative action by black neoconservatives seem to transform "us" into "them" and vice versa.

The effect of these changes on higher education has been profound. Clark Kerr notes in his foreword to *The Racial Crisis in American Higher Education* (Altbach and Lomotey 1991:vii), "While the numbers are better, the relations [between races] are worse. . . . The number of racial incidents on campuses is increasing. Both the lash and the backlash are getting stronger."

Conflicts about how to interpret these changes, which are first of all conflicts between races, have been an important aspect of race relations during the 1980s and early 1990s. At the moment, neoconservatives occupy the high moral ground in discussions of race relations in higher education. Their critique of what has gone wrong and their vision of a color-blind future at the university has set the tone for current debate.

Conservative and neoconservative critics of higher education are fond of saying that the university has lost its vision of a liberal education. They insist that a liberal education ought to be consistent with the basic principles of democracy—individual rights, a rational exchange of ideas, and the pursuit of knowledge apart from politics. Instead, they argue, the university serves up a regimen of closed-mindedness, bigotry, intolerance, and inequality.[2] According to conservatives, the most fundamental and cherished reserves of the academy—meritocracy in admissions, a curriculum of classics, peer review in faculty hiring and promotion, and academic standards—have been tainted. The metaphors they use for the decline they perceive, a "closing" of the mind" (Bloom 1987), "illiberalism" (D'Souza 1991b), and "killing the spirit" (P. Smith 1990), are widely diffused in popular discussions of higher education. In tirades against feminism, ethnic studies, cultural relativism, the left, and popular culture—"young people know that rock music has the beat of sexual intercourse" (Bloom 1987:73)—conservatives have appealed for a return to the basics, the "great books," classical music, and "serious" reading.

The most central and recurring theme of conservative disappointment with the university is race. Conservative scholars characterize black studies courses as "rap sessions," scold university administrators for caving in to "minority terrorism," and complain that admissions policies set double standards, meritocratic ones for whites and Asians and preferential policies for other "less qualified" minorities. The university, say conservatives, has so deteriorated that race has become a defining and exaggerated feature of campus intellectual, cultural, social, and political life. Conservative exposés of the "truth" inside the university allege that white students, faculty, and administrators are cowed into submission by minority bullies who demand curricular changes, more faculty and student diversity, and increased institutional support services for themselves.

Conservative analysts suggest that "underrepresented minorities" are not solely responsible for the decline in higher education. Rather, in what is viewed as further evidence, conservatives allege that minorities have ganged up with a crew of other "victims"—an assortment of other disenfranchised special interest groups, including feminists, lesbians, gays, the disabled, and their various "liberal sympathizers"—to press a political agenda on university officials. By conservative accounts, all of the major contemporary issues pandemic in the 1980s—renewed controversy over preferential admissions policies, the "new racism," "fighting words," policies against hate crimes on campus, faculty diversity, non-Western civilization course requirements, and the debate over political correctness—were imbued with the same disturbing pattern of racial dynamics, an allegedly increasing and lopsided emphasis on minority concerns at the cost of democratic principles of fairness and equity.

The increasingly polarized nature of racial politics at the university has set the stage for repeated political confrontation between liberals and their allies, on the one side, and conservatives, on the other. In the debate over revamping the "core curriculum" at the university, for example, minorities, feminists, gays, and liberals/radicals argued that reading only the classics—"dead white men"—was irrelevant to their own social experience. The guardians of the core, most of whom were white men, insisted that the classics were a necessary part of the diet for a liberal arts education and that, moreover, worthy non-Western philosophy was practically nonexistent.

A recent concern at the university has been the issue of "political correctness," or PC. Conservatives charge that minority domination has brought about a chill in the intellectual climate, that administrative policies, academic scholarship, and intellectual exchange are evaluated on the basis of politics rather than nonpartisan standards. According to conservatives, white men are de facto "politically incorrect" while minorities and their liberal allies are "politically correct."

Yet the suggestion that university policies of admissions, curriculum, and faculty hiring and promotion are the result of a minority "takeover" is absurd. The professoriate in American universities continues to be dominated by whites, who constitute 90 percent of the faculty; racial minorities make up the remaining 10 percent (National Center for Education Statistics 1990:5). And although some universities, particularly the University of California's Berkeley and Los Angeles campuses, have made dramatic gains in diversifying their undergraduate populations, minorities are still a tiny fraction of national undergraduate enrollment.[3]

Conservative arguments about minority "bullies," though inaccurate, *seem* all the more compelling because of the particular ways in which the topic of race is overlapped with rhetoric about social problems in higher education. Conservative arguments invoke popular sentiments about race—resentment, for example—without being explicitly derogatory or degrading or appearing to be outwardly racist. Conservative disenchantment thus cannot be understood as white resentment toward the increasing numbers of minority students and minority faculty in the university.

Affirmative Action: The Tail Wagging the Dog

Nowhere are conservative protests about higher education more clear than in contemporary discussions of affirmative action. If race has been the primary leitmotif of conservative criticism, then affirmative action is the concrete embodiment of all that has gone wrong at the university. For conservatives, affirmative action, or, more specifically, a preferential policy for underrepresented minorities, is an outstanding example of liberal ideals translated into wrong-headed social policy.

Affirmative action, say its critics, privileges the "less qualified" at the expense of the "more qualified" on the basis of race. In addition, conservatives suggest that affirmative action hurts rather than helps "less qualified" minorities, who may gain admission to the university but then find they cannot succeed in the competitive world of undergraduate academics.

Conservative antidotes for affirmative action practices and, more generally, for the alleged decline in higher education emphasize aggressive policies aimed at "de-racializing" the university.[4] On this agenda, university admissions should be based strictly on merit or, at the very least, on the class background of the applicant, and not on his or her race; hiring and promotion of faculty should be

independent of *any* racial considerations; and campus student organizations founded on common racial identities—for example, African American student associations, La Raza groups, Asian/Pacific
Islander student organizations—should not be recognized as campus
organizations or receive any campus funding because such organizations tend to encourage racial segregation, not racial integration.

Transforming Affirmative Action

In the late 1980s and early 1990s conservative calls for "de-racialization" have fomented rancorous debate but have otherwise had little
effect on actual policy at the university. Conservative discourses on
de-racialization, however, have made some headway at the university, particularly in the arena of affirmative action policy in undergraduate admissions.

In the late 1980s, for example, officials from both the University
of California, Berkeley, and the University of California, Los Angeles, drastically revised their undergraduate admissions policy.
Both schools announced that underrepresented minorities who met
minimum University of California eligibility requirements would
no longer be automatically accepted for admission. Berkeley and
UCLA's abandonment of what were popularly referred to as "race-
based" guaranteed admission policies—which selected student applicants in part on the basis of their racial background—received
mainly rave reviews. In 1989 UCLA inaugurated a new admissions
policy, under which guaranteed race-based "affirmative action" was
abolished. Previously, "UC-eligible" minorities had been guaranteed
admission to UCLA. But under the new system, underrepresented
minorities no longer enjoyed guaranteed admission or what University of California officials refer to as a policy of "total protection." At
Berkeley in 1990, similarly, a revamped admissions policy ended
guaranteed admission for UC-eligible underrepresented minorities.
In addition to abandoning the policy of total protection, the new
policy established a new category of admissions based on socioeconomic status, in which students were to be selected partly on the
basis of their class background or the socioeconomic status of their
family.

Class and racial preferences in university admissions are obviously not mutually exclusive—it is possible to take into account
both race and class in the selection of applicants. But as the shifts

at Berkeley and UCLA suggest, university admissions policy has moved decisively away from the language of racial preference. Before 1989, race was a pivotal factor among several others (grades, test scores, etc.) for admission to Berkeley and UCLA; after 1989, the *official* policies of both campuses dropped guaranteed admission for underrepresented minorities who met minimum University of California eligibility requirements.[5]

At many of the top private universities in the United States, admissions officials like to say that they "take race into account," but they never describe their admissions policies as race-based. They interpret race-based admissions policies to mean that applicants are admitted exclusively on the basis of their racial background. Several admissions officers point out that such programs, also known as "set-asides," were judged to be illegal in the 1978 Supreme Court decision on *Bakke* (*Regents of the University of California* 1978). Instead, admissions officers at many private schools describe race as "one among several factors" that are taken into consideration during the selection process. At Harvard, for example, making race a factor in admissions means that minority students, along with legacies (children of alumni) and athletes, receive "tips," or preference, in the admissions process. In addition, minority applicant files are reviewed by a third reader, a member of the admissions staff of a racial background similar to that of the applicant.

Although tips or preferences for class or socioeconomic background are not always formally inscribed in admissions policy at private universities, the rhetoric of class has become increasingly important, particularly when the discussion turns to Asian American applicants. In the early 1980s the administration at Brown University, for example, proposed either to exclude Asian Americans from affirmative action admissions procedures or, alternatively, to divide the Asian American applicants into a low socioeconomic status (SES) pool, eligible for affirmative action, and a non–affirmative action pool. At Harvard, although Asian American students have been eligible for minority "tips" since 1976, a Harvard admissions officer explained to me in 1989 that "only working-class Asians" were given special preference in the admissions process.[6]

The practice of using class criteria to differentiate which Asians are eligible for affirmative action programs and/or minority preference and which are not surely reflects the wide range of socioeconomic status among Asian Americans in the United States. Such practices, however, also dramatize the difficulty admissions officers have in deciding whether Asian Americans deserve any special consideration, that is, preference based on race or class, in admission decisions. Some admissions officers, pointing to large numbers of Asian applicants to their school, feel that Asian Americans should receive no special consideration in the admissions process. Others argue that Asian Americans are a socioeconomically diverse population and that Asian American applicants from working-class backgrounds should be included in affirmative action admissions programs. No one, however, argues that Asian American applicants should be eligible for strict racial preference in admission.

Explicit policy changes that move away from race-based policies, along with an appreciable rise in rhetoric and language about class in affirmative action policy (particularly with regard to Asian American applicants), are in line with conservative calls for deracialization. But the increasing emphasis on class and diminishing emphasis on race in university admissions policy is paradoxical. Although conservatives have been at the vanguard of class-based affirmative action, it has been liberal university officials and faculty, not their conservative critics, who have established and implemented these preferences in admissions policy.

This book analyzes how and why liberal officials refashioned affirmative action policy in university admissions. Conservative renderings might suggest that liberals finally buckled under the accumulated weight of conservative attacks. Alternatively, liberal interpretations might defend the reconstruction of affirmative action as "progressive" policy designed to preserve the intent and spirit of racial preference. But neither interpretation accurately describes what really happened. I argue that these changes in affirmative action, regardless of who has taken credit for them, grew out of fluid discourse(s) on racial minorities in higher education in which the main issues were pivotally constructed in, and encapsulated by, the debate over Asian admissions. I am not suggesting that discourse itself, as opposed to people, changed popular ideas about affirmative action. The question is not who changed affirmative action but, rather, what were the conditions under which change was possible.

In stating the problem this way, I do not mean to imply that certain social and historical conditions were by themselves responsible for the transformation in affirmative action beliefs and practices. Many among those who are sympathetic to affirmative action policies have suggested that the climate of conservative backlash, begun during the Reagan presidency and nurtured through the

Bush administration, explains the current wave of anti–affirmative action sentiment. Such an explanation is incomplete. What is missing is an understanding of how and why liberals, driven by a desire to "save" preferential policies, transformed affirmative action.

The explanation for changes in affirmative action transcends the boundaries of conservative and liberal political interests. In saying that we need to understand the conditions under which racial politics has changed, I am referring not just to changes in political climate, positions, and interests but to the allegations, claims, and rhetoric about climate, positions, and interests. Discursive changes in racial politics are key for comprehending liberal positions on affirmative action. A discursive reading of Asian admissions, moreover, helps illuminate the larger picture as well: the ways in which the "us" and "them" of race politics shifted in the 1980s. Perhaps most important, I argue that the shift in the basic organizing principle of affirmative action ought to be viewed not as a series of political victories for one side or another but as evidence of a profound crisis in how educational policymakers, as well as intellectuals from different political camps, contend with racial differences in academic achievement.

Asian Admissions: From Discrimination to Affirmative Action

This book focuses on a recent and controversial social problem—charges that the most selective universities and colleges in the United States used quotas and ceilings to limit the enrollment of Asian Americans. But it is not a book about whether such schools actually used quotas or ceilings; nor is it a book about how many more or how many fewer Asian Americans should have been admitted to college during the 1980s. Rather, this book examines how discourse over Asian admissions facilitated a shift in affirmative action in higher education. I use the term "facilitated," as opposed to "caused" or "forced," in an effort to connote how changes in the public understanding of affirmative action policies were nourished by the language and rhetoric of the debate over Asian admissions.

Between 1983 and 1986, Asian Americans accused many of the leading institutions of higher education in the United States—including Brown, Harvard, Princeton, Stanford, Yale, the University of California, Berkeley, and the University of California, Los Angeles—of intentionally discriminating against Asian American applicants. All of the universities denied that their admissions policies were discriminatory in this way. They argued instead that Asian American applicants were either overrepresented or not qualified for admission to their university. But media reports, featuring sympathetic stories about Asian American applicants with dazzling academic and extracurricular records who could not gain admission to the top schools, suggested otherwise.

In-house reviews of admissions policy at most of the elite schools produced mixed results. Brown University conceded that there was a "serious problem" and Stanford found "unconscious bias." Self-studies at Cornell,[7] Princeton, and Harvard found no evidence of bias. At Berkeley, several state agencies, including the state auditor general and the California Senate Subcommittee on Higher Education, stepped in to examine the allegations of bias against Asians in university admissions policies. In 1989 Berkeley's chancellor, Ira Michael Heyman, publicly apologized to the Asian American community for "disadvantaging Asians" in the admissions process. At the federal level, the Justice and Education departments undertook investigations of discrimination against Asian Americans in university admissions. In 1990, after two years of study, the Education Department's Office of Civil Rights cleared Harvard of discrimination against Asians but ordered UCLA to offer admission to five Asian Americans who were judged to have been unfairly rejected by the graduate program in mathematics.

Beginning in late 1988 conservatives and neoconservatives suggested that discrimination against Asian Americans was symptomatic of a deeper problem at the university: affirmative action. According to conservatives, discrimination against Asians was the logical and inevitable outcome of preferences for "other" minorities (that is, blacks and Chicanos/Latinos). Although Asian Americans were quick to denounce conservative attacks on affirmative action, it appears that blaming affirmative action for discrimination against Asians has been a fruitful political venue for continuing conservative claims.

Asian admissions is an outstanding example of a "shifting discourse"—in which the central focus of debate changes as participants redefine and rearticulate others' definition of the problem (Takagi 1990). In the first period of the controversy, 1983–1986, complaints by Asian Americans of quotas and ceilings at the elite universities defined Asian admissions as a problem of racial discrimination; in the second period, 1987–1988, university officials' response to charges of discrimination shifted the focus of the debate to issues of diversity and meritocracy in admissions; and in the third and final period, 1989–1990, conservatives and neoconservatives shifted the center of the debate once more, to affirmative action.

This periodization of the controversy is not a strict one. I have organized my discussion in terms of these three periods as a means of establishing the primary patterns and rhythms of discourse in the controversy. Thus although the three centers of discourse, discrimination, diversity, and affirmative action, are representative of a particular period, they are not wholly consigned to that period.

One quick and easy explanation of complaints about Asian admissions is that racist college administrators decided to find ways to limit the number of Asian students pursuing higher education. Such an argument resonates with the charge frequently made by writers on the left that the right has been the main culprit in the "take-aways" from the racial gains of the 1960s and 1970s. The history of the Asian admissions controversy suggests that this explanation may be too facile. Social movements do not simply take away social programs: they participate in transforming our understanding of a social problem or policy, sometimes by challenging our frames of reference or by redefining through language and rhetoric the way in which we see the issues. Often we cannot fully see or anticipate the consequences of such changes in discourse.

The construction of a discourse around admissions, which ultimately led to a liberal critique of affirmative action, was in large measure framed by university officials and Asian Americans. This study of Asian admissions thus makes the broader argument that a full comprehension of racial politics in the 1980s requires the inclusion of liberals in the account.

The central theme of the book is that shifting discourse about Asian admissions facilitated a subtle but decisive shift in public and intellectual discourse about, and at some universities, in practices of, affirmative action. The crux of this shift was that affirmative action, typically conceptualized and executed as racially based preferences, increasingly tilted toward a rhetoric of class. The move away from race in admissions policy is historically significant as a reflection of a much broader retreat from race in American politics. The defining characteristic of this disturbing development in post-1960s race relations is evidenced in the growing reluctance by politicians, academicians, policy analysts, and the American public to define contemporary social problems explicitly as racial problems.

I develop my argument about the retreat from race in the course of presenting the history and development of the Asian admissions controversy. Two related subthemes highlight different aspects of the Asian admissions debate. Both are integral to understanding why Asian admissions moved from being a debate focused on discrimination to one focused on affirmative action and preferential policies.

The first subtheme is that Asian American students and faculty have been, and continue to be, peripheral to racial politics in higher education. Although Asian American students may have been active participants *in* racial politics, Asian American experiences are for the most part not defined *by* racial politics. Instead, racial politics in higher education are determined and shaped by black experiences, on the one hand, and white experiences, on the other. Asians are perceived to be either like whites or not like whites; or, alternatively, like blacks or not like blacks. In a sense, Asian Americans have functioned as a wild card in the racial politics of higher education—their educational experiences could be and have been incorporated into arguments both for and against discrimination, diversity, and affirmative action.

Asian Americans constitute the fastest-growing minority group in higher education, and issues that affect them often hold consequences or implications for others—blacks, Hispanics, whites, and Native Americans. It is therefore crucial to evaluate the position of Asian Americans in discourses about race in higher education. Put another way, what is being said about "them" is also a statement about the "others." In the case of the admissions controversy, what started out as an almost exclusive concern of Asian Americans evolved into an issue that held profound consequences for other underrepresented minorities.

A second subtheme is that facts and statistics were less important than what people made of them. This truism was frequently noted by many of the participants, and yet facts and statistics were often at the very center of constructing and deconstructing others' claims. I estimate that at least one million dollars was spent by a combination of campus, state, and federal institutions to compile, reorganize, and analyze voluminous amounts of admissions data in order to ferret out discrimination against Asian American applicants. However, because the core of the debate over admissions pivoted not on the facts per se but on interpretation of the facts, all of the official investigations of Asian admissions generated further controversy in spite of their attempts to put the controversy to rest. Despite the central position of facts in the debate, their significance depended on the particular contexts in which they were created and used. Indeed, the failure of facts and statistics to clear up the controversy only serves to reinforce the key importance of the rhetoric and language about Asian admissions.

Facts and statistics of course remain an important part of the Asian admissions controversy, but my intention is to show that they are constructions in that same way that different interpretations of the facts are constructions. The difference between a statistic such as an admission rate and an interpretive claim about the admission rate lies not in the relative validity of each but in the more privileged status we assign to the former.

The Social Construction of Race Relations

The phrase "retreat from race" will evoke comparison with the "declining significance of race." But my argument is radically different from the one laid out by William J. Wilson (1978). Whereas Wilson treats the declining significance of race as *structural change*—in the economy, in occupational markets, in the black class structure—I examine the retreat from race as a *discursive strategy* about race relations and racism. In adopting a constructionist approach to the analysis of racial politics, this book, unlike Wilson's, does not problematize the *origins* of the declining significance of race; rather, it problematizes the *idea* of the declining significance of race.

There are also more obvious differences in scope and subject that set this book apart from Wilson's. He locates a century and a half of race relations within the context of political economy; I examine how seven years of debate about Asian American students in higher education ushered in a change in discourse about affirmative action. Wilson argues that over time, class has become a more potent explanatory variable than racial oppression in explaining black life chances; my argument is that in the 1980s, public discourse about racial problems in higher education became increasingly articulated in language and rhetoric about class. Finally, as I will discuss in the concluding chapter, I am more skeptical than Wilson (1978, 1988) that the abandonment of race-specific policies—in affirmative action programs, for instance—is an appropriate policy course toward the attainment of racial equality.

My general disagreement with Wilson over how to approach the study of race relations applies to a majority of his critics as well.[8] In the debate that followed publication of his 1978 book, many of Wilson's critics sought to undermine the main thesis of the book by challenging the validity of his assertions—for example, the growing income gap and differentiation of classes within the black community, the notion of "progress" for the black middle class, the ineffectiveness of affirmative action for the black "underclass." The weakness of these criticisms is that they chip away at the validity of the details of Wilson's argument, leaving untouched his refusal to distinguish between race as a constructed ideology—common sense and popular thought, stereotypes, race relations theory—on the one hand, and race as a structural effect—of arrangements of economic and political power—on the other. I find myself in the peculiar position of being in general agreement with Wilson about the declining significance of race—in this case, illustrated by the controversy over Asian admissions and its effect on affirmative action—but, unlike Wilson, I conceptualize the decline as ideological and, hence, contingent rather than given, constructed rather than structured.

In parting with Wilson, this book joins with a small but growing group of studies that treat race relations, racial antagonism, and racial identity as socially constructed realities produced and articulated through social interaction and political struggle.[9] Two broad thematic projects, stated here in simplified terms, characterize the breadth of constructionist concerns about race and racism. One theme, which concerns the historical development and contemporary practices and understandings of race, is that race, racism, and race relations are central and vital issues, albeit sometimes hidden from plain view, in the discourses of everyday life. David Theo Goldberg (1990a:xv), for example, suggests, "Of the oppressive social configurations confronting any concern with modernism, modernization, and their postmodern beyond, racisms are among the most pressing. They are in both senses of the term embedded— hidden and anchored. Racist discourse touches very nearly all, though some among us may choose to ignore its articulation."

A second theme, loosely focused on the question of what is to be done about racism and race relations, is that social and political attempts to confront racism(s) must first manage a theoretical understanding of a complex set of issues regarding identity and difference. Identities, for example, including those defined by racial discourse, are never singular, but always multiple. The task before us, suggests Homi Bhabha (1990:208), is to grapple with the multiplicity of identities: "What remains to be thought is the repetitious desire to recognize ourselves doubly, as at once, decentered in the solidary processes of the political group, and yet, ourself as a consciously committed, even individuated, agent of change—the bearer of belief."

Such complex notions of identity have been recognized by feminists for some time. Teresa de Lauretis (1986:9) notes, "What is emerging in feminist writings is, [instead,] the concept of a multiple, shifting, and often self-contradictory identity, a subject that is not divided in, but rather at odds with, language; an identity made up of heterogeneous and heteronomous representations of gender, race, and class, and often indeed across languages and cultures." Similarly, Linda Alcoff (1988), arguing against an essentialized notion of the category "woman," favors post-structuralist descriptions of the subject as partial, multiple, and contradictory.

In the humanities—particularly in literature, literary theory, literary criticism, and feminist theory—where constructionist (and deconstructionist, semiotic, and postmodern) analyses of race are more common than in the social sciences, numerous writers have theorized about one or both of these themes. An eclectic group of writers and cultural critics, including Roland Barthes (1972), Ralph Ellison (1952), Frantz Fanon (1967), David Theo Goldberg (1990b), Barbara Christian (1990), Henry Louis Gates (1986), Trinh T. Minh-ha (1989), Homi Bhabha (1990), and Michelle Wallace (1990), have located racial issues—the production of racial subjects, the analysis of racial discourse(s), and issues of racial identity and racial difference—at the center of their commentary and analyses of contemporary society.

In the social sciences, constructionist interpretations of race analyze social movements and social problems, not literary texts.[10] Michael Omi and Howard Winant (1986:68), in their ground-breaking argument for a theory of racial formation, propose race "as an unstable and 'decentered' complex of social meanings constantly being transformed by political struggles." According to Omi and Winant, one transformation was the formation of radical discourse by minority movements during the 1960s; a second, the start of a racial backlash, was the appropriation of that radical discourse—what they describe as rearticulation—by neoconservatives during the 1970s and early 1980s.

In keeping with Omi and Winant, this book is an in-depth study of how conservatives and liberals rearticulated a particular social problem, Asian admissions, in the second half of the 1980s. In contrast to Omi and Winant, however, I place far more emphasis on the provisional nature of discourse and rhetoric—as opposed to political interests defined by social movements—in the transformation of racial ideology. I do not mean to suggest that social movements and their political interests are not a crucial part of discursive change. But in the controversy over Asian admissions, claims by the different participants—Asian Americans, university officials, and neoconservatives—can often be read in multiple and contradictory ways as expressions of different political interests. That liberals, not conservatives, were pivotal in "the retreat from race," for example, illustrates an awkwardness in reading political interests out of discursive struggles.

Though their research focuses on race relations in Britain, not the United States, Stuart Hall, Chas Critcher, Tony Jefferson, John Clarke, and Brian Roberts (1978:327) examine the crime of mugging as a social phenomenon "from the perspective of the society in which it occurs." Through a richly detailed analysis of media portrayals of mugging, the authors explain how and why mugging came to be defined as a *racial* social problem—a black crime. But this is only a starting point. Hall and his colleagues go behind the criminal act of mugging to the social conditions that produce such acts— "black youth can only be properly understood as a class fraction" while racism is the "specific mechanism which 'reproduces' the black labour force" (Hall et al. 1978:389). Other writers associated with Hall and the Centre for Contemporary Cultural Studies in Birmingham, England, have similarly located race relations within a nexus of socially and political contested meaning.[11] Paul Gilroy (1982) explores the construction of Rastafarian music as a medium of expression for black working-class youth in Britain. He critically examines why these cultural expressions of race and class take the form they do, and how they are transformed and under what conditions. Gilroy, like Hall, anchors the cultural expression of black youth—through music—in the structural conditions of the existence of black youth in British society. Though I am sympathetic to such endeavors, I am not convinced that the social construction of an issue or problem—be it mugging or reggae—from black youth experiences is consistent with a simultaneous theoretical move to root that problem or issue in conditions, whether they be economic, political, social, or racial. The problem, of course, is where we draw the line in constructing—in defining social problems or in defining the conditions that contextualize social problems.[12]

Although I argue that the retreat from race can be viewed as the product of shifting discourse about Asian admissions, I do not argue that changes in affirmative action should be viewed as the articulation of other conditions, for example, class relations. Race does function, as Hall (1978:394) has stated, as "the modality in which class is lived." Rather, I would argue that while it is relatively easy to see the effects of race constituted at different levels of the social formation, by comparison, it is difficult to see exactly how changes in ideology about race are *determined* by structural positions in the social formation.

Much research in Asian American history has focused on the fully legitimate tasks of reclaiming, documenting, and analyzing the variety of Asian American experiences (Chan 1986; Ichioka 1988; Takaki 1989; Okihiro 1991). This book will, I hope, be read as a contribution to such efforts. Asian American students, faculty, and community activists developed and sustained claims of discrimination against some of the most elite colleges in the nation. Perceptions of Asian American students by university officials and conservatives shaped the contours of the debate over university admissions.

But this book should not be read primarily as an appreciative account of Asian American activities in the admissions controversy or as a vehicle for hearing new voices. Rather, my intent is to present an analysis of how contests about Asian Americans in this critical debate in higher education were figurative in the transformation of affirmative action.

This book also seeks to expand the borders of the field of Asian American studies by insisting on its engagement with contemporary race relations theory and practices. Claims of discrimination against Asian Americans in higher education do not make sense outside the larger context of race relations in higher education. In turn, the comparison of Asian American experiences with those of others challenges race relations theorists to rethink how racial politics have moved beyond black and white.

Approaching the Study of Asian Admissions

While researching this book, I found that when I told people that I was studying the controversy over Asian admissions, their response was typically swift and conclusive. Some, shaking their heads, asked, "Do they [Asian Americans] really have much of a case to make? I mean, there are so many of them. . . ."[13] Others nodded their approval, demanding, "How did those universities think they could get away with all that . . . quotas and stuff?"[14] A few people held back their reaction, first asking for my "expert" sociological opinion based on my evaluation of the evidence. I saw the disappointment register in all of their faces when I explained that my book was not about amassing evidence to condemn or acquit university officials, but instead was focused on discourse about affirmative action and racial politics in higher education. They were much more interested in an answer to the direct question "Does Harvard discriminate against Asians?"

It is nearly impossible in such a debate not to take sides. Many of the issues involved a call for partisanship: Are you for or against supplemental criteria? What is the best way to measure discrimination, by opportunity or outcome? Should private universities be openly accountable to the public? Should Asian Americans, or any other group for that matter, be part of the admissions process? Is discrimination against Asians the result of affirmative action? These questions are important because they bear directly on university policy. I do not have simple answers. Nor is my goal simply to describe what the "right" or "good" admission policy would look like. This book is not an evaluation of policy as much as it is an analysis of the politics of policy.

I gathered official reports, statistical tables, and media reports to familiarize myself with the debate. As I read over these materials, I found that at some points I murmured a soft "yes" before going on to the next paragraph or section. In effect, I was keeping a mental score of who was ahead, the university or Asian Americans. Each time either side scored what I thought was a decisive point, I cheered for it from my desk chair. But over the years, as the "game" wore on, it seemed as if the game itself had changed. New teams and different players were introduced, game strategies shifted, the stakes of the game changed, and it became increasingly difficult to keep score.

I expect that most readers will not be able to resist taking sides in the debate—at some point. It is not necessary that one be "neutral" on issues related to Asian admissions. But I want to suggest that taking sides should illuminate, not obscure, the meaning and importance of discourse about Asian admissions for how we now think about affirmative action in higher education.

My approach to the study of this debate has been to examine comparatively claims and counterclaims concerning discrimination against Asian Americans at both private and public universities. Throughout, I am concerned more with the viability of claims than with whether or not they are valid. Thus I refrain from "jumping in" the debate to aruge with a participant about the accuracy of a statistic.

My presentation of the history of the debate is both descriptive and interpretive. I have estimated the scope of the debate, distinguished various arguments and the statistical reasoning used by different participants, and evaluated the significance and meaning of shifting discourse about Asian admissions within the context of contemporary racial politics in higher education. In my account I have relied on both quantitative and qualitative information drawn from three main sources.

First, to understand how participants constructed the problem of Asian admissions in different ways, I conducted sixty interviews with key participants in the debate. Between 1988 and 1991 I interviewed Asian American students, faculty, and community activists; admissions officers at Berkeley, Brown, Harvard, Princeton, Stanford, UCLA, and Yale; various other university administrators;[15] members of Congress; and federal officials from the Department of Education. The interviews ranged from one to three hours. Some individuals were re-interviewed, in several cases, once or twice, and in two cases, three and four times.

A second source of information for this study was a comprehensive assortment of public discourse on Asian admissions from 1983 to 1991, which includes (a) primary documents—meeting transcripts, official university memos, press releases, reports, correspondence of participants in the controversy, and summary reports of the investigations conducted by faculty committees, state agencies, and federal departments; and (b) secondary accounts—media reports, scholarly and popular articles, and editorial commentary.

Third, I launched this project in 1988 with a survey of admissions officers at thirty of the top public and private universities in the United States.[16] To estimate the scope of the problem of Asian admissions, I asked three questions—whether Asian admissions was considered an "issue," whether students and/or faculty had pressured the university to investigate the issue, and how the university had responded, if at all. In addition I solicited admissions officers for the names of other individuals who might be knowledgeable about Asian admissions.

Of the admissions officers at the universities that I discuss in this book—Berkeley, Brown, Harvard, Princeton, Stanford, and UCLA—only one, Stanford's, responded to this initial query. From officials at universities that were not in the center of public discourse about Asian admissions, however, I received many responses. Various officials described Asian admissions as an "issue of concern" even though no specific complaints had been raised at their university. Only a few officials described Asian admissions as a "non-issue."[17] Many sent me their most recent statistical summaries of admission and enrollment of Asian Americans and/or described their school's minority recruitment and academic support services that targeted Asian Americans.

The responses and nonresponses to my survey in 1988 provided me with an early hint of an issue that would resurface again and again as the controversy continued to unfold over the next several years: public access to admissions data. I found that those universities least afflicted by the controversy were the most responsive and generous with admissions data; those at the center of the controversy were comparatively stingy or unresponsive. The issue of access to data has been a persistent trouble spot for university officials and their critics because the top private universities, including those in the center of the Asian admissions controversy, do not publish admissions statistics by race and achievement. Availability of admissions data is for obvious reasons an important factor in the kinds of claims that are put forward and, more generally, in the level of controversy. It is difficult to press claims of discrimination if no data are available.

From my survey and my reading of the public discourse, I surmised that Asian admissions emerged as a controversy where competition for admission has been the keenest—at highly selective colleges and universities. This book, then, focuses on the development of the controversy at those schools. The degree to which each school is discussed varies, however, reflecting the uneven development of claims and public discourse at different schools.

My coverage of events at Berkeley is extensive for two reasons. One is that Berkeley was the site of the most protracted and embittered struggle between university officials and Asian Americans. At Brown, Princeton, and Stanford, questions about Asian admissions were more or less resolved within six months. At Berkeley, the struggle between officials and Asian Americans lasted five years. A second reason for the focus on Berkeley is that claims by Asian Americans and university officials are documentable there, whereas they are not at other schools. Princeton, Stanford, and Harvard have refused to release the details of their in-house investigations. Without such reports it is impossible to examine the logic and evidence on which they based their conclusions. In contrast, Berkeley officials were comparatively forthcoming and open with admissions information. Owing to its willingness to "open its books" to the public, Berkeley quickly became the center of claims and media attention, particularly after 1986.

The five narrative chapters of the book should be read as an extended argument. Each chapter represents a piece of the explanation of the ways in which Asian admissions has been an important discursive social problem for the transformation of affirmative action. Chapter 2 examines the development of Asian American claims of discrimination at Berkeley, Brown, Harvard, Princeton, Stanford, and UCLA. Chapter 3 analyzes how university officials shifted the debate to focus on diversity while simultaneously responding to Asian American charges of discrimination. Continuing the discussion of diversity and meritocracy, Chapter 4 analyzes how external reviews of the Asian admissions problem by state and federal agencies—the undertaking of extensive quantitative studies—attempted to settle the debate through empirical study. Instead, such reviews had the unintended effect of fueling the conflict by providing participants with yet more data over which to disagree. Chapter 5 examines neoconservative intervention and reconstruction of Asian admissions as an affirmative action problem. Chapter 6 looks at liberal responses to neoconservative claims, in particular, changes in admissions policy at Berkeley and UCLA. In the final chapter I explore the theoretical, political, and policy implications of the shift in affirmation action from race to class.

CHAPTER 2

Clamor at the Gates: Discrimination, 1983–1986

*B*y 1980, the demographic warning signals were already in place. In the previous decade the population of Asian Americans in the United States had more than doubled in size.[1] During that same period, whites, blacks, Hispanics, and Native Americans had experienced comparatively modest gains in population.[2] In higher education, the rise in the Asian American population in turn fueled tremendous growth in the number of Asian American students attending college. Between 1970 and 1980 Asian Americans were the fastest-growing minority in undergraduate enrollment at U.S. colleges and universities (Wang 1987). Between 1976 and 1982 Asian American undergraduate enrollment climbed 62 percent while Hispanic enrollment grew 32 percent, white enrollment grew 5 percent, and black enrollment rose 1.3 percent.[3]

In 1981 the *New York Times* warned that the rapid increase in Asian American students was causing problems at Berkeley (Turner 1981). Asian American undergraduates complained of being "pushed into" certain academic fields because of counselors' recommendations or, perhaps more directly, because of language difficulties. According to Watson M. Laetsch, vice chancellor for undergraduate affairs, Asian American students at Berkeley found the requirements in the social sciences and humanities "frustrating" (Turner 1981). In 1966, 5.2 percent of the undergraduate enrollment at Berkeley was Asian. By 1980 the figure had quadrupled—Asian American students constituted 20 percent of 21,000 undergraduates.

At other universities, especially among the elite schools, increases in the enrollment of Asian Americans were far less dramatic. But many of the elite private universities experienced a rapid rise in the number of Asian American applicants, even if such increases were not ultimately reflected in enrollment patterns. At Harvard, Asian enrollment rose from 5.5 percent in 1979 to 8.5 percent in 1982 (U.S. Department of Education 1990). At Stanford, figures for Asian American enrollment are not available before 1983, when Asians made up 7 percent of the freshman class. Between 1983 and 1985, Asian American enrollment at Stanford rose to 8 percent (Fetter 1991).[4]

Increases in Asian American enrollment in higher education came at a time when affirmative action programs appeared to be making promising gains in black and Hispanic enrollments. The pace of black and Hispanic enrollment during the 1970s and 1980s, however, was not as large as for Asian Americans. Compared with Asian American enrollment, black and Hispanic gains through affirmative action often appeared modest.

In late 1982, the *New York Times* reported that minority access to higher education had "flattened out" (Fiske 1982). The concern focused on black, Hispanic, and Native American enrollment—not Asian American enrollment. Minority enrollment—including Asian Americans—rose from 6.4 percent in 1960 to 13.8 percent in 1977. From 1977 to 1981, however, overall minority enrollment remained "steady" at 13 percent, with black enrollment at about 10 percent, of all students (Fiske 1982). But in the fall of 1982, numerous colleges and universities reported discouraging news: fewer numbers of minority freshman—blacks, in particular—had enrolled for classes.[5] According to the *New York Times*, the decline in black freshman was "sharply evident" at Ivy League and other expensive colleges (Fiske 1982). At Cornell University, the number of entering minority students had dropped 10 percent. Similarly, at Harvard, minority enrollment fell 7 percent between 1981 and 1982.

Elias Blake, Jr., then president of Clark College and head of the National Advisory Committee on Black Higher Education and Black Colleges, told the *New York Times* that the problem was to avoid a backslide: "There were tremendous gains in a short period of time, and most people tended to assume that, once they got started, they would be continuous. But, this didn't happen. The progress got stalled, and no one I know is talking about continuing the climb. Most of our energy is going into trying to avoid regression" (Fiske 1982).

It is in this context—on the one hand, declining black enrollment, and on the other, demographic pressure from an expanding Asian American population—that charges of discrimination against Asian American applicants emerged at several of the highly selective colleges and universities in the United States. In the early 1980s, Asian American admissions surfaced as a local campus issue at Berkeley, Brown, Harvard, Princeton, Stanford, and UCLA. In the beginning, Asian admissions was not a particularly flashy topic in higher education. Racism toward minority students and faculty, divestment of university funds in South Africa, and burgeoning demands for multiculturalism were the issues of the day. But by the end of 1986, Asian admissions was national news.

This chapter examines the development of discrimination charges at Berkeley, Brown, Harvard, Princeton, and Stanford. In all instances, it was Asian Americans—students, faculty, and professionals from the outside community—who initiated and advanced claims of discrimination in undergraduate admissions. In some cases, existing organizations—student groups, for example—levied charges against the university administration. In one instance, a group of Asian American professionals and faculty members established a new organization to confront the admissions office at the local university.

Asian Americans issued two basic complaints. One was that the admission rate of Asian Americans was lower than that of whites. In other words, Asians were less likely to gain admission than whites. A second claim was that enrollments of Asian Americans had not risen in proportion to increases in the number of Asian American applicants.

Campus, local, and national media contributed to the efforts of these organizations by publicizing their claims. Though the tone of news reporting was not always sympathetic or partisan in this early period, the act of *reporting* complaints by Asian Americans seemed to confer at least a limited degree of legitimacy on their activities. Media coverage of Asian American charges of discrimination serve as a kind of bellwether of the development of the controversy. In 1983, when the first charges were raised, media reports were local and sporadic. But by 1986 the national print and voice media were running features on the problem of discrimination against Asian American applicants.

At some universities, Asian Americans made charges of discrimination outright—accusing university officials of using illegal quotas and ceilings—to limit Asian American enrollment. At other schools, Asian American students and/or faculty concerned about possible discrimination against Asian applicants requested reviews of undergraduate admissions policies.

Charges of discrimination were framed by prevailing understandings of race and racism in higher education. Public discourse about race was dominated by two major concerns in liberal thought during the post-1960s period: equality of outcomes and equality of individual opportunity. The principle of equality of outcomes is associated with preferential policies for "underrepresented" groups—minorities and women—in short, affirmative action. In contrast, equality of opportunity is linked with public policies that encourage individual competition for jobs or admission slots without regard to an individual's membership in a particular racial, gender, or other "disadvantaged" collectivity.

Public discourse about Asian admissions reflected both principles of equality used to measure bias and discrimination in admissions policy. One notion of equity—a parity-based argument—suggested that Asian Americans, like blacks and other minorities, were a racially disadvantaged group in the university admissions process. The concept of parity is typically featured in arguments about *equal outcomes* in higher education: the representation of racial groups in the university should be proportionate to their representation in the population. In the case of Asian admissions, several groups charged that the admission of Asian Americans had not kept pace with increases in the size of the Asian American applicant pool. A second notion of equity—based on individual merit and competition—suggested that Asian American applicants, unlike other minorities, were academically competitive with white applicants. Issues of individual merit and competition are characteristic of arguments over the *equal access* of minorities to higher education: individuals from different racial groups should be evaluated by the same criteria. Asian American activists charged that admissions criteria—for example, personal ratings—were biased against Asian American applicants.

The construction of discrimination charges by Asian Americans was sometimes contradictory. Arguments that Asians were a disadvantaged racial minority in admissions did not always seem consistent with claims that Asians were academically competitive with whites. But these various, if conflicting, accusations of discrimination were probably less reflective of differences among Asian Americans activists than of the inherent conflict between the principles of equal access and equal outcomes.

Berkeley, 1984: Asian Enrollment

In late 1984, Professor L. Ling-chi Wang made a discovery while scanning reports from the Office of Admission and Financial Aid. Sitting in his office around the corner from the Asian American Studies office at Berkeley, he double-checked the figures in the reports. He was looking at fall 1984 admissions and enrollment data by race for the University of California, Berkeley. Wang was surprised to see that the absolute number of newly enrolled Asians had dropped from 1,303 in 1983 to 1,031 in 1984, a 21 percent drop in a single year. The figures were surprising to him, because key enrollment indicators projected a steady and continuous rise in Asian American enrollment at Berkeley through 1990.[6] As early as 1981, the *New York Times* had reported that Berkeley officials expected Asian American enrollment to climb steadily and to constitute 40 percent of the entering freshman class by 1990 (Turner 1981).

Until the spring of 1984 Professor Wang had not been in the habit of reviewing admissions and enrollment statistics. For the past three years, however, he had had an uneasy feeling that something was wrong. In 1981, when Berkeley was about to switch from the quarter system to the semester system, Wang took part in a series of faculty meetings, organized by Vice Chancellor for Undergraduate Affairs Watson M. Laetsch. The purpose of the meetings was to discuss how Berkeley's conversion to semesters might provide an opportunity to enhance and improve undergraduate education. As chairman of Ethnic Studies and as a member of the Asian American Studies faculty, Wang attended, along with faculty members from several other departments on campus. The general discussion on undergraduate education occasionally singled out Asians as "problem" students. Wang recalled, "It was during the course of these discussions that I began to feel very uncomfortable that all these people from different departments are saying things about Asians. So for instance, some English department professor said that we should do something about these Asian students who are really deficient in the English language . . . 'they should not be here at all; just because they are good in math and science doesn't mean they make good undergraduate students.'"[7]

In 1981–82, Asians constituted 80 percent of immigrant student enrollment at Berkeley. The Basic Skills Task Force, convened by Vice Chancellor Laetsch in the early 1980s, advised the administration on how to improve services to immigrant students. Asians were not eligible for admission through EOP, but the university hoped that the Basic Skills Task Force would address the special academic issues of the largely Asian population of immigrant students who had been admitted through regular admission channels. Wang, along with other faculty from Asian American Studies, the director of the Campus Learning Center, and the director of the Office of Student Research, conducted two campus studies to identify student needs and to suggest ways that those needs might be addressed by the university. The Basic Skills Task Force concluded that language deficiency played an important role in Asian students' decisions on majors and their ability to gain access to academic services. The university responded by establishing the Immigrant Student Project to look more closely at the problems and needs of immigrant students.

In early 1984 Professor Wang began to hear rumors from faculty and staff, some of whom were employed within the chancellor's office, about a possible restriction on incoming English as a Second Language (ESL) students. He was furious. He knew that any restriction on foreign students would have a disproportionate impact on Asian immigrant applicants. A private lunch meeting with Vice Chancellor Laetsch failed to dispel Wang's suspicions. Wang recalled that Laetsch, "assured me that whatever policy changes being made would be, in his own words, racially neutral. But somehow, I just did not trust what he was telling me. So, I decided that I would look at the admissions data for fall."[8]

In late October 1984, when the fall 1984 admissions data were made available, Wang decided the rumors that he had heard were true. He said, "I was really shocked. They obviously did something. I didn't know at that time what they did. I felt that something had to be done."[9]

East Coast Institutions: "Admissions Impossible"

Professor Wang's findings at Berkeley were not surprising to the members of the East Coast Asian Student Union (ECASU), a network of Asian American student organizations from eastern colleges and universities, including Brown, Harvard, Princeton, and Yale. In 1983, the Joint Admissions Task Force of ECASU surveyed twenty-five universities about their admissions rates by race. The results of the survey, published in an article entitled "Admissions Impossible" (Ho and Chin 1983), found that the number of Asian American applicants had soared between 1978 and 1983, but that Asian enrollment had barely increased. The two undergraduate authors of the article, Fred Ho and Margaret M. Chin, suggested that an "alarming barrier" was in place to keep Asian Americans from "seeking higher education and better lives" (Ho and Chin 1983).

The findings of the ECASU survey were published in an Asian American periodical virtually unknown outside the Asian American community. This accusation of discrimination at eastern colleges was soon supplemented, however, by several local reports and inquiries of discrimination at exclusive private schools. Asian American students confronted the Brown University administration with charges of discrimination in 1983. In 1985 concerned Asian American students at Princeton inquired about Asian enrollment there. And at Stanford a faculty investigation began in 1986 in response to persistent inquiries from an Asian American undergraduate.

Brown: Prima Facie Case of Racial Discrimination

At Brown University, as at other elite colleges on the East Coast, undergraduate students have the opportunity to participate in the admissions process. Their role in admissions ranges from reading files to helping with recruitment to, in some cases, conducting interviews. At Brown, minority students, including Asian Americans, play a crucial role in the recruitment of prospective minority applicants. During the fall recruiting season, minority students travel back to their former high schools to meet and talk with groups of potential applicants.

For the minority student recruiter, working in the admissions office can be both exciting and glamorous. Students are entrusted with the important role of presenting the "Brown experience" to the outside world. In addition, minority students have a certain expertise that other admissions officers do not—minority recruiters are "insiders" in their home communities. In addition to traveling on behalf of Brown, recruiters may read and comment on applicant files once they are received in the admission office.

As "insiders," several Asian American student recruiters in the Brown admissions office were dismayed by what they saw and heard during the early 1980s. In October 1983 the Asian American Students Association (AASA) published a thirty-page report charging the university with discriminatory bias in admissions policy. The report said that after four years of failed meetings between the Asian community and Brown officials, the Asian American Students Association was finally resorting to a public documentation of "a prima facie case of racial discrimination against Asian Americans in the Brown University admissions process" (AASA 1983:1).

The student group, citing a 750 percent increase in the Asian applicant pool between 1979 and 1987 and steadily declining admission rates (44 percent in 1979 to 14 percent in 1987), found the widening gap between the size of the applicant pool and the admit rate "shocking" (AASA 1983:6).

An increase in applications, of course, does not necessarily translate into an increase in *eligible* applicants. Was the growing Asian applicant pool a qualified group? The Asian American Students Association, drawing on statistics from the Brown admissions office, found that among Asian and white *applicants* to Brown, the average Asian SAT verbal score was lower than the white average. The average Asian SAT math score, however, was higher than the white average. Similarly, among those students *admitted* to Brown, Asians on the average had lower verbal scores but higher math scores than whites. On the basis of percentile ranks of applicants and admits, Asians uniformly ranked higher than whites in both the applicant and admit pools.

If Asian applicants were qualified for admission to Brown, the AASA report asked, why did Asian admission rates fall between 1979 and 1987? Brown admissions officers suggested four possible explanations: Asians were not academically diverse, there were financial constraints in major areas of study popular with Asian Americans, Asians were "overrepresented," and that a growing applicant pool required tighter controls in the admissions process.

The AASA report responded point by point to these justifications and rejected each. Among their arguments, the students insisted that Asian Americans were not all pre-med applicants; that financial limitations ought to affect all groups equally and that no particular group should bear the burden of the cuts; that Asian Americans were in all likelihood, underrepresented, not overrepresented, and that parity arguments were singling out Asian Americans for disadvantage; and that tightening admissions controls could not explain the gap between enrollment increases and admission rates of Asian Americans.

The AASA rejoinders on underrepresentation and parity raised the problem of how to define equity directly. For example, according to the AASA (1983), Asians were probably underrepresented relative to whites at Brown because the overall high school graduation rate for Asians (68.8 percent in 1970) was higher than that of whites (52.3 percent). From the AASA's point of view, if Asians were more likely than whites to graduate from high school, then, by extension, Asians should be more likely than whites to gain admission to college. The question of parity obviously hinges on specific comparisons.

The AASA argument against using parity to assess equity in admissions was provocative. The students suggested that although officials were willing to limit Asian enrollment, they would not be willing to limit the enrollment of others, for example, Jewish applicants. The AASA report (1983:20) noted,

> Furthermore, one could only imagine the outcry from all sectors of the community if Brown decided to reduce its 25–30 percent Jewish student population down to the 3 percent that Jews represent in the national population. And if this isn't ridiculous enough, try limiting the number of alumni sons and daughters in the University to their overall national representation. The point here is not that we wish to cut either the number of Jewish students or Alumni children but that this argument which Brown uses to justify limiting acceptance of Asian Americans is invalid and inconsistent.

Brown officials suggested two possible "remedies" for Asian admissions: either to remove Asian American applicants from affirmative action considerations or to exclude some portion of the Asian American applicant pool from affirmative action. The AASA bristled at both suggestions because it believed that the relationship of Asian American applicants to affirmative action at Brown was only part of the problem. We will return to the university response in Chapter 3.

In the following year, the Corporation Committee on Minority Affairs (COMA) at Brown decided in favor of the students. Arguing that evidence of an equal chance of admission means equal admissions rates, COMA (1984) concluded: "An extremely serious situation exists and . . . immediate remedial measures are called for." On the basis of the AASA report, testimony by admissions staff, and additional documentary evidence, COMA (1984) found that "Asian American applicants have been treated unfairly in the admissions process. While in this report we do not claim intentionally unfair treatment on the part of individuals or in the stated admission policies of the University, the admission practices used to implement these policies have resulted in such unfair treatment."

Harvard: Asians the Least Likely to Be Admitted

Although Harvard is mentioned by Ho and Chin (1983) as one among several elite institutions where the Asian applicant pool increased with no concomitant increase in Asian admissions, there was no formal protest or complaint lodged by the Asian American Association (AAA) against the university. Margaret Chin (class of '84) recalled, "We never had a case where it came up that we wanted to actually protest. So the only time that we had a list of demands for certain things for minority students was when we wanted them [Harvard] to sponsor events actually for minority prefreshman week."[10]

The Asian American Association, a student organization at Harvard, wanted the Harvard admissions office to ensure recruitment for inner-city minority students and to retain Asian Americans within the minority category. In addition, the AAA demanded that the university increase the number of minority professors and provide courses in ethnic studies. The demands did not include a specific claim concerning falling admission rates for Asian Americans.

That Asian American students at Harvard never formally protested against the school's admissions policy has not stilled claims that a problem exists.[11] Jane Bock (1981), in her senior sociology thesis on admissions, found that Asians were "considerably disadvantaged" in the admissions process compared with whites.[12] In 1980 Asians had the lowest rate of admission to Harvard of any racial group. The overall admit rate was 15.5 percent, and minority rates were 26.5 percent for blacks, 21.6 percent for Native Americans, 24.6 percent for Hispanics, and 13.1 percent for Asians. Moreover, according to Bock, "In general, Asians were required to have higher high school class rank, SAT scores, and admissions officers' overall ratings than whites to be admitted. Applicants who went to prep school, were potential varsity athletes, and whose fathers went to Harvard were disproportionately admitted; these attributes more often apply to whites than to Asians. The findings indicated that a race blind policy would admit more Asian Americans than the present 'affirmative action' program does" (1981:4.13). Similarly, David Karen (1985) suggested that Asians were "very disadvantaged" in the Harvard admissions process. He noted, "Except among those whose average test scores are above 700, Asians are admitted at percentages lower than whites. Not only, then, are Asians being admitted overall at rates lower than whites, but the very categories that seem to provide large advantages for whites are not terribly consequential for Asians. Going to a prep school almost doubles the chances that a white applicant will be admitted, while the Asian applicant's chances actually decline" (Karen 1985:318).

The Harvard affirmative action program, which was held up as a model for the University of California in the 1978 Supreme Court decision on *Bakke*, does not employ a separate admissions process or a quota system for minorities and whites. Indeed, there is no "minority admissions program" per se at Harvard. There is regular recruitment machinery that relies on Harvard's reputation as a top school, including a national network of alumni organized into Harvard clubs in addition to admissions officers and recruiters who are currently enrolled students. The undergraduate Minority Recruitment Program, organized by minority student activists in the late 1960s, supplements the efforts of the regular recruiting machinery by recruiting working-class minority applicants to Harvard. As such, the affirmative action program at Harvard is an effort to enlarge the pool of *applicants* to include working-class minority students. All applicants, minority or not, are evaluated under the same criteria. Affirmative action at Harvard therefore refers to recruitment policy, not admissions policy.

Bock's criticism of affirmative action at Harvard was that the program failed to recognize that Asian students come from both middle-class and working-class backgrounds. She reports that students from the AAA were concerned about mixing working-class and middle-class Asians in the applicant pool: "It seemed that recruitment might actually be hurting the chances of working class Asian Americans. Visits to working class high schools seemed ineffective; recruitment served only to increase the number of applicants in the affluent pool, argued the students. The introduction of more affluent applicants made the Asian pool more competitive, diminishing the chances of the few working class Asian applicants that there were" (1981:3.2).

Bock's criticism of Harvard's process of affirmative action was balanced by the more sanguine finding that the number of working-class Asian students was rising. She noted, "While the data bore out the Asian student recruiters' worries that recruitment has increased the competition within the Asian pool, the major goal of the students—to increase the number of Asian working class students—is being met" (Bock 1981:4.14).

If during Bock's tenure as a student at Harvard the AAA

claimed that the *class* character of Asian applicants was lopsided in favor of middle-class applicants, several years later members of the AAA were more concerned with differential admission rates. AAA members at Harvard after 1983 saw their school as one among many elite institutions that "capped" Asian admissions at around 12 percent of an entering class. Margaret M. Chin recalled:

> I started working in the admissions office in the 1981–82 academic year. I was doing recruitment for them, going around to different cities, especially New York City and San Francisco and Boston, recruiting in schools where they normally don't recruit, inner cities, where the populations are minority. That's how I started getting involved in it. And then I met other students at different schools via the ECASU network and we started talking about Asian admissions, and apparently at Brown and Princeton, there was a lot of research done before . . . as well as at Harvard, about what was going on with Asian students and their admission rates. At Harvard, there was a thesis that one of the presidents of the AAA wrote on the admissions process. Every year we found the admission rate for Asian Americans was dropping, although the number of applicants was rising. By 1983–84, it felt like three or four years straight, there had been something going on.[13]

Like their counterparts at Brown, Asian American students at Harvard were active in minority recruitment through their student organization. Minority recruiters, drawn from the various minority student organizations, are responsible for contacting potential applicants and traveling to inner cities to talk with prospective students and their families during the fall recruiting season. Two recruiters from each of the minority groups are paid for their work,[14] and the rest of the work is performed by volunteers. Bock described the work as "exhausting": "Students are expected to attend several training sessions before they leave, submit budget requests, arrange their itinerary, miss a week of classes, visit three high schools a day, hold night meetings, develop contacts in Asian community groups, confer with alumni, host a reception, write recommendations and a report when they return, and maintain correspondence with students they meet on their trips" (1981:3.7).

Because Asian students played an active role in the recruitment process at Harvard, their queries to admissions officers about Asian admissions were not routed through the bureaucracy as official complaints, as had been the case at Berkeley. Rather, queries about Asian admissions were raised directly by student recruiters with regular admissions office staff. Margaret M. Chin, co-author of "Admissions Impossible" and a former Harvard recruiter, recalled:

> [The staff's] argument was that every year we [Harvard] admit more and more Asian Americans, you know, the number just keeps rising, and there's nothing we can do about the admissions rate. But then we kept saying, "Well, how come the admissions rate is lower for Asian Americans?" And our admissions office always just said, "Well, every year we admit so many others, the numbers that apply obviously just aren't qualified and you don't know." So we did a little research and found out that people that were applying, were actually more qualified than anybody else.[15]

At both Harvard and Brown, charges of discrimination were raised by Asian American students knowledgeable about the admissions process. Not satisfied with the results of discussions held internally within the admissions office, the students "went public" with their complaints, in the form of a report at Brown and the publication of an article that named Harvard as one among several schools using "quotas" against Asian Americans.

Berkeley: The Asian American Task Force on University Admissions

At Berkeley, Professor Wang shared his shocking findings with prominent leaders of the Asian American community in the Bay Area. The group, which included lawyers, judges, academics, and community leaders, met during the fall of 1984 to discuss the implications of Wang's discoveries. At its first meeting, the group, calling itself the Asian American Task Force on University Admissions (hereafter referred to as the task force or AATF) took up its first project: investigation of the 1984 decline in Berkeley's Asian enrollment. In addition the task force planned to review the impact on Asian American applicants of recently announced changes in admissions policy.

Unlike the Asian American student organizations at Brown and Harvard, the members of the task force were not insiders in the admissions office. Asian American student recruiters at East Coast schools freely "borrowed" (they prefer to describe their borrowing as "photocopying") admissions data. In contrast, the task force was dependent on the willingness of the Berkeley administration to make admissions data public. The first act of the task force was to

send a letter to the chancellor's office requesting university cooperation with the investigation. Chancellor Ira Michael Heyman pledged
his cooperation and designated Vice Chancellor Laetsch as the official university liaison to the task force. The vice chancellor, in turn,
delegated the responsibility to the assistant vice chancellor for undergraduate affairs, B. (Bud) Thomas Travers.

Headed by two co-chairs, Lillian Sing, a San Francisco County
judge, and Ken Kawaichi, an Alameda County judge, the task force
spent the next six months researching the fall 1984 decline in Asian
admissions at Berkeley. The group's findings, released in June 1985,
attributed the decline in Asian admissions to a "series of deliberate
policy changes" (AATF 1985a). According to the task force, the university instituted these policy changes knowing that they would reduce Asian American freshman enrollment at Berkeley. Task force
members made four specific criticisms.

First, they charged that two policy changes, unannounced by
the university, were intentionally discriminatory against Asians: a
minimum SAT verbal test score of 400 for immigrants (subsequently
known as the "SAT 400 memo"; see Chapter 4), and the automatic
redirection of applications of Asian American students eligible for
the Educational Opportunity Program (EOP) to other University of
California campuses.[16] According to the report, "The [fall 1984 implementation of the] decision to temporarily employ a minimum SAT
verbal score to disqualify applicants and to redirect EOP students
who were not 'underrepresented minorities' (a euphemism for
Asians) . . . precipitated an unfair and devastating impact on many
unsuspecting victims—those Asian applicants who were either recent immigrants or poor and disadvantaged" (AATF 1985a:8).

This claim echoed a concern shared by Brown students about
Asian Americans and affirmative action. According to the task force,
the decision at Berkeley to redirect Asian EOP students to other University of California campuses effectively excluded Asians from the
Berkeley EOP program. According to Professor Wang, this exclusion
transformed EOP into a strictly *race-based* program for which only
"underrepresented minorities" (blacks and Hispanics) were eligible.
In contrast, the AASA at Brown *sought* a race-based affirmative action program, but not one that would exclude Asians. The AASA
report criticized plans by the Brown administration to consider only
low-income Asian applicants for affirmative action programs. The
AASA felt that all Asians, regardless of income level, should be considered.

Second, the task force argued that the decline in Asian enrollment and the drop in the Asian admission rate (from 47.4 percent of Asian applicants admitted in 1983 to 34.4 percent in 1984, compared with 61.1 percent and 48.1 percent for whites) were contrary to earlier predictions by the chancellor's office. The report noted, "The decline occurred in a period, 1979–84, when several key enrollment trend indicators, such as college-going rate, UC eligibility pool, application rate, and admission rate, instead suggested an accelerated increase in Asian American admissions. . . . The average rate of annual increase for Asian applicants between 1979 and 1984 is 21.4 percent while the rate for whites in the same period rose only 3 percent" (AATF 1985a:6).

This claim is identical to those made by ECASU and the Brown AASA that the admission rate of Asian American applicants had not kept pace with increases in the size of applicant pools. Similarly, both the task force and the Brown AASA complained that Asian admission rates were persistently lower than white admission rates.

The task force's third claim held that the introduction of a new admissions policy for the entering fall 1985 class, the two-tiered system, discriminated against Asians. In the two-tier system (see Table 2.1), applicants to Berkeley would be admitted on the basis of either strict academic criteria or a combination of strict academic plus supplemental criteria.

Through Tier 1, 50 percent of the entering class would be selected from the pool of UC-eligible students on the basis of strict academic criteria: grades and test scores.[17] The Academic Index, a newly created measure for ranking students based on strict academic criteria, was equal to the sum of the applicant's grade point average (GPA, multiplied by 1,000), SAT verbal and math scores, and three achievement test scores.

Through Tier 2, the remaining 50 percent of the entering class was to be admitted through one of two broad categories: supplemental or complemental. Supplemental category students were admitted on the basis of the Academic Index and various other criteria: the personal essay and extracurricular activities, California residency, exemption from Subject A (writing requirement), extra European foreign language courses, extra science or math courses, and attendance at a high school that does not offer honors courses. Those admitted through the complemental category were UC-eligible affirmative action students, athletes, and "special talent" students.

Table 2.1. University of California, Berkeley, Admissions, 1985–1986

Basis of admission	% of freshman class admitted, 1985	% of freshman class admitted, 1986
Tier 1	50%	40%
Strict academic criteria as measured by the Academic Index score (AIS)*		
Tier 2	50%	60%
AIS plus		
a. Supplemental criteria		
1. Essay		
2. California residency		
3. Exemption from Subject A		
4. Extra foreign languages		
5. Extra science or math		
6. Attendance at a high school with no honors courses		
b. Complemental categories (Students who meet minimum UC eligibility)		
Affirmative action students		
Athletes		
Special talent students		

*AIS = 1,000 × GPA + SAT Verbal + SAT Math + ACH1 + ACH2 + ACH3. Range of the AIS = 1,000–8,000.

    The task force said that the new policy was biased in two ways. First, the so-called a–f subject requirements (history, English, math, science, foreign language, and elective courses)—essentially prerequisites for University of California eligibility in the first tier—systematically disadvantaged Asians whose foreign language was English. The task force argued that "strict adherence to the a–f subject requirements will unfairly deny admission to those highly qualified graduates who happen to be recent immigrants" (AATF 1985a:11).

    According to the task force, a second source of bias lay hidden in the supplemental criteria. The report stated, "Not only are these criteria far more rigorous than the a–f requirements, they contain built-in biases that automatically put most recent immigrants and refugees at a disadvantaged position. Criteria such as four years of college preparatory English, four years of one foreign language or two years each of two foreign languages, exemption from Subject A, and demonstration of leadership, character, motivation, and accomplishments in extra-curricular activities are unfair to most recent immigrants" (AATF 1985:12).

Criticisms of the new policy at Berkeley were similar to claims made by the Brown AASA and ECASU concerning "subjective" criteria for admission. The Brown analogue to supplemental criteria at Berkeley were the subjective reviews by admissions officers of interviews with prospective students. The Brown AASA report claimed that Asians were academically as qualified as whites and therefore that "the disparity in Asian to White acceptances must lie in the subjective personality assessment of applicants" (AASA 1983:7).

Fourth, the task force insisted the university violated the public trust in two ways: by not announcing the policy changes, to give all applicants advance notice of changes, and by not including Asians in the decision-making process about policy that would directly affect them: "Asians were excluded from the process through which the new admission and redirection policy for Fall 1985 was formulated. . . . These exclusionary policy decisions were inconsistent with the publicly announced policies of the University, and they were made without justification and adequate input from the affected groups, and were carried out without public knowledge" (AATF 1985a:9–10). This criticism of the decision-making process in admissions was similarly made by the Brown AASA. There, the AASA concluded its report on admissions bias with the recommendation that an admissions review committee be granted wider influence and review powers in the admissions process. The task force accused Berkeley of implementing unfair admissions policies *and* additionally faulted the university for leaving Asians out of the decision-making process.

The task force report concluded with recommendations in three areas—admissions policy, the participation of Asians in policymaking, and curriculum. Regarding admissions policy, the task force members recommended that the EOP redirection policy be abolished immediately. Further, they suggested that the university move away from the use of "unreliable" indicators of academic performance, specifically, the SAT test. The task force recommended that the use of additional criteria be reevaluated and additionally that the university permit flexible application of the a–f subject requirements.

A second set of recommendations focused on the relationship

between the university and Asian Americans. The task force insisted that in order to "maintain the public trust" the university "must include Asian representatives in all committees or task forces that formulate, monitor or evaluate admissions policies" (AATF 1985a). In addition, the task force urged Berkeley to provide full cooperation with a statewide Asian community task force on Asian American concerns in higher education. Last, the task force recommended that given the ethnic diversity within the Asian community, the university should "in consultation with the Asian American community" refine the "other Asian" category on admissions applications so that the "cultural diversity and distinctive needs of each Asian subgroup" could be "recognized and better served."

The task force's third set of recommendations urged the university to take proactive steps in the curriculum. The task force called on the College Entrance Examination Board (CEEB) to develop Asian-language tests, and short of that, the university "should take appropriate steps to make sure that immigrant students are not penalized by the non-availability of proficiency tests in the Asian languages." The task force also requested that the university "teach those students with a language or mathematics deficiency instead of trying to use the pretext of their unpreparedness for UC work to exclude these otherwise excellent students." Toward that end, the task force recommended that the university "minimally appoint" one ladder-rank (tenured or tenure-track) faculty member to take charge of developing a coordinated language instruction program for students from Asia, Mexico, and Latin America. Finally, the task force demanded the university remedy any unfair rejections or redirects of students that were the result of the policy changes made in 1984.

Stanford: Why Don't More Asians Get In?

In 1983, during his junior year at Stanford, Jeffrey Au wondered why Asian Americans were not considered eligible for affirmative action recruitment in admissions. Au, a political science major, recalled that when he put this question to the Stanford admissions office he was told that Asians were not considered "underrepresented" because so many Asians were already applying to Stanford. Au thought he heard someone from the Stanford admissions office say that as many as 30 percent of applicants to Stanford were Asian.[18]

On the issue of Asians and racial preferences in undergraduate recruitment, Au agreed with the admissions office. If the proportion of Asian applicants to Stanford was as high as 30 percent, excluding Asians from racial preference in recruitment seemed justifiable. He could not understand, however, why Asians were responsible for as much as one-third of all applications but made up less than one-tenth of enrollment at Stanford.[19]

Au decided to raise his question directly with the admissions office. In 1985, he wrote a series of letters to the dean of admissions, Jean Fetter, inquiring about Asian American applications, enrollment, and admissions and suggesting that there might be evidence of discrimination and bias. As a result of this correspondence, Dean Fetter presented Au's questions and arguments before the oversight committee of the faculty academic senate. The faculty senate, in turn, appointed a subcommittee of the Committee on Undergraduate Admissions and Financial Aid to examine the matter more closely.

The subcommittee consisted of the dean of undergraduate admissions, the associate provost and registrar of the University, two faculty members, and an undergraduate student. According to Au, all of the subcommittee's statistical data and most of its analysis was provided by the Office of Undergraduate Admissions.

Au was never a member of the subcommittee investigating Asian admissions deliberations, but he was concerned that the committee's work was conducted under a shroud of "confidentiality." Shortly after the subcommittee began its investigation, Au was appointed by the academic senate to fill a student vacancy on the parent committee of the subcommittee, the Committee on Undergraduate Admissions and Financial Aid (C-UAFA). But Au recalled that even as a member of C-UAFA, he was not entitled to full access to admissions data or privy to the deliberations of the subcommittee. He received a copy of the subcommittee's thirty-page confidential report and a two-page summary of the report that was incorporated into C-UAFA's annual report to the faculty senate. But according to Au, because the report was never publicly released, neither the data nor the analysis of data has ever been independently analyzed by officials, academics, or researchers outside the Stanford admissions office.

The subcommittee spent approximately six months analyzing admissions data before concluding that Au had been right—there was some evidence of bias. The report stated, "No factor we considered can explain completely the discrepancy in admission rates between Asian Americans and whites" (*Campus Report* 1986). Although the subcommittee decided that "unconscious bias" by admissions officers in rating personality traits might have disadvantaged Asian American applicants, it also elected not to investigate the bias because "the analysis required would be formidable" (*Campus Report* 1986).

But Au was still not satisfied. He felt that the subcommittee had dodged the question of the cause of differences in white and Asian admission rates. In a letter to the subcommittee chairman, Au (1986) wrote, "My primary objection to the Subcommittee's conclusions, as they stand, is that they not only fail to resolve several key questions, but they also serve to perpetuate admittedly unsubstantiated racial stereotypes. In the absence of conclusive data, to surmise or even imply that Asian Americans, as a group, are somehow significantly and systematically deficient in terms of 'subjective' criteria, merely because some alternative hypotheses for low Asian admit rates have been disproven, seems to exacerbate rather than alleviate problems of inaccurate racial stereotyping."

Au joined in C-UAFA's unanimous adoption of the subcommittee's policy recommendations to improve admissions practices at Stanford although he objected to some of the conclusions and analysis contained in the subcommittee report. The report, or perhaps the investigation itself, seemed to have a positive impact on Asian admissions at Stanford. In 1986, the year the report was released, the Asian admission rate was 89 percent of the white admission rate, compared with 66–70 percent between 1982 and 1985. And every year since the report was released, Asian enrollment has increased at Stanford.

Unlike at Berkeley and Brown, where Asian American organizations publicized charges of discrimination against the university, Au acted as a solo lobbyist at Stanford. Talks between university officials and Asian Americans broke down at both Berkeley and Brown, but this was not the case at Stanford. Au, in fact, was one of three student members of C-UAFA. The AASA at Brown was pivotal in conducting the research and raising charges of discrimination, but there was no comparable organized *student* drive at Stanford. At Brown, Asian American student recruiters in the admissions office photocopied copies of various statistics on admission rates, enrollment, and qualifications, which formed the basis for the AASA report charging discrimination. No analogous mechanisms for student participation in admissions existed at Stanford. Instead students worked as members of the subcommittee, reviewing data and policies to address the question of bias against Asians.

But as at Berkeley, Brown, and Harvard, public access to data was also an issue at Stanford. Asian American student organizations had no inside access to the Stanford admissions office as did students at Brown. Several years after the subcommittee report was completed, members of an Asian American student organization complained that they could not gain access to admissions data. They said that their repeated requests for data on admission by ethnicity, test scores, and grade point average during the mid-1980s were always denied by admissions office staff. The Stanford student Elsa Tsutaoka recalled in 1990 that the admissions office claimed it did not keep admissions data by ethnicity and could not in any event supply students with the information, for reasons of confidentiality.[20]

Princeton: Student Inquiries Prompt Explanation

In 1985, after hearing rumors of "ceilings" on Asian American enrollment at other schools, a group of concerned Asian American students at Princeton was curious to know whether a problem existed at their school. They approached individual faculty members for help in determining how to broach the issue with the Princeton administration. In addition, the students hoped the faculty could help them gain access to, and analyze, admissions statistics. The resulting faculty group, all but one of whom were Asian American, opened a dialogue with the dean of the college, Ann Girgus, and the dean of admissions, Anthony Cummings. The faculty group, acting as a broker between the students and the admission office, met several times with campus administrators. Based on their evaluation of the data, the Princeton faculty group decided that Asian American applicants were "treated fairly within the context of Princeton's overall admissions framework." Professor Uwe Reinhardt, the only non-Asian member of the faculty committee, recalled, "We had several meetings at which the administration tried to interpret the statistics to us. They were quite informative, and, I think, sort of laid the matter to rest, maybe not totally in the minds of the students, or not totally in the minds of anyone, but basically the feeling was certainly on my part, a point had been made given the way Princeton functions."[21]

In comparison with Jeffrey Au's correspondence with the dean, which led to a formal investigation by a standing committee of the academic senate at Stanford, the inquiry into Asian admissions at Princeton was relatively informal. At Princeton, there was no final written report of a faculty committee and no formal presentation on the issue before a general assembly of the faculty. Rather, the issue of Asian admissions came and went through discussions between students/faculty and administrators. Certainly compared with the extended claims of discrimination at Berkeley and Brown, the problem of Asian admissions at Princeton seemed barely to get off the ground before the issue was quickly resolved.

Berkeley: Stalemate

In June 1985, the task force investigating Berkeley's Asian admissions distributed its report to university officials and the local media. A brief follow-up meeting between Berkeley administrators and the task force was tense and, according to one member of the task force, "unproductive."[22] Those attending the meeting included Chancellor Heyman, Vice Chancellor Laetsch, Assistant Vice Chancellor Travers, the director of the Office of Student Research Austin Frank, and Professor Wang and six other members of the task force.[23] Heyman's faculty assistant argued on behalf of the administration that admissions policy was not within the purview of the administration but, rather, was the responsibility of the academic senate. The meeting resulted in a stalemate. Both the task force and the chancellor were steadfast in their positions. Each side was angry with the other's allegations. The task force felt that the administration was not taking the allegations of bias in a "serious manner," and the chancellor was unhappy over being labeled a racist. Wang recalled, "We all left kind of disgusted because we didn't get anything, . . . we had worked very hard for six months and [even] so Heyman [only] said that he would give a formal response."[24]

Early Media Reaction to the Task Force

Professor Wang recalled that at first local media were unenthusiastic about the task force report. According to Wang, several reporters did not agree with the task force's charges of discrimination. One journalist commented that discrimination against Asians was unlikely, given that a quarter of the freshman class at Berkeley was Asian.[25]

Overall the initial tone of local media reports of the task force's 1985 report was lukewarm. Especially when compared with the tone of later reporting, these first articles were relatively nonpartisan. The *Daily Californian*, Berkeley's school paper, did not even cover the story. The *San Francisco Chronicle* covered the story, but placed the term "bias" in quotation marks, suggesting that the charges were not fully warranted. The headline ran, "Asian Americans Talk of UC Berkeley 'Bias'" (Hsu 1985). In subsequent articles over the next several years, the *Chronicle* would remove the quotation marks.

Evelyn Hsu (1985), the author of the article, listed task force charges concerning redirection, the SAT verbal minimum (the SAT 400 memo), and declining enrollments. Each charge was flatly refuted by the Berkeley officials who were quoted. The article reported that according to Travers, the SAT verbal minimum was never implemented, the move to redirect both Asians and whites to other campuses was necessitated by the demand for slots at Berkeley, and the decline in Asian enrollment was due to an overall decline in the size of the freshman class coupled with an effort to increase black, Hispanic, and Native American enrollment.

Similarly, an article in the *San Francisco Examiner* on the task force's claims presented a cursory list of allegations and, after each, offered rebuttals by university officials from the public information office and the office of the vice chancellor for undergraduate affairs (Garrison 1985). The other major local paper, located in the East Bay, the *Tribune*, reported the task force charges with a summary of the UC response (Bay City Service News 1985). All three papers noted that Chancellor Heyman would officially respond to the charges within a week.

Heyman's official response might have been anticipated by the piecemeal responses offered by Travers, Laetsch, and Ray Colvig, director of the Office of Public Information, in these first articles. Did the university discriminate against Asian Americans? Absolutely not, said university administrators. At this point, the issue of Asian admissions handled by the office of Vice Chancellor Laetsch. Other senior officials knew little or nothing of the details of the dispute, and the Berkeley administration assumed that the vice chancellor had the situation "under control." Patrick Hayashi, the first Asian American assistant to the chancellor, who was appointed in July

1986, recalled that the chancellor did not even broach the topic of Asian admissions with him until September 1986.[26] Similarly, Roderic Park, executive vice chancellor at Berkeley, recalled that Laetsch assured everyone in the chancellor's office that the university was "in the right."[27]

Berkeley's Official Response: Cumulative Errors

The university delivered its formal response in late July 1985. The response was based on a set of tables from the Office of Student Research. Director Austin Frank suggested that there were cumulative statistical errors in the task force report. He noted, "The Office has reviewed these tables in whole or in part and finds errors in varying degrees of magnitude in all tables except Table 18. In several instances the office is incorrectly cited as the data source and data in the tables do not agree with the data we have. Attached are annotated copies of the tables attributed to OSR. Elements known to be wrong in the tables are circled and occasionally the correct numbers have been written in to indicate the magnitude of the errors" (Frank 1985).

The errors discovered by the OSR varied but included incorrect totals, incorrect table titles, incorrect citation of OSR as the table source, and computational errors. In some cases, Filipino students were incorrectly counted as part of total Asian American admissions. In a few instances, the errors were trivial; total counts of over 8,000 students were off by 2 cases. But the Office of Student Research, while ferreting out errors in the tables, did not detail the substantive implications of the various kinds of errors in the task force report. Did the errors undermine the empirical evidence offered by the task force on declining enrollments of Asian American students? Were the errors statistical manipulations designed to weigh against the university? Frank's 1985 memo did not directly respond to such questions. But a letter from Assistant Vice Chancellor Travers to the task force did. Citing Frank's table corrections, the vice chancellor wrote, "Many of the errors appear relatively minor if taken individually; however, as a whole they provide an unsound basis for the analysis contained in the report" (Travers 1985). It seemed to the task force that the university was hoping to dismiss its claims on technicalities.

The official university response did not sit well with the task force. Professor Wang was pleased to see that Asian enrollment for fall 1985 had gone up from the previous year to 26.9 percent, but he remained dissatisfied that there was still no explanation for the 1984 decline. On behalf of the task force, he sent a memo to the administration pointing out that the issues raised by the task force concerning the 1984 freshman class were unresolved. He noted, "The task force is disappointed that the University response failed to address the causes of the sharp decline and the findings identified in the report. Instead, the response resorted to highlighting some inconsequential clerical and mathematical errors in an effort to minimize or dismiss the main findings and issue raised" (AATF 1985b). Calling for continued dialogue, the task force urged the university to include Asian Americans in the admissions decision-making process.

But Berkeley officials made no move to do so. As far as Vice Chancellor Laetsch was concerned, the issue of Asian admissions was over. But he was wrong. He did not anticipate that Asian admissions at Berkeley, along with charges of bias at other elite universities, would become national news in 1986.

Throughout 1986 the task force continued to accuse the university of bias in 1984 and, in addition, raised new questions of bias and discrimination in admissions for fall 1986. At the close of the year, David Gardner, president of the nine-campus UC system, in an attempt to explain and justify University of California admissions policies to a reporter, sparked further controversy when he commented that the university needed a "better ethnic mix" (*San Diego Union* 1986). In response to Gardner's comments, the task force redoubled its efforts to publicize charges of discrimination against Berkeley. Finally, in January 1987, Assistant Vice Chancellor Travers issued Berkeley's second rebuttal to task force charges of discrimination. What were the events that transpired during 1986 that escalated, rather than quieted, this controversy?

Asian Admissions: From Local Problem to National Issue

Several events stimulated wide public discussion of Asian American admissions during 1986. In May 1986, Asian admissions was one of several issues featured at a conference on anti-Asian violence held at Berkeley's law school. Although the main theme of the conference was violence against Asians, a few panels focused on other topics of interest to Asian Americans, including one on "closing the door to higher education." The three panelists, among them Professor Wang, discussed college admissions procedures in California. The next day, the story in the *Tribune* featured the panel and not the conference. The headline ran, "Asians Say Bias in Education Troubles Them," and the opening line of the article read, "Violence against Asians may be a flashier topic, but discrimination against them in education is as much a problem, says a University of California at Berkeley Professor" (Gust 1986).

Professor Wang's comments centered on admissions. He was quoted in the *Tribune* article as saying, "The university, as far as I can see, each year uses different kinds of mechanisms to affect the enrollment . . . so UC Berkeley will not be over-run with a so-called Asian invasion" (Gust 1986). "Over-run" was Wang's blunt term for what university officials would later describe as "overrepresentation" of Asians. The *Tribune* article reported that public relations director Ray Colvig, "admitted that UC has been trying to cut back on Asian enrollments" (Gust 1986). According to Colvig, the university was trying to reduce its overall student load from 31,000 students to 29,000 students (Gust 1986). And toward that goal, Colvig noted, "Berkeley has been trying to cut down all but 'underrepresented' minorities—such as blacks, Hispanics, and American Indians" (Gust 1986). According to Colvig, "Out of about 3,000–4,000 of our freshman, we were running about 30 percent Asian . . . The Asians are far, far overrepresented in terms of percentage of the population" (Gust 1986).

Then, in the fall of 1986, Asian admissions was a featured topic of discussion at a systemwide meeting of the nine campuses of the University of California. A scheduled debate on admissions featuring Wang and Laetsch ended in embarrassment for Berkeley. Laetsch, unable to attend the meeting, sent his assistant Travers. But the debate was not an even match. Recalled Professor Wang, "It was pathetic . . . he just didn't have a chance at all."[28]

Changes in Policy and Renewed Charges of Bias

Enrollment figures released in late 1986 showed yet another drop in the proportion of Asian American students at Berkeley. The fall 1986 enrollment figures showed a drop in the proportion of Asian American enrollment from 26.2 percent (1,005 Asian Americans) of the freshman class in 1985 to 25.8 percent in 1986 (875 Asian Americans). There had now been two precipitous drops in the admission rate of Asian Americans, one in 1984 and the other in 1986. Also in the fall, a memo from the director of undergraduate admissions, Robert Bailey, reported that there were 3,003 first-year students in the UC system with GPAs of 3.9 or higher who were not accepted at Berkeley but had been redirected to another campus. The memo explained that "in most cases, if a 4.0 applicant had two or more test scores under 600, they were not retained" (Bailey 1986).

The unexpected drop in the admission rate of Asian American students in 1986 along with Bailey's memo angered Professor Wang. A third revelation, that the university had changed the percentages of the entering class admitted through Tier 1 and Tier 2, only increased his dismay. The proportion of students admitted through Tier 1 and Tier 2 had been 60 and 40 percent, respectively. From 1985 to 1986, the percentage of the class admitted under the first tier dropped from 60 percent to 50 percent. In effect this change meant that a greater proportion of the entering class had entered via Tier 2 and thus had been judged on the basis of objective *and* supplemental criteria. The overall shift from 1984 to 1986 represented an increasing reliance on the supplemental criteria, which the task force believed were unfair to Asian American applicants.

A lengthy article that appeared in the *Berkeley Graduate* in November 1986 chronicled changes in policy since 1984 and indicted the university for disadvantaging Asians (Lye 1986). The article described a number of complicated changes in admissions policy and said that the two factors most responsible for the decline in Asian admissions were the elimination of Asians from EOP in 1984 and the trend toward giving increasing weight to subjective criteria and language skills.

The *Berkeley Graduate* reported that the university "without any prior notification" decided in fall 1984 not to admit any EOP applicants who were not "underrepresented minorities"—that is, blacks, Hispanics, and Native Americans (Lye 1986). The article went on to explain that the establishment of EOP in 1964 was designed to admit those students who were UC-eligible, but not necessarily competitive. But in 1984, the rules changed so that EOP students who could not "make the admissions cut with everyone else" were redirected, that is, sent to other campuses. Wang told the *Berkeley Graduate* reporter, "Now there are two classes of Asian applicants. Disadvantaged Asians can't get in, only advantaged" (Lye 1986). The article reported that the university had initiated the EOP redirect policy in

1984 because of the large number of applicants that year. Speaking for the university, Travers explained the dilemma this way: "Had we let in all the EOP students, they would have filled half the freshman class" (Lye 1986). But the *Berkeley Graduate* concluded that such policy changes disproportionately affected Asian applicants—white EOP applicants were more likely to be admitted than Asian EOP applicants.

A second major area of discrimination, according to the article, was the use of supplemental criteria in admissions. Referring to the increasing use of subjective criteria, Wang told the reporter, "We all know that Asian parents don't allow their children to participate in extracurricular activities, they insist that they stay home and study" (Lye 1986). The *Berkeley Graduate*, echoing task force claims, went on to point out that some of the "additional" criteria required by the university for admission to the second tier were redundant and punitive toward Asians. For example, in addition to the personal essay, the fulfillment of the Subject A English language requirement was also considered part of "additional criteria" (Lye 1986).

Throughout 1986, various university officials offered explanations for particular decisions or policies related to admissions in interviews with the media. As already noted, university spokesperson Colvig called Asians "overrepresented" in his defense of Berkeley policies. Leonard V. Kuhi, dean of the College of Letters and Science and chair of the Admissions Study Group, at first denied any knowledge of the SAT verbal minimum (the SAT 400 memo) and later recalled discussing such a policy only once (Lye 1986). And Assistant Vice Chancellor Travers dismissed the idea of a discriminatory ceiling on Asian admissions, saying it was a matter of competition. But these explanations did little to quiet the growing controversy.

When the *Daily Californian* reported on October 31, 1986, that the Justice Department was conducting an inquiry into the allegations that Berkeley admissions policy discriminated against Asian American applicants, neither Travers nor Assistant Dean for Undergraduate Admissions Richard Shaw knew of the investigation. Both Travers and Shaw denied that Berkeley's admissions policy was discriminatory toward Asians. In the November issue of the *Berkeley Graduate*, the Civil Rights Education chief, Nathaniel Douglas, explained that the Justice Department "expresses an interest in all discrimination controversies, but in order to launch a formal investigation—which would require the university to open all its books—the Department must first receive a written civil rights complaint. So far, none has been received" (Lye 1986).

If the Justice Department was not officially conducting an investigation, certainly the threat that such a step might be taken heightened the seriousness of the controversy. The issue of discrimination against Asians, which first pitted university officials from the chancellor's inner circle against the Asian American task force, was now broadened by the threat of a federal investigation of the university.

Media scrutiny of Berkeley admissions policies was interrupted briefly in November 1986 with the announcement by officials at Stanford University that Asian Americans there were being accepted at lower rates than whites despite equal academic qualifications. The faculty committee report, following months of investigation, found "unaccountably lower admission rates for Asians than for whites" (*Stanford Observer* 1986). One recommendation of the faculty committee was to establish a "training program on unconscious stereotyping" as part of the regular training program for admissions staff (*Stanford Observer* 1986). In addition, as a result of the report, a special assistant dean, responsible for Asian staff, was appointed.

From the Daily Californian to the New York Times

The release of the Stanford report along with prior allegations made at other schools contributed to a reinforcement in the public mind of Asian admissions as a social problem of national scope. Further supporting that image were a number of important media reports on Asian admissions that began to appear in the closing months of 1986.

Numerous articles on admissions had already appeared in local and school newspapers associated with Berkeley, Brown, Harvard, Princeton, and Stanford. But the appearance of feature-length pieces on Asian admissions from November 1986 through the early months of 1987 in the *Chronicle of Higher Education*, the *New York Times*, the *Los Angeles Times*, the *Washington Post*, and elsewhere suggested that the issue was no longer "local" problem. Headlines such as "Asian Students Fear Top Colleges Use Quotas" (Biemiller 1986), "Is There a 'Ceiling' Under the Table?" (Lye 1986), "Colleges Accused of Bias to Stem Asians' Gains" (Lindsey 1987), and "Do Colleges Set Asian Quotas?" (Salholz 1987) alerted the public to Asian American complaints of discrimination. Unlike the reserved and cautious headlines appearing in mid-1985, these sounded a clear alarm. Even an article devoted to other features of Asian American student life by Jay

Mathews (1985) for the *Washington Post*, "Asian American Students Creating New Mainstream," included a detailed discussion of the task force claims, university counterclaims, and a picture of Professor Wang.

Taken together, the media reports presented a canvas of possible systematic and broad-based discrimination against Asian Americans that, if true, would have far-reaching consequences. According to the *Chronicle of Higher Education*, the evidence for discrimination against Asian Americans was ambiguous (Biemiller 1986)—but the fact that the evidence was not plainly incontrovertible was disturbing.

Professor Wang's disappointment over the initial news coverage of Asian admissions vanished in November 1986 when the *Chronicle of Higher Education* provided a survey of the charges of bias by Asian Americans (including charges by the task force) and explanations offered by various university administrators across the country. Officials from Harvard to Berkeley emphatically denied willful intent to discriminate against Asian applicants. Wang, along with Professor Don T. Nakanishi of UCLA, faulted the top schools for unexplainable gaps between enrollment statistics, admission rates, and the demographic rise in qualified Asian American applicants. Nakanishi commented, "I think a lot of elite institutions have defined a certain number of Asians they should have on campus, and that has discriminatory outcomes. There's the argument that the Asian admissions pool is not deep, but any study shows Asians are better qualified on traditional academic measures" (Biemiller 1986).

Fred Jewett, dean of Harvard College and former admissions director at Harvard, responded to the allegation of a ceiling on Asian admissions, saying, "Harvard has a record of being quite receptive to Asian students. . . . They are an extraordinarily talented group. The academic interests of Asian students are heavily weighted toward science, which makes competition or admission in that area a little more difficult. And to some degree, the university seeks a broad national population, which could have an effect on Asian applicants at the margins—because so many come from California, Hawaii, and New York. I get no sense that there has been systematic discrimination" (Biemiller 1986).

In late 1986 Professor Wang suggested to the *New York Times* that discrimination against Asians bore an uncanny resemblance to the Jewish quotas employed by Harvard, Yale, and Princeton in the 1920s. Apparently the comparison with Jewish quotas struck gold with the media. Asian admissions moved to center stage. Professor

Wang recalled, "So, I linked the Asian issue to the Jewish quota. When that article hit, all four networks—CNN, NBC, CBS, and ABC—all called."[29]

Thus by the end of 1986 Asian admissions had made its debut in the national news as a thorny social problem in higher education. What was the problem? The media framed the issue simply enough with a single nagging question: Do the top universities in the United States use quotas or ceilings to discriminate against Asian American applicants?

The specific claims on both sides were clear. Asian applicants were alleged to be victims of discrimination by the top educational institutions in the country. At Harvard, the proportion of Asian students in the freshman class (approximately 10 to 12 percent) remained constant in spite of a virtual demographic explosion in the number of Asian applicants. At Berkeley, there had been a precipitous drop in Asian American enrollment in 1984, and following the change in admissions criteria in 1986, an unprecedented drop in the admission rate of Asian Americans. The counterclaims were also clear. University officials adamantly defended their admissions practices and insisted that there was no systematic bias. According to them, the findings that had provoked charges of bias were the result of either statistical flukes or specific features of the Asian American applicant pool.

Race and Equity

Asian American claims of discrimination cast Asian admissions into the thicket of public discussion on race and equity in higher education. The year 1986 was one in which educators and civil rights leaders expressed deep concern over the plight of minorities, particularly blacks, in American universities. One concern, sparked by a series of racial incidents on college campuses around the country, was the alarming rise in racist incidents directed against blacks. These incidents included violent fights between black and white students at the University of Massachusetts, Amherst, following the World Series; threats by "Aryan Collegiates" at the University of Texas against black students; and a Ku Klux Klan–style cross burning in front of a black sorority at the University of Alabama, Tuscaloosa (Williams 1986).

Outright violence was not the only problem. Black students

from dozens of colleges across the country spoke of verbal harassment, insults, and social isolation at school. Declining black enrollment and high drop-out rates for black students since the 1970s at the nation's colleges reinforced individual accounts of alienation.

Though several reasons have been offered for the upswing in racism, one of those most often cited was affirmative action. Dennis Wyn of the U.S. Department of Justice told the *New York Times*, "We have seen resentment on the part of white students who perceive that black students have been given a 'free ride' so to speak. White students often feel that blacks have gained admission through affirmative action, that they don't have the ability to compete academically or to be evaluated objectively on their own merit" (Williams 1986).

The backlash against affirmative action was hardly a new phenomenon in 1986. The years since the *Bakke* decision in 1978 had witnessed a rising tide of public skepticism about affirmative action. How did the plight of Asian Americans clamoring at the front doors of higher education fit with the public discussion of racism in higher education?

The racial politics of Asian admissions, not the least of which were the implications of the claims of discrimination for blacks, Hispanics, and Native Americans, were far from clear in 1986. On the one hand, claims about admissions bias suggested that Asian students shared with black students the insult of discrimination on the basis of race. On the other hand, the admissions claims also included the argument that Asians were *better* qualified than whites for admission, a claim not often made by commentators on the black experience in higher education. In later years, Asian admissions would, over the protest of the task force and others, become an important launching pad for renewed scrutiny of affirmative action. But in 1986, the assertion that Asians were turned away from the doors of higher education because they were *Asian* underscored the issue's racial dimension.

In December 1986, David Gardner reinforced the view that Asian admissions was a *racial* problem. His remarks, expressing his perspective as the University of California's highest-ranking official, acted as a kind of bellwether of systemwide thinking on Asian admissions. Until then, all counterclaims to task force charges of discrimination had been offered by administrators at the Berkeley campus.

Gardner made several key points in an interview with the *San*

Diego Union (1986). First, as had all of the administrators at Berkeley, he denied the charges of discrimination. Instead, Gardner argued, there were proportionately more Asians at the university than in the general population of the state of California. Second, suggesting that Asians had been admitted at the expense of the "truly" underrepresented, he tied Asian admissions to black and Hispanic admissions. And third, he stated that whites were slightly underrepresented at Berkeley. His counterclaims to the charges of bias, to which we will return in Chapter 3, represent an important turning point in the development of Asian admissions claims activity. Gardner suggested that admissions was a *racial* problem, but not in the same way that the task force had constructed the issue. In Gardner's view, not only were Asians not victims of discrimination, but they were threatening the enrollment of "real" underrepresented students (blacks and Hispanics).

Conflicting Notions of Equity in Asian Admissions Rhetoric

The concept of equity is central to the definition of all social problems, racial or not. Groups mobilize to make various claims because they perceive that they have been "wronged" or because they feel some condition must be rectified. They evaluate the degree and extent of the "wrong" on the basis of some notion of what is fair, just, and equitable. Asian admissions is no exception to this general feature of the production of claims and counterclaims about social problems.

In the case of Asian admissions, although the specific claims varied from school to school, a distinctive feature of claims on admissions from 1983 to 1986 is the reference to two, sometimes conflicting, notions of equity, parity and individual academic competition. The concept of parity is defined by reference to a *group*. For example, university administrators frequently refer to a group as "over-" or "under-"represented at the university, relative to the percentage or proportion of that *group* in the general population. In contrast with parity, assessments of equity based on the process of individual academic competition are predicated on an evaluation of *individual* attributes, for example, comparing individual Asian American SAT scores with individual white SAT scores. Thus parity as a concept references *group* attributes; academic competitiveness references *individual* achievement.

Charges of discrimination by Asian Americans embraced both notions of equity. Task force and ECASU arguments that Asian enrollments or admission rates were low when compared with whites, for example, were based on the assumption that Asian students were academically competitive with white students. The claim by ECASU that Asian admissions (enrollment or admission rate) had not kept pace with increases in the size of the applicant pool was based on the claim that the pool of Asian applicants was an academically competitive one. Similarly, task force claims about plunging admission rates for Asian Americans was based on the assumption that the Asian applicant pool was as likely to gain admission to Berkeley as was the white applicant pool. In other words, equal applicant pools ought to produce equal admission rates. The critical question asks whether the Asian pool of applicants is as qualified as the white applicant pool. The answer, according to the task force, was a resounding yes. The task force, the Brown AASA, and ECASU insisted that Asian applicants were academically competitive with white applicants.

But the task force also argued that academic competitiveness should not be the *sole* criteria for admission. The task force, ECASU, the AASA at Brown, and AAA at Harvard all strongly supported affirmative action as a means of redressing past wrongs against the historically "underrepresented" minorities.

Although the task force and ECASU turned to academic competitiveness of Asians to justify their claims of discrimination, they also pivoted toward parity arguments at times. One of the claims of the task force was that Asian Americans ought to be included in the admissions decision-making process. In other words, groups affected by policy ought to be represented during deliberations about policy. In calling for Asian participation in decision making, the task force invoked a notion of equity based on parity, or reference to the *group.*

Berkeley officials also embraced both notions of equity. Officials agreed that academic competitiveness was important in order to gain admission to the top schools. At Berkeley, the Academic Index score provided admissions officers with a measure of individual academic competitiveness. But Berkeley administrators also argued that Asians were overrepresented—a parity argument—to justify their admissions policies, particularly when Asians were compared with other minorities who were "underrepresented." University officials' responses will be examined in more depth in the next chapter.

For both sides, evaluations of equity, whether they were drawn from parity or academic competition, engendered important statistical and methodological questions that emerged in the later years of the admissions controversy. Two examples illustrate the types of problems inherent in each type of evaluation. Regarding the question of parity, the methodological issue concerns what group should be used as the standard. Should the proportion of blacks in the Berkeley's entering class be compared with black high school graduates in California? Black high school graduates in the Bay Area? Black high school graduates who are also UC-eligible? Each comparison group yields different parity estimates and, in some cases, may yield wildly different evaluations of whether black admissions are above, below, or on par with admissions for the comparison population. The problem with parity statistics is deciding *who* should be compared with *whom*. My own calculations suggest that, at minimum, there are 24 possible estimates of parity to evaluate a claim of discrimination.[30]

Practical methodological issues also stem from invoking academic competition as the basis for equity in admissions. Task force claims that Asian and white applicant pools to Berkeley ought to produce similar admission rates for each group are based on the premise that the pools are comparable, that is, that the pools have similar mean SAT scores, GPAs, and other academic credentials. The critical question is whether the two applicant pools are comparable. The task force says yes. But some claimants, such as ECASU, insist that the Asian pool is *more* qualified than the white pool. Although logically a more qualified pool can be expected to produce more admitted applicants, is it still justifiable to compare the more qualified pool with the less qualified pool? More to the point, in the period 1984–1986, black students did not compete with Asian students for admission to Berkeley because the applicant pools were evaluated in different "tiers" in the admissions process. Thus a critical question in evaluating academic competitiveness is with *whom* we should compare the Asian applicant pool to determine if the admission rate is too high, too low, or about right.

Chronicling Asian American charges of discrimination against various elite schools between 1983 and 1986 illustrates the awkwardness of locating Asian admissions within a racially based politics in higher education. Although the claims of discrimination identify Asian applicants as *racially* disadvantaged subjects, the rebuttals by university officials construct Asians as (nonracial) *advantaged* subjects. And from the perspective of many admissions officers and university officials, Asians were *not* minorities, racial or otherwise.

When compared with debates on the role of minorities in higher education during the 1960s and 1970s, the charges of discrimination against Asians set the political stage for interesting reversals. Whereas two decades earlier minorities and liberals had invoked parity arguments to justify creating affirmative action programs to rectify "past wrongs," in the mid-1980s, university officials—from President Gardner of the University of California to Dean Jewett of Harvard University—appealed to parity as the first line of defense against the charges that their schools were racially discriminatory toward Asian applicants. Yet the notion of merit-based advancement in higher education, encapsulated in the principle of individual academic competition, was frequently, if gingerly, used by Asian American critics of university admissions policy.

The point is not that the university officials leaned on parity arguments while the task force trumpeted individual academic competition. Rather, arguments on both sides—by university officials and by the various Asian organizations—routinely espoused, though sometimes in an implicit manner, *both* notions of equity. As a result, there is both ambiguity and irony in the way discrimination claims were framed in discourse about Asian admissions. Asian Americans were not the only ones to put forward contradictory notions of equity in their definition of the problem. But the framing of charges of discrimination between 1983 and 1986 turn out to be fertile ground for the reinterpretation and reconstruction of Asian admissions in later years.

CHAPTER 3

Diversity, Merit, and the Model Minority: "Good But Not Exceptional Students"

*B*etween 1987 and mid-1988, public discourse about Asian American admissions shifted from a focus on charges of discrimination to a focus on issues of diversity and meritocracy in admissions policy. University officials initiated this shift in the course of responding to charges of discriminatory quotas and ceilings against Asian American applicants. They made two broad countercharges. First, many officials claimed that Asian American students were overrepresented in U.S. universities. The *New York Times* reported that a Princeton faculty member, after rejecting an Asian American applicant, said to his colleagues, "You have to admit, there are a lot" (Winerip 1985). Second, several key university administrators charged that Asian American students, though qualified, were not competitive enough to gain admission to the elite schools. According to many officials, Asian American students were "flat" and "not well rounded."

Although arguments from university officials rejecting Asian American claims came at different times—for example, in 1983 at Brown, in 1985 at Princeton, and in 1988 at Harvard—the main public debate occurred in 1987 and 1988. Berkeley, where escalating tensions between the task force and the administration drew national attention, became the center of public debate.

University officials' claims about Asian American students often borrowed rhetoric from general debates about the state of contemporary higher education. Assertions that Asian American students were narrowly concentrated in technical fields and hence poor all-around candidates for the top schools mirrored concerns about excellence and merit in higher education. Similarly, claims that Asian Americans had more than their share of admissions slots reflected, and contributed to, increasing public anxiety about racial balance and diversity in undergraduate education. Several university officials insisted that merit and diversity were nice ideals in theory that did not work in practice.

The shift in the admissions debate from discrimination to diversity and meritocracy also brought into sharp relief an important change in the popular image of Asian Americans as a "model minority." Asian Americans, so frequently praised as diligent, hardworking super-students, increasingly found themselves cast as a homogeneous pool of narrow-minded, overly technical science majors. This flip-flop in image from "model minority" to academic nerd was a direct result of broader public arguments about discrimination, diversity, and meritocracy in higher education.

Racial Politics and the Model Minority

In the mid-1960s social scientists and journalists lauded Asian Americans for their successful entry into the mainstream of American life and labeled them a "model minority." William Petersen (1966), in a seminal article published in the *New York Times Magazine*, said this about Japanese Americans: "By any criterion of good citizenship that we choose, the Japanese Americans are better than any other group in our society, including native-born whites."

A core piece of the model minority image was Asian Americans' level of educational achievement (see Table 3.1). In 1960, educational attainment among Chinese Americans and Japanese Americans was on par with whites and well above that of blacks. But by 1980, Asian American subgroups boasted the highest level of educational achievement of all racial groups in the United States.

Popular images and stereotypes of minority groups, positive or negative, are constructed as racial politics within a historical context. The concept of the model minority was born in the midst of the tumultuous racial change of the 1960s. Against the backdrop of rioting in black ghettos, the "long hot summers" of the late 1960s, and mass public demonstrations for civil rights, Asian Americans ap-

Table 3.1. Median Levels of Educational Achievement, 1960–1980

	1960	1970	1980
Japanese	12.1	12.5	12.9
Chinese	11.1	12.5	13.4
Filipino	n.a.	12.2	14.1
Asian Indian	n.a.	n.a.	16.1
Korean	n.a.	n.a.	13.0
Vietnamese	n.a.	n.a.	12.4
White	10.9	12.1*	12.5
Black	8.2	9.8	12.0

Source: Compiled from U.S. Bureau of the Census, *Census of Population, 1960, 1970, 1980*, Subject Reports PC(1)1C, PC(2)1G, PC(2)1B, PC80-2-1E (Washington, D.C.: Government Printing Office); and U.S. Bureau of the Census, *Statistical Abstract of the United States, 1991*, 11th ed. (Washington, D.C.: Government Printing Office).
*Whites in non-Southern states.

peared to be a relatively quiescent minority. There were no Asian American counterparts to fiery black political leaders such as H. Rap Brown, Malcolm X, Stokely Carmichael, and Martin Luther King, Jr., nor was there an Asian American equivalent of, for example, the Black Panthers.

To many whites, Asian American achievement sounded an encouraging note in what was otherwise a threatening and uncertain period of racial politics. Angered by black criticism of the "white establishment," some whites pointed to Asian American achievement as evidence that racial minorities could get ahead in America, if only they would "try." There were numerous media stories featuring Asian American "Horatio Algers"—Vietnamese immigrants who became class valedictorians, Koreans who built thriving businesses from scratch, Chinese and Japanese who overcame a legacy of discrimination and went on to become doctors, lawyers, and other professionals. Black critics responded that invidious comparisons between black rage in the cities and Asian achievement in schools was unfair. According to some, the black experience was a deeper and more complicated oppression than the Asian experience, and comparisons between Asians and blacks were therefore misleading. As Martin Luther King said, "we would pull ourselves up by our bootstraps if we had boots."

Some Asian Americans were quick to disown the "model minority" label; they charged that the concept was inaccurate, ahistorical, and racially biased.[1] But despite their protests, the popular image of Asian Americans as a hard-working, diligent, and family-oriented minority lingered through the 1980s. The stereotype cannot be waved away as media hype. With respect to college admissions, Asian Americans have dazzled administrators and admissions officers with their impressive grade point averages and high SAT scores. In California, for example, on the basis of strict academic criteria alone, Asians are the best-prepared group to enter the UC system.[2] Across the country, Asian Americans have been the fastest-growing sector of the applicant pool to the top colleges and universities since the early 1980s.[3] According to the standards deployed by university admissions officers, the quality of the Asian American college applicant pool has been excellent.[4] Anna Quindlen (1987), a *New York Times* reporter, summed it up this way: "Asian American students have a special place in the American consciousness right now. They are perceived as intelligent, diligent, and mature, with a strong sense of responsibility."

But the educational achievement of Asian American students was, and continues to be, followed by a wave of reaction. The image of Asian Americans as diligent super-students has often kindled resentment in other students. Sometimes called "damned curve raisers," a term applied first to Jewish students at elite East Coast colleges during the 1920s and 1930s, Asian American students have increasingly found themselves taking the brunt of campus racial jokes.

In the late 1980s, white students' anxiety about Asian American students combined nineteenth-century racist stereotypes of Asians as "hordes" of "unfair competition" with contemporary images. Articles in the popular press reported that some white students claimed that M.I.T. stood for Made in Taiwan and that U.C.L.A. stood for University of Caucasians Living Among Asians.[5] At some schools, high concentrations of Asian Americans in math and science earned the local elevators in those buildings the name "The Orient Express." On many college campuses, college seniors only half-jokingly advised freshmen to avoid classes with high Asian enrollments.[6] Their advice was based on the belief that white students "don't have a chance" against all that Asian American "unfair competition."

White students' resentment toward Asian Americans resonated with American corporate dread of Sony, Mitsubishi, and Toyota. As the dollar plunged against the yen, so did white tolerance of Asians across the Pacific. The emergence of a phenomenon known as "Japan bashing" in the late 1980s only reinforced popular anxiety that American corporations and schools were losing their competitive edge against Japan. Fear that the Japanese were "taking over" was fueled by a Japanese investment spree in American corporate icons ranging from Rockefeller Center in New York to Pebble Beach in California.[7]

White nervousness about the model minority was humorously captured by the cartoonist Gary Trudeau. A nationally syndicated Doonesbury strip shows Kim, a National Merit scholar, talking with her high school teacher (Trudeau 1989). The teacher, offering congratulations on her achievement, says, "It's very good news for the school, it demonstrates that the failure of so many kids to learn here isn't just the school's fault. It reaffirms the importance of discipline and personal motivation." Kim responds that not everyone in the community agrees. In the last panel, Kim's parents are talking with some neighbors, who are pleading, "She's throwing off the curve for the whole school! Couldn't you get her to watch more TV?" (Trudeau 1989).

If, as Trudeau suggested, white students and their parents were apprehensive about competing against Asian American "whiz kids" in school, university officials held a different perspective. They, unlike the anxious white parents depicted by Trudeau, insisted that the achievement of Asian American students be critically evaluated against the need for more diversity in higher education. The *Los Angeles Times* noted: "It is inevitable, say UC administrators, that as the number of blacks and Latinos is increased to meet the legislative mandate, the Asian and white populations on campus will be squeezed" (L. Mathews 1987). Other officials suggested that Asian American students were simply not sufficiently qualified to gain admission to the top schools. One Harvard administrator explained, "family pressures make more marginal students apply" (Bell 1985).

Overrepresentation, Merit, and Diversity

In their discourse about Asian admissions, university officials persistently sounded themes of overrepresentation, merit, and diversity. Although the specific claims of varied considerably, they shared several general characteristics.

First, from both public and private universities, the response to accusations of discrimination was the same: administration officials unequivocally denied the charges. Formal investigations produced mixed results. At Brown and Stanford, university-sponsored studies conceded that the admissions process was biased against Asian American applicants. At Princeton, a university committee found no evidence of bias. At Harvard, no investigation was performed by an independent faculty committee, but admissions officers conducted an in-house study and found no evidence of bias. At UCLA, similarly, there was no faculty committee investigation, but top administrators assured the public that there had been no foul play. At Berkeley, where the controversy had been the most embittered, investigations by two different faculty committees took over three years to conclude that there was no systematic bias against Asian American applicants.

Second, regardless of the outcome of the investigations, university officials responded by parlaying facts about Asian American admissions into broad public discussion of diversity and merit. Some administrators denied that they used quotas to limit the number of Asian Americans in each freshman class, and they used different statistics to argue that Asians were in fact overrepresented at the university. Others accepted the figures used by Asian American critics but insisted that differential admission rates of whites and Asians were statistically explainable. Still other officials conceded that their policies were discriminatory but denied that the policies were meant to be so.

In their analysis of the facts of admissions, university officials cited two interdependent levels of evaluation in the admissions process and, correspondingly, used two types of arguments to refute charges of discrimination. One level concerned the individual *merit* of student applicants. All of the elite public and private universities in the United States admit students on the basis of "objective" criteria (grades, test scores, and indicators of academic achievement) *and* "subjective" criteria (extracurricular activities, personal interviews, personal essays). Although the relative importance of objective to subjective criteria varies considerably from school to school, the important point is that all of the top schools use "subjective" criteria to evaluate applicants. At the highly selective private schools, admissions officers rate students' leadership qualities and creative potential on the basis of essays and individual interviews. Other schools, Berkeley, for example, use a set of "selection criteria" tain features of an individual application. According to some university officials, Asian American students often did not score high enough on the objective, the subjective, or both parts of the evaluation to gain admission. In other words, Asian American students were outflanked by others in the individual competition for admission slots. The charge that some Asian Americans students were not good enough to get into the top schools was at odds with Asian American claims about the quality of these students. Claims by university officials, in turn, spurred an angry reaction from some Asian American students and faculty.

A second level of evaluation was the "admissions context," which refers to the fluid use of criteria by admissions officers to select a composite group of students for the freshman class. Within an admissions context, students are selected on the basis of their contribution to the composition of the class as a whole as well as on the basis of their individual accomplishments. All of the admissions officers I interviewed stressed the importance of "building" an entering class of individuals with mixed talents who hail from a variety of social backgrounds. For example, the official register of Harvard and Radcliffe, a publication for prospective applicants that describes the Harvard admissions process as "complex, subjective, and sometimes difficult to comprehend," states: "we believe that a mixture of particular excellences will produce the most stimulating intellectual environment and satisfying educational experience for all" (Official Register 1988).

Bob Lee, director of minority affairs and former admissions officer at Brown University, felt that the Ivy league depiction of the "ideal class" was more fable than fact. He said, "admissions at Brown, and I suspect everywhere else, is an extraordinarily mystified system. It's very ideological in the sense that it's kind of the ideology of creating the ideal class, you know it's this kind of mythic notion."[8]

Without exception, all of the top public and private universities use the term *diversity* to describe the ideal mix of a freshman class. Marvin Bressler, chair of the Princeton sociology department, told a reporter for *Newsweek*, "the concept universities love beyond all others is diversity. But it's a highly flexible word" (Salholz 1987). The term is a relatively recent addition to the lexicon of college admissions. The concept of constructing a class of mixed talents *and* races is a relatively recent phenomenon, as well, a legacy of the civil rights movement of the 1960s.

But the use of supplemental criteria to make admissions decisions is not new. The introduction of additional criteria (such as regional diversity) in college admissions has been traced to efforts by administrators at the Big Three (Harvard, Yale and Princeton) to limit Jewish enrollment during the 1920s.[9] At Berkeley, officials explained that selection criteria were introduced in an era in which the demand for slots exceeded supply. Among the elite private schools, admissions officials feel the use of additional criteria allows them to select the "cream" of athletes, children of alumni, creative talents, student leaders, and disadvantaged students.

Third and finally, as in the 1983–1986 period, facts and statistics continued to be an important part of claims. University officials countered Asian American charges of discrimination with a barrage of facts about enrollment and admissions. Sometimes officials made these data public; more often, they did not. Citing confidentiality, most of the private schools refuse to provide detailed admissions data by race and qualification.[10] As a result, availability and access to the facts continued to be a sore point.

The facts and statistics used by university officials were the same ones used by their Asian American critics. Yet one side reached conclusions very different from those of the other side. The exchange of claims between representatives of the university and Asian Americans suggests that although the debate was quite technical, facts alone were insufficient for a resolution of differences between the two sides.

Each of these features of officials' discourse—counterclaims; the rhetoric of overrepresentation, merit and diversity; and efforts to shift the discourse from discrimination to diversity—are evident in the local responses to Asian American claims of discrimination.

Brown: Academic Balance

Brown University was the first school to receive and respond to complaints of discrimination against Asian Americans. Jim Rogers, director of admissions at Brown, dismissed the claims. Many Asian American applicants, he said, were turned away from Brown because of their choice of major, not because of their race. Rogers explained to the reporter Michael Winerip (1985) of the *New York Times*, "The vast majority of Asian Americans applying here, 70–75 percent, are premedical students. The question is not one of race, it's academic balance."

But Asian American students and staff at Brown insisted that discussions about Asian American applicants in the admissions office were often racial. Grace Tsuang, a former member of the Minority Review Committee in the admissions office recalled that "some outrageous things were said."[11] According to Tsuang, admissions officers described Asian applicants "as having bad profiles, they don't have enough extracurriculars to be admitted at a high rate, and they're all pre-meds."[12]

In the spring of 1983, the Brown Asian American Students Association presented its "prima facie" case of racial discrimination to the Board of Trustees, the governing body of Brown University. The trustees, in turn, delegated the Committee on Minority Affairs to review AASA complaints. COMA initially sided with Rogers, not the AASA. According to Bob Lee, then assistant dean, COMA members, composed mainly of black alumni and a few white faculty members, challenged both the data and the conclusions of the AASA presenters. But a reluctant COMA agreed to conduct a formal investigation of the AASA charges. All of the black members of COMA, however, refused to sit on the investigation committee. As a result, the COMA investigation committee was composed of white faculty members, student representatives, and one black faculty member who was not a member of COMA.

The findings of the COMA-sponsored investigation vindicated AASA claims of discrimination (COMA 1984). The COMA report concluded that differential admission rates between whites and Asians constituted an "extremely serious" problem, as were the attitudes of some officials in the admissions office. According to Bob Lee, admissions officers interviewed by faculty investigators confirmed many of the allegations and charges of racial discrimination raised by the AASA. In one instance, Director Rogers is alleged to have quipped that the task of shrinking the admitted class could be accomplished by cutting the first ten Kims off the top of the list. In addition to the COMA investigation, a separate study by the Committee on Admission and Financial Aid (CAFA) also confirmed AASA complaints of discrimination.

COMA made seven recommendations, including policy revision, annual training of admissions officers to be responsive to the social, cultural, and economic backgrounds of minority applicants, and improved public accessibility to admissions statistics and data. Although the recommendations did not prompt any major shifts in the organization of Brown admissions, there were some important developments. For example, COMA recommended regular evaluations of the admissions process and provisions for Asian American participation in the admissions process. Though the Brown AASA would have liked Rogers to be replaced, this was not one of the final recommendations of COMA. Director Rogers continued to head Brown admissions until 1988, when he resigned to work in the private sector and was replaced by Dean Eric Widmer.

Stanford: Latent Bias

A faculty committee investigating bias against Asian American applicants at Stanford reached a conclusion similar to COMA's at Brown. In late 1986, after investigating Jeffrey Au's inquiries about Asian admissions, the Committee on Undergraduate Admissions and Financial Aid (C-UAFA) began a self-study of the school's admissions practices. The committee found "unaccountably lower admissions rates for Asians than whites," though there was no evidence of "implicit quotas or conscious discrimination" (*Stanford Observer* 1986). Addressing the academic senate, the chair of C-UAFA referred to the problem as one of "latent" bias against Asian Americans and promised that such bias would be removed from the Stanford admissions process. Thus at Stanford, as was the case at Brown, differences in admission rates between whites and Asian Americans were interpreted as hard evidence of bias.

Stanford officials, like many administrators at elite universities, speak about their school in tones of pride and loyalty. Jean Fetter, dean of admissions at Stanford, was no exception. In 1986, just after the C-UAFA findings were released, she accepted the findings but was reluctant to assign blame to the institution or to any individuals associated with the university.[13] When Professor Harumi Befu wrote a letter to the *Campus Report* suggesting that the university owed an apology to Asian Americans, he was summoned to a private meeting with Fetter and several other school officials and told he had "no right to say things like that."[14] According to Befu, Fetter said, "Why do we have to apologize? We did nothing wrong."[15] Then as now, the actual C-UAFA report remains confidential. Professor Befu recalled that without adequate facts, he was unable to engage Fetter in a debate. Frustrated by the lack of evidence and her challenge, Befu remembered, 'Well, what kind of a discussion is this? She knows all the cards I have and I don't know the cards she has. You can't play a game like that. So, I said, 'Well, there's not much to talk about' and I left. I thought of writing to the *Campus Report* once more reporting on this meeting, but I thought it would be counterproductive."[16]

Princeton: Not Enough Asian Alumni

In contrast with the findings at both Brown and Stanford, a faculty-student investigation at Princeton in 1985 reached a different conclusion. Whereas at Stanford different admission rates for whites and Asians were taken as evidence of bias, the same differences were not interpreted as bias at Princeton.

At Princeton, as at most of the Ivy League schools, admissions is divided into two general areas of evaluation: academic criteria and nonacademic criteria. Professor Reinhardt, a member of a group of faculty concerned about Asian admissions, explained, "A university such as ours will have preferred candidates that are preferred for one reason or another reason, which would mean if academics were the same, we would prefer such and such, and the preference criteria are alumni. You'd rather have a hockey player with a B average than a nerd with an A average who can't play hockey."[17]

The Princeton in-house study found that for four of the five years between 1981 and 1985, Asian American applicants were rated higher than whites in the academic portion of the evaluation. Asian Americans were rated "below average," however, in the nonacademic portion of the evaluation for the five-year period. Thus, according to the Princeton study, the difference between the overall Asian and white admission rates was explainable by factors other than bias. Anthony Cummings, director of admissions at Princeton, told the *New York Times* in 1985, "One of the things that worked against Asian American applicants is that they are underrepresented among groups given preference for general undergraduate admission—such as athletes, blacks and the children of alumni" (Winerip 1985). The admission rate of alumni children at Princeton was approximately 48 percent, the overall admit rate of white students was 17 percent, and the overall admit rate of Asian Americans was lower still, 14 percent (Winerip 1985).

The explanations offered by Director Rogers at Brown and Director Cummings at Princeton prefigured the basic arguments in public debate over admissions between 1987 and mid-1988. The problem, according to Rogers and Cummings, was that discrimination against Asians should have been evaluated within the context of a broad framework of admissions. In this context, Asians were not members of any preference groups. In addition, private school officials such as Cummings and Rogers believed another part of the explanation for the differential between Asian and white admission rates lay in the poor performance by Asian students in the subjective evaluations by admissions officers. Because elite private schools do not admit on the basis of grades and tests scores alone, students must be rated highly on both subjective and objective criteria in order to gain admission.

Harvard: Statistical Fiction

Between 1986 and 1987, commentators on Asian admissions, journalists and academics alike, frequently mentioned Harvard. But Harvard, like other private universities, was not the lightening rod of controversy that Berkeley was. Linda Mathews (1987), reporting for the *Los Angeles Times Magazine*, commented: "Oddly, though their Asian American populations lag far behind the University of California's in actual numbers and percentages, the private universities have been spared the harsh criticism directed at the UC system."

A partial explanation for Harvard's buoyancy in the public discourse on admissions may be its policy that admission rates by race and other qualifications (such as SAT scores) are confidential.[18] But though the Harvard admissions office has exempted itself from close scrutiny by outsiders, the university has hardly escaped public debate.

Several writers were skeptical about Harvard's admissions policies because Asian American enrollment remained suspiciously constant through the first half of the 1980s. In early 1987 Professor Wang told the *New York Times*, "As soon as admissions of Asian students began reaching 10 or 12 percent, suddenly a red light went on. At Berkeley, Stanford, MIT, Yale, in fact all of the Ivy League schools, admission of Asian Americans has either stabilized or gone down" (Lindsey 1987). Ben Wattenberg (1987) of the *Washington Times* posed the question: "Does Harvard discriminate against admitting potential Nobel Prize winners?" His answer: "My recent reading offers a roundabout answer: probably so." Wattenberg (1987) profiled a University of Houston physicist, Chin-wu Chu, a competitor for the Nobel Prize for research on superconductivity. The problem, according to Wattenberg, was that future generations of Chus might not have the same chance of admission to Harvard as their white counterparts. Wattenberg lamented that Harvard would lose its status as a world-class university by denying admission to world-class scholars.

More concrete charges of discrimination were marshaled by John Bunzel, a senior research fellow at the Hoover Institution, and Jeffrey Au, the Stanford undergraduate who had prompted Stanford's self-study of admissions. Having managed to gain access to 1982 Harvard admissions data, Bunzel and Au discovered differential white and Asian admission rates. According to Bunzel and Au (1987) the Asian admission rate was 74 percent of the white rate. More disturbing, Bunzel and Au argued that Asian American applicants had to be better qualified than whites in order to gain admission to Harvard. Among those admitted, "the figures suggest that in order to be offered admission, Asian Americans had to score an average 112 points higher on the SAT than the Caucasians who were admitted" (Bunzel and Au 1987:55).

In 1985 Susie Chao, a junior at Harvard who would later join the admissions office as director of minority recruitment, told the *New York Times* that admissions officers from Harvard, Yale, and Princeton met with Asian American faculty and students to discuss Asian admissions in early 1985. She recalled, "we discussed why certain Asian Americans' folders seemed kind of flat, all science and math" (Winerip 1985). In 1986 Dean Fred Jewett told the *Chronicle of Higher Education*, "Harvard has always rejected some valedictorians in favor of those who bring other talents—we are choosing people who bring talents underrepresented in the applicant pool" (Biemiller 1986). Denying charges of a possible ceiling on Asian admissions, Jewett offered several explanations for the 1985 differential admission rate of Asians (12.5 percent) and whites (15.9 percent). "Arguments over numbers ignore a whole range of personal qualities," Jewett said. He also suggested that because Asian American applicants were concentrated in California, Hawaii, and New York, Harvard's quest for a broad national population might have a disproportionate impact on these applicants. Finally, according to Jewett, Harvard's use of alumni preferences were also a possible explanation for different white and Asian admission rates.

Two years later, officials from the admissions office statistically confirmed Jewett's alumni preferences explanation. In early 1988, in a two-page statement on Asian American admissions that called claims of discrimination "media speculation," Director of Minority Recruitment Susie Chao and Dean of Admissions William Fitzsimmons rejected accusations of discriminatory admissions practices as statistical fiction (Chao and Fitzsimmons 1988). They argued that differences between white and Asian admit rates disappeared after controlling for extracurricular activities and alumni status: "While Asian Americans are slightly stronger than whites on academic criteria, they are slightly less strong on extracurricular criteria. In addition, there are few Asian-Americans in our applicant pool who are alumni/ae children or prospective varsity athletes. When all these factors are taken into account, the difference in admission rates for the two groups disappears" (Chao and Fitzsimmons 1988:1).

Berkeley officials too argued that differences in admission rates were a statistical fluke—in this case a product of preferences for the "underrepresented," not alumni children. Obviously a key difference between the admissions practices of these two schools was that alumni preferences were an important factor at Harvard but nonexistent at Berkeley. Also, unlike Berkeley officials, Chao and Fitzsimmons did not issue the countercharge that Asians were overrepresented among Harvard undergraduates. These two officials disagreed with the notion of Asian overrepresentation. Chao and Fitzsimmons (1988:1) wrote, "Some recent articles contend that the increasing numbers of Asian American students at selective colleges reduce diversity in the student body. Nothing could be further from the truth. Asian Americans bring with them an enormous breadth of individual talents. The admissions committee understands and is sensitive to the cultural differences and great diversity within the Asian American community, which spans many countries of origin, languages, and sub-groups." In dissociating themselves from the overrepresentation claim and in interpreting differential admission rates as a bogus indicator of discrimination, Harvard officials hewed a position on the problem of Asian admissions distinct from those adopted by the other elite schools.

Diversity, 1987–1988

The themes of overrepresentation and academic merit became most pronounced in 1987 and 1988 during the public discussion of Asian

American student admissions at Berkeley. Assistant Vice Chancellor Travers had expected the flap over Asian admissions to fade quietly after the university issued its eight-page response to the task force report in 1985. The next year, various Berkeley officials defended the school's admissions policies in response to regular inquiries from the media. Frank Baratta, research coordinator of admissions services for the University of California, cited what would become a recurring theme: "Asians are overrepresented by three times their high-school population" (Biemiller 1986). The task force maintained, however, that parity—that is, an Asian admissions rate that reflected the fact that Asians constituted 6 percent of the state population—ought not be viewed as an upper limit on Asian American enrollment at Berkeley.

In 1987, after nearly two years of persistent debate over Asian admissions, Travers, now one of the main spokespersons on the issue for Berkeley, issued a second explanation of the admissions problem. His fourteen-page letter, addressed to the Asian American community and interested parties, staunchly defended university admissions policy. Travers recalled that he wrote the 1987 letter because "the thing that troubled me was that a lot of what was being said in my mind demeaned a lot of the qualities and success of Asians at Berkeley. And so one thing I tried to do was to say, okay, you have concerns about this or that policy or what is happening, or whatever, but also be aware about the success of Asian students at Berkeley, both historically and at the particular point in time that we were looking at."[19] Travers (1987) called the controversy a "public misunderstanding" that he hoped would be cleared up by his letter.

The letter boasted that the University of California had the second-highest enrollment of Asian Americans in the United States: "Ours is a success story: we have a rich and talented pool of applicants from which to draw upon to fill our freshman class. The caliber of our students attests to our excellent results in admitting and encouraging students from all ethnic groups to choose Berkeley for their undergraduate studies" (Travers 1987).

Travers's (1987) primary explanation for the drop in Asian admissions was that "Cal began reducing its freshman class size and coincidentally experienced a drop in the overall number of Asian students who were admitted and who accepted." Citing data on the freshman class entering the College of Letters and Science and the College of Engineering at Berkeley in the fall of 1986, Travers found that on the basis of strict academic criteria (i.e., the Academic Index score, for which the top score is 8,000), there was "no difference for students with 7000 or more, between the percent of Asian and the percent of whites admitted to either college." He also found that among those admitted for the fall of 1987 through Tier 2, in which students were evaluated on the basis of objective and supplemental criteria, Asians and whites had equivalent admission rates, at 37 percent. According to Travers, this showed "that fears that Asian students would be discriminated against on the basis of these criteria are unfounded."

University officials defended the supplemental criteria as part of their solution to the more general problem facing the UC system. That problem was to maintain what President David Gardner called a "desirable ethnic mix" in an era of unprecedented demand for admission. In late 1986, in an interview with the *San Diego Union*, President Gardner explicitly linked Asian admissions and diversity: "Twenty to twenty-five percent of our undergraduate enrollment are Asian Americans, while they represent 6 percent of the population of the state. This is part of a much larger and more complicated issue, and I think it's only within the context of that larger picture that I can give you a reasoned response. The number of black and Hispanic youth enrolled in the University of California is not below their rate of UC eligibility but it is below their rate of proportional representation with the high school graduation pool" (*San Diego Union* 1986).

Since 1974, the University of California had been governed by a state legislative resolution recommending that the ethnic mix of the student body match the ethnic mix of the state's high school graduates.[20] The goal of proportional representation of ethnic minorities had been satisfied for Asian American students, but was difficult to attain for black and Hispanic students. Travers suggested that the university in effect had its hands tied on the issue of proportional representation. He told the *Chronicle of Higher Education*, "We could fill up half the freshman class with Asians, but that wouldn't be acceptable to the legislature" (Biemiller 1986).

At Berkeley, university officials argued that growth in demand for admission slots was mainly an *Asian American* demand. White student admissions had declined at Berkeley in the face of what appeared to be a growing and well-qualified Asian applicant pool.[21] According to the task force, it was the declining white student population at Berkeley that really worried administration officials. Henry Der, a member of the task force and the executive director of Chinese for Affirmative Action, suggested, "Berkeley has the chance of being a major Asian university. Does that scare people? It shakes the socks off their feet" (Nakao 1987). Travers fueled such task force suspicions, saying, "If we keep getting extremely well prepared Asians, and we are, we may get to the point where whites are an affirmative action group" (Nakao 1987).

Other university officials argued that the supplemental criteria added diversity to the freshman class because students needed more than good grades and high test scores to attend Berkeley. Vice Chancellor Laetsch told the *Los Angeles Times* that the supplemental criteria added "some necessary human element" to admissions decisions: "If we had a system based purely on the Academic Index, we'd get a very homogenous student body. And we'd be putting our faith in standardized tests whose value is often in dispute. We'd be rejecting some students whose test scores were only a few points lower than those who were admitted; the system would be based on very fine and meaningless gradations. Using the supplemental criteria, we think we get the better, more interesting students—not just the good test takers" (L. Mathews 1987).

Members of the task force rejected Travers's assertion that the supplemental criteria were fair;[22] they argued that the criteria were intentionally aimed at limiting the number of Asian students at Berkeley. Henry Der criticized what Laetsch extolled as the "human element" of supplemental criteria as administrative "latitude" in admissions decisions (L. Mathews 1987). Task force co-chair Ken Kawaichi charged university officials with clinging to an "idealized" picture of the racial mix of a campus. He accused them of believing that a campus "should be predominantly white, maybe 70 percent" (L. Mathews 1987).

Still upset at what they felt was an unfair shift toward supplemental criteria in 1986, task force members were further angered by the 1987 policy changes. They renewed their objections of 1985: the supplemental criteria were difficult for Asian immigrant students to meet. In particular, the task force protested the decision to award supplemental criteria points for foreign language study and exemption from Subject A. Der explained, "In the 1960s, admission to UC was based on high school grade point averages. In the 1970s, UC began to take into consideration SAT scores. We could live with that. . . . But in the 1980s, we've seen UC start paying attention to so-called supplemental criteria, which means subjective criteria. That change works to the detriment of Asian-American applicants, so it's very valid to raise the question of whether admissions criteria are being manipulated to keep our numbers down" (L. Mathews 1987).

University officials continued to insist that Asian "overrepresentation" be viewed within the context of racial diversity of the student body. Gardner had outlined the limited set of options in late 1986: either the application of quotas or the application of supplemental criteria. Rejecting the possibility of quotas, Gardner said, "If we continue on the present path, it inevitably will lead to quotas, so I don't wish to continue on this path. It seems to me that we need to take account of more variables in the backgrounds of these people than ethnicity and grades" (*San Diego Union* 1986).

The task force bristled at what it believed were unacceptable choices offered by Gardner. Professor Wang (1986), in a letter to Gardner, commented, "Even though you forthrightly spoke out against 'any form of ethnic quota system' and against any admissions criteria aimed at 'punishing Asians,' the gist of your comments in fact points to the need to reduce the so-called 'overrepresentation' of Asians."

The problem of Asian admissions refused to go away. Explanations by Gardner and Travers, intended to defuse the controversy, only seemed to inflame it further. Neither the media nor the task force members were satisfied with the explanations offered. The task force continued to assert that admissions policies at Berkeley discriminated against Asians; university officials defended themselves by saying that the real problem was that Asian overrepresentation was undermining diversity. The supplemental criteria formed the great barrier between university claims of diversity and task force claims of discrimination.

The Media as Participant in Asian Admissions

Media accounts of the issue often leaned favorably in the direction of claims by Asian Americans, a fact duly noted by Harvard officials in their 1988 memo (Chao and Fitzsimmons 1988). In the first half of 1987, articles with headlines such as "Colleges Accused of Bias to Stem Asians' Gains" (Lindsey 1987), "Thorny Debate at UC: Too Many Brainy Asians?" (Nakao 1987), and "When Being Best Isn't Good Enough" (L. Mathews 1987) filled the pages of the *New York Times*, the *Los Angeles Times*, and the *San Francisco Examiner*. Although some writers strove to present a balanced view of claims by Asian Americans and the counterclaims by university officials, many abandoned neutrality.

A prime example of media support for the task force position on supplemental criteria, mentioned by university officials and members of the task force alike, were the sympathetic news stories of highly talented Asian American individuals who had been rejected by Berkeley. Perhaps the best-known case of media coverage angled to feature the "human interest" side of Asian admissions featured a young man named Yat-pang Au. Yat-pang's case may not be a convincing example of anti-Asian discrimination, but the zeal and tenor with which journalists covered his rejection from Berkeley made him a cause célèbre, bringing the issues involved into the public spotlight.

Yat-pang, the eldest son of immigrant parents, accumulated an impressive Academic Index score of 7,210 out of 8,000. His academic prowess was matched by an inspiring set of extracurriculars—he ran track, taught math to fifth-graders, and was a student leader in the math and science clubs at San Jose's Gunderson High School. In spite of his stellar high school record, Yat-pang could not gain admission to Berkeley's School of Engineering. The Los Angeles Times Magazine reported it this way: "And yet one goal, the honor he had most coveted to cap his high school years, eluded Yat-pang. He was rejected by the University of California, Berkeley. At least ten other students from Gunderson High will be entering Berkeley this fall, but not Yat-pang" (L. Mathews 1987).

Under Tier 1 criteria, Yat-pang's Academic Index score was shy of the 7,550 points necessary to gain admission to the engineering school. But Yat-pang felt that he should have been admitted through Tier 2 when supplemental criteria were taken into account. Pointing to his array of extracurricular activities, Yat-pang told the Los Angeles Times, "I am not a nerd" (L. Mathews 1987). Laetsch responded that Yat-Pang was a "good but not exceptional student" and warned that "you play in that sandbox, you have to understand you're taking a chance" (L. Mathews 1987).

Privately, many university officials were unhappy with their public image in the Yat-pang case. Later that year, in an unpublished report on Asian admissions, Professor Scott Lynn would label the Yat-pang incident a case of "slanted journalism" (see Chapter 4). He chided the Los Angeles Times for leaving out "the fact that 7 applicants (3 Asians and 4 whites) were denied [entry to the School of Engineering] who had Academic Index scores higher than Mr. Au's, and that the only admission of an applicant with a lower academic index score was by affirmative action" (Lynn Committee 1987).[23]

The elite private schools found themselves, perhaps inadvertently, snared in the net of media scrutiny cast over Berkeley. Task force criticisms at Berkeley were easily extendable to other elite universities and colleges. Officials from private schools hastily distinguished their admissions process from that of other schools, particularly the University of California, saying, "We don't use formulas."[24] But all of the top private schools used (and use) nonacademic criteria as a basis for admission. That admissions officers from private universities were mute when it came to describing how they made fine distinctions among the best and brightest applicants may have contributed to popular perception of their culpability. Although these officers openly described the admissions process—for example, the number of times a file was read and by whom—they said it was impossible to detail the actual decision making in admissions. By that, they meant that the decision to admit a student was dependent on a combination of factors, including a student's "overall profile" in the context of constructing a diverse class. In contrast to the University of California, where diversity often referred to the *racial* mix of a class, private school administrators used diversity to refer to a broad range of attributes an individual applicant might have—including alumni status, socioeconomic status, race, and athletic prowess.

Though often sympathetic to the task force, media accounts were quick to pick up the juxtaposition of merit and diversity suggested by many different university administrators. At about the same time that Travers issued Berkeley's second denial of university wrongdoing, the *New York Times* reported that "officials at some institutions, who did not want to be publicly identified, say that they oppose the use of quotas for moral reasons but that the influx of Asian students is causing a growing problem for some academic policy makers. Among other things, they say, it threatens efforts to maintain a diverse student body, especially in engineering and science classes that are especially popular among students with Chinese, Japanese, Korean, Vietnamese and other Asian backgrounds" (Lindsey 1987).

Offering the public a short and pithy discourse of contrasting images of the problem—discrimination and diversity, pure meritocracy and supplemental criteria, Asian nerds and Asian whiz kids—news articles and editorials with headlines such as "Everyone Needs Affirmative Action" (Alleyne 1987) and "When White Guilt Won't Matter Anymore" (Raspberry 1987) warned that blacks and whites would be the losers in unfettered competition with Asians. The fresh concern for diversity rather than discrimination was echoed by the Harvard sociologist Professor emeritus David Riesman, who told *Newsweek*, "Stanford could become 40 percent Jewish, 40 percent Asian American and 10 percent requisite black. You'd have a pure meritocracy, and that would create problems for diversity and alumni" (Salholz 1987).

Whites were not the only ones who seemed more concerned with diversity than with discrimination. Dorothy Gilliam (1987) of the *Washington Post* cited the former Nixon official William "Mo" Marumoto's claim that Asian American students didn't add to the diversity of a class because "Most non-Asian kids are into sports, student government, etc., . . . but most Asian students are just hitting the books and not having a well-balanced school life."

Rhetoric about Merit: Transforming the Model Minority

I have noted that the "model minority" image of Asian American students was born in a period of exceptional racial change and uncertainty. But the racial politics of the 1960s were not the racial politics of the mid-1980s. In the mid-1980s, racial problems continued to plague American institutions, but there was no indication, as there had been in the 1960s, that the United States was at the edge of a racial apocalypse.

The presence of minority students, their campus organizations, and ethnic studies courses was a stark contrast to the predominantly white campuses of the 1960s. The greater racial diversity of the 1980s, however, was not necessarily a sign of a healthy campus racial climate. Though overall minority enrollment was growing, black enrollment was declining. After peaking in 1976 at 10 percent of total undergraduate enrollment, the numbers of blacks at the nation's colleges fell during the 1980s. Blacks constituted 9.7 percent of all undergraduates in 1984, declining to 9.2 percent in 1987 (National Center for Education Statistics 1989). Native American enrollment, like black enrollment, also declined in the 1980s, while Hispanic enrollment grew modestly, and Asian enrollments boomed (Fiske 1987).

It was the decline in black enrollment that troubled college administrators, one of whom said, "There is a perception that blacks and other minorities are no longer welcome on college campuses" (Fiske 1987). The downward trend in black enrollment led some to question university commitment to affirmative action, particularly in student admissions and faculty hiring. Many black students and faculty viewed the black enrollment problem as emblematic of a sweeping retrenchment from affirmative action that began with the 1978 *Bakke* decision. At many colleges, including several elite schools, minority students and some minority faculty demanded that administrators preserve student affirmative action programs, redouble college efforts to recruit minority faculty, and reexamine the college curriculum.

Conflicts about race on college campuses occurred in the midst of persistent concerns over student academic achievement. University faculty and administrators complained of declining academic standards. They pointed to curriculum changes, the presence of illiterate or near-illiterate college students, grade inflation, and what some called "canon revisionism." By 1988, debates over revising the "canon" were highly symbolic of a litany of complaints and anxieties about the state of higher education. One writer lamented, "By the 1970s, no one was just reading anymore; everyone was deconstructing" (Atlas 1990).

Explanations for the "decline" in higher education varied. Some blamed television, others blamed rising numbers of minority students, and still others suggested that the new education represented by the movement to reform the teachings of Western Civilization at many universities had taken away from instruction in the "basics." Neoconservative critics charged that replacing the "great books" with new literature—drawn from the social experiences of minorities—was eliminating the very foundation of learning at the university.

The combination of the nascent but developing mood for a "return to the basics" and the demands by minority students for institutional change on racial issues prompted an unwieldy juxtaposition of images and rhetoric with which university officials responded to Asian admissions. Besieged by demands from the right and the left to change the university, administrators constructed their account of Asian admissions out of a limited set of terms and categories: nonwhite and white, diversity and merit, strict academic and nonacademic criteria. With little ideological space within which they

could maneuver their claims about Asian admissions, university officials struggled to frame Asian achievement while justifying levels of
Asian enrollment/admission. The result was different thematic combinations in their counterclaims. Some officials stressed the institutional context of diversity, others pointed to the competitive
deficiencies of Asian American applicants.

Taken together, the responses of university officials to charges
of discrimination in admissions sketched a highly critical public por-
trait of Asian American students. Praise turned into criticism, and
words of encouragement drifted toward platitudes. The new discursive rhetoric about Asian American students combined criticism
with old stereotypes. Once set on an academic pedestal, a model for
other minorities and even for white students, Asian American students joined the ranks of the "good but not exceptional" in school.
Praise for Asian American students was now routinely accompanied
by qualifying statements. They were diligent, but too narrowly focused; strongly dedicated to the pursuit of education, but to a fault,
and at the exclusion of other activities; hardworking, but lacking in
creativity. Perhaps inadvertently, the rhetoric used by well-intentioned university representatives to preserve diversity and define
merit provided the institutional voice for white students and their
parents to express trepidation about Asian American achievement.
In the context of the debate over Asian admissions, university administrators, through their rebuttals to claims of discrimination,
gave official "voice" to the popular "nerd" image of Asian American
students.

Rhetoric about Diversity: The Asian American
"Nerd" versus Affirmative Action

It would be inaccurate to conclude from this discussion that the response by university administrators to the charges of discrimination
was a monolithic effort to shift the discourse to diversity. In their
framing of counterclaims, all of the officials defined the Asian admissions problem in terms of diversity and individual merit or
achievement. Beyond that general agreement on how to situate the
problem, university officials held quite different interpretations of
diversity, merit, and the relationship of both to Asian American applicants.

To officials from Berkeley and UCLA, diversity was closely

bound up with affirmative action. In their admissions process, diversity and affirmative action were two related principles governing selection. For these officials, affirmative action was practically synonymous with the 1974 State Assembly resolution promoting minority representation at the University of California proportionate to the minority mix in the state's high school graduating class. By "diversity" officials meant a broad mix of different types of students—urban/rural students, disabled students, athletes, musicians—but according to the 1974 resolution, a diverse mix should also be reflective of the racial composition of the state's high school graduation class.

At the private schools, diversity and affirmative action were two distinct and nonoverlapping parts of the admissions process: recruitment and selection. Affirmative action was a program to recruit *applicants* for the freshman class. Diversity was a measure of the range of talents in the freshman class. Admissions officers at the highly selective private universities applied the term "diversity" to a broad range of characteristics of applicants—soccer player, musician, legacy (child of an alumnus/a), artist, future mechanical engineer, underrepresented minority—a list of individual characteristics identifying an applicant's social and racial background, past accomplishments, and future plans. In short, what constituted diversity at Harvard might fail to meet Univesity of California standards, and vice versa.

University officials had no shared methodology for evaluating how individual applicants contributed to diversity. Although all of the schools used objective and subjective criteria to evaluate an applicant, they interpreted and applied their criteria in different ways. In a decision imposed by their "boss," the Regents of the University of California, both Berkeley and UCLA were required to admit between 40 and 60 percent of the entering class through Tier 1. Berkeley and UCLA were the only schools to have explicit minimum eligibility requirements, an issue to which I shall return in Chapter 7. Berkeley, using the only formula-based index among all of the top schools, and UCLA admit some students strictly on the basis of grade point average and test scores. Eschewing formulas, private schools such as Stanford do not admit any students "purely by the numbers." Instead, the highly selective private schools distinguish their objective and subjective criteria in different ways. Subjective criteria are called "personal achievement" at Stanford, are known as "personal qualities" at Harvard, and fall under the categories of "special skills" and "capacity for involvement, commitment, and personal growth" at Yale. In contrast, admissions officers at Berkeley and UCLA calculated what in Harvard's process would be "personal qualities" as actual points based on, for example, family background (Educational Opportunity Program eligibility, worth 200 points) and the personal essay (worth up to 500 points).

All of the schools have an affirmative action policy to ensure racial diversity, although again there are enormous differences in the application of policy. At the private schools, affirmative action is a *recruitment* policy only. Berkeley and UCLA interpreted affirmative action as a *recruitment and enrollment policy*. Moreover, which racial groups were included under the aegis of affirmative action varied. At Harvard, an Asian student from a working-class background was a candidate for affirmative action; the same student was ineligible for Berkeley's affirmative action program from 1984 to 1989.

But there is a constancy beyond these differences in officials' interpretation of diversity. Asian American students were at odds with university goals of diversity, in terms of either, and sometimes both, academic achievement and racial mix of the student body. Harvard's Dean Jewett, in a justification for lower Asian American admission rates (compared with whites), noted, "a terribly high proportion of the Asian students are heading toward the sciences" (Bell 1985).

Conflicting Claims

Because of the differences in how they conceptualized diversity and affirmative action, university officials offered counterclaims that were sometimes inconsistent with one another. For example, several officials charged that Asians had more than their fair share of slots and were "overrepresented" at the university; Harvard officials openly disagreed. At Berkeley, President Gardner called Asians overrepresented but Assistant Vice Chancellor Travers praised Asian enrollment at Berkeley as a "success story." Some officials described Asian applicants as "flat" or not well-rounded; others claimed Asians were not well-rounded because of their proclivity for math and science majors. Other officials—in the case of Yat-pang Au, Berkeley officials—contended that Asian applicants, though well-rounded, were not competitive enough to gain admission to Berkeley. Still other officials suggested that Asian applicants were every bit as competitive as whites but that their subjective ratings were lowered by letters of recommendation from high school counselors and teachers containing well-intentioned but left-handed compliments.

University officials thus delivered a mixed bag of claims about Asian American applicants. There were claims for *and* against the belief that Asians undermine diversity. And there were claims for *and* against the assumption that Asian Americans were competitive with white students. Although it might seem that these were empirical questions for which there ought to have been clear-cut answers—for example, either Asians were or were not competitive with whites—such debate did not seem to interest university officials. Rather, administrators developed a "theoretical discourse," to use Habermas's phrase, collated from different types of arguments—diversity and merit—which did not contest their opponents' facts, but instead contested Asian Americans' interpretation of the facts.[25] Indeed, university officials constructed their conflicting claims with the very same facts used by their Asian American critics (Takagi 1990). Thus the construction of university officials' discourse about merit and diversity reflected conflicting claims and, more important, accommodated wide differences in interpretation by officials.

University officials responded to Asian American charges of discrimination in three main ways. One argument raised by numerous officials was a parity-based notion of equity—Asian American students were overrepresented at the university compared with their proportions in the general population. A second argument, often used in concert with the overrepresentation argument, was that Asian American students were qualified but not competitive students. Some university officials perceived Asian students as lacking in a diversity of interests—"all science and math," "not enough extracurriculars," "below average in personal ratings." Frequently, the notion that Asians were "good but not exceptional" students was linked with the more general argument that Asian American admissions threatened racial diversity—for example, black enrollment—at the university. Finally, a third response to the charges of discrimination, one that was invoked by Princeton in 1985 and fully explicated by Harvard in 1988, was that private school preferences for groups other than Asians explained and justified the fact that Asians were less likely than whites to gain admission to the university.

These responses, in turn, contributed to a reshaping of the

popular image of Asian American students as a "model minority." Although this popular image of Asian students had been a good fit with racial politics in higher education in the 1960s, it was less viable in the context of the 1980s. Once viewed as academic "darlings," Asian American students had lost ground two decades later. In the context of declining black enrollment, anxiety about racist incidents in higher education, concern over academic "standards," and increased demographic pressure from Asian Americans to gain access to higher education, the place of Asian American students was in flux and uncertain. The "model minority" image was modulated downward into a more critical view of Asian students through discourse about Asian American admissions. Characterizations of Asian students by university officials as "overrepresented" and "good but not exceptional" furnished the critical rhetoric.

CHAPTER 4

The Tyranny of Facts: State and Federal Reviews

*D*avid Gardner once remarked about Asian admissions, "If you think you know the answer, then you don't understand the problem." The University of California president was referring to the daunting task of balancing demographic changes in the college-going population with diversity on the one hand, merit on the other, to frame an admissions policy that was nondiscriminatory toward Asian American students. By 1987 definitions of the problem of Asian admissions and answers to it were awash in numbers, statistics, and facts.

Public discourse on Asian admissions between 1987 and 1988 reveals both a conflict in interpretation and a struggle to define and analyze facts. Nowhere was this conflict in interpretation more apparent than at Berkeley, where Asian Americans attempted to shift the discourse back to discrimination through external reviews of the controversy by state agencies. State reviews were then complemented by two federal inquiries, one by the Justice Department and the other by the Office of Civil Rights of the Department of Education. In the stalemate over how best to define Asian admissions—as a discrimination problem or a diversity problem—the facts and statistics of the controversy seemed to be increasingly important to both Asian Americans and university officials. Perhaps most significant, the impasse in interpretation of the controversy, during which the national media provided extensive coverage of the issues, offered neoconservatives an important opportunity to link affirmative action with Asian admissions.

The shift in the focus of public debate troubled task force members. Though they tried to get the discussion back on track toward the issue of discrimination, they were mostly unsuccessful. Every time Berkeley officials issued a statement or an explanation of Asian admissions, the task force quickly responded, often point by point. But additional task force statistics did not seem to blunt administration claims about diversity. As a result, the details of task force rejoinders languished against university claims about Asian over-representation and the need for well-rounded students in higher education.

By late 1987 the task force moved to politicize the issue. Frustrated by what it viewed as a lack of action on the part of a stubborn university, the task force decided to pressure Berkeley officials "from above." While simultaneously issuing memos detailing its arguments, the task force successfully lobbied for investigations of Asian admissions by the California state legislature and the Regents of the University of California. In sharp contrast to the in-house studies conducted by admissions officers and faculty at other schools, the announcement of outside reviews of undergraduate admissions by state agencies suggested that the issue had slipped out of the control of the Berkeley administration.

But Berkeley officials did not believe they had lost control of the issue. Rather, they hoped that outside reviews would provide an "objective" evaluation of the issue, and thus they greeted the announcement of external reviews with outward enthusiasm. Assistant Vice Chancellor Bud Travers told the *Daily Californian*, "We welcome the opportunity to have an outside review group with credibility taking a look at the information . . . I think it is going to dispel a lot of myths" (Kazmin 1987).

A year later, in 1988, after a major review by the auditor general, a hearing on University of California admissions by a state legislative committee, two special sessions on admissions by the Regents, one aborted faculty committee investigation and another in-progress faculty review, the question of Asian admissions was far from settled. The combination of ongoing external reviews by the state legislature with persistent and unyielding counterclaims by university officials about diversity ensured Asian admissions a spot in the national news through 1988. That widespread news coverage, in turn, was cited by the federal Department of Justice in late 1988 when it announced formal investigations of allegations of discrimination against Asian Americans at UCLA and Harvard.

Encouraged by its political success with the state legislature, the task force shifted the focus of its complaints from discrimination to the politics of admission decisions. The task force charged that university policymakers had been unfair to Asian Americans not only in the outcomes of their decisions but also in the process of decision making. Charging university officials with willful neglect of Asian American concerns, the task force demanded that university officials make amends by including Asian Americans in the review process of admissions policy.

Asian American attempts to shift public discourse about admissions back to discrimination marked an unexpected and ironic twist in the controversy. Although claims about Asian admissions pivoted on the facts, the availability and analysis of more facts deepened rather than quelled controversy.

Facts and statistics became increasingly prominent in the debate between 1987 and 1988. The external reviews supplied new mountains of data—facts, tables, charts, and statistics—much of which was incorporated into claims on both sides. But more statistics produced less consensus. The production of more data generated more complex and confusing arguments about the meaning of a statistical analysis of Asian American admissions. One writer drily observed that the auditor general's study had "yielded a slew of new data, about which both sides can now disagree" (Lye 1986).

But as the statistics became more abundant and more confusing, the discourse about facts and statistics became clearer. The chasm between university officials and their Asian American critics was qualitative, not quantitative. In the face of sharply different value judgments about how best to define discrimination and diversity, the numbers became increasingly irrelevant.

New Strategy by the Task Force

Professor Wang saw the issue of diversity as a university ploy designed to divert public attention away from the 1984 decline in Asian admissions at Berkeley. Not satisfied with Travers's explanation of the problem in 1987, Wang circulated Travers's letter along with his own comments to colleagues on the Berkeley campus and to members of the Asian American community in the San Francisco Bay Area. In his comments, Wang criticized Travers for conducting only "selected research" and for not including Asian American staff or faculty in the research process. Wang (n.d.) predicted, "Instead of clarifying the issue and putting the controversy to rest, it [Travers's memo] may very well generate more controversies and distrust."

The official task force response to Travers's letter began by complimenting the assistant vice chancellor for releasing the 1986 data on admissions and enrollment and providing an explanation of Berkeley's "supplemental criteria" (Sing and Kawaichi 1987a). But most of the response was devoted to a point-by-point criticism of Travers's letter. "We are plainly disappointed with the report," wrote the task force leaders. Point one criticized the university for using selective data in its review of admissions. Travers's memo claimed that Asian enrollment had risen steadily at Berkeley. According to the task force, the university's analysis failed to include data for 1983 that helped substantiate a decline in Asian enrollment from 1983 to 1986. Point two blasted the university for failing to address the disproportionate decline between 1983 and 1984 in Asian enrollment and the 1984 decision to redirect all Asian EOP students to other UC campuses, "two crucial issues raised by the 1985 task force report." Point three criticized the university for having altered the admissions criteria or screening process every year since 1983 and expressed concern that "the unsettling condition makes it exceedingly perplexing for aspiring Asian high school students who must prepare themselves to meet the changing requirements." Point four charged that the research undertaken by Travers's staff for the memo was completed "apparently without the input of the Asian American faculty." The task force argued that "meaningful participation of Asian American faculty will help dispel growing distrust over UC Berkeley's handling of Asian American affairs." In point five, the task force expressed its "shock and dismay" that no Asian Americans had been appointed to the admissions and enrollment committee.

The task force concluded its criticism of Travers's letter by calling for "an independent, comprehensive study on the issue with significant Asian American input, much as the Stanford University faculty did last November in response to charges of racial discrimination against Asians" (Sing and Kawaichi 1987a).

Bypassing the Vice Chancellor's Office

The task force was also still bothered by David Gardner's comments in his December 1986 interview with the *San Diego Union* about Asian American overrepresentation at the university. At the request of the task force, President Gardner agreed to a meeting in early March 1987 to discuss Asian admissions and other concerns relating to Asian Americans at the University of California. Also present at the meeting were Berkeley Chancellor Ira Heyman, Vice Chancellor for Undergraduate Affairs Watson Laetsch, UC Regent Yori Wada, and Julius Krevans, chancellor of the University of California, San Francisco. Task force members took the opportunity to express their concerns about Asian admissions directly to Gardner and urged the Berkeley administration to publicize widely changes in admissions procedures and criteria and to include Asian Americans representation in admissions decision making.

Although the meeting did not produce any major shifts in position on either side, Lillian Sing, co-chair of the task force, told the media, "We've opened a dialogue" (*East/West* 1987). According to *East/West*, an Asian American community newspaper reporting on the meeting, "President Gardner reaffirmed his commitment to accommodate all UC-eligible students somewhere within the UC system, and to increase the numbers of underrepresented ethnic groups." On the matter of Asian admissions, Gardner "assured the group that Asian overrepresentation was not an issue" (*East/West* 1987).

The task force felt that Berkeley officials were dragging their heels. Two years had passed since the group had first made its charges of discrimination. In contrast, faculty investigations at Brown, Stanford, and Princeton had been concluded within a relatively short period of time, six months or less. From the perspective of the task force, UC administrators, from the president's office down to the assistant vice chancellor at Berkeley, were dodging the real issue, the decline in Asian enrollment in 1984. Angry that officials stubbornly continued to defend university admissions policy, the task force adopted a new strategy. In response to what they interpreted as the administrators' change in the subject of discourse, from discrimination to diversity, the task force sought outside reviews from state agencies on the charges of discrimination. In essence, this strategy was designed to recapture the public debate and refocus public attention on the charges of discrimination. In its first flex of political muscle, the task force approached the state legislature.

Taking It to the State Capital

In the spring of 1987, as a result of successful lobbying by the task force, two state-sponsored investigations were begun at Berkeley. Assemblyman Art Agnos (D-San Francisco) and Senate Pro Tempore leader David Roberti (D-Burbank) announced that they were requesting an investigation into Asian admissions at Berkeley by the state auditor general. Assemblyman Agnos said, "We want everybody to be treated fairly without any kind of bias. Nobody is pointing any fingers yet, we're just asking questions" (Hickey 1987). In a separate announcement, Assemblyman Tom Hayden, chair of the State Assembly Education Committee, called for subcommittee hearings on admissions to be held in Los Angeles later that spring (Hickey 1987). (Ultimately these hearings were held in January 1988, in Sacramento.) In addition to these two formal reviews of UC admissions, *East/West* reported that members of the task force had met with the Speaker of the Assembly, Willie Brown, to discuss several issues related to Asian Americans and higher education in California (Hickey 1987).

At the same time that the auditor general's office was conducting its research, a faculty committee at Berkeley was constituted to investigate Asian admissions. The Subcommittee on Asian-American Admissions, part of the Committee on Admissions and Enrollment and chaired by Professor Scott Lynn, began its work in May 1987. Unlike its parent committee, the subcommittee included an Asian American member, Chang-lin Tien, who, was specially appointed. In keeping with the spirit of "open dialogue" initiated by Gardner's March meeting with the task force, the committee invited the task force to discuss its concerns and its reactions to the work of the committee. At a dinner meeting over the summer the task force presented its case to the committee. Task force co-chairs Kawaichi and Sing expressed their eagerness to work with the Lynn committee and requested that the task force be allowed to discuss the committee's findings before official publication of its report. Professor Wang warned the committee to avoid becoming too immersed in the statistics of Asian admissions. He noted, "Just to set the record straight, there is no dispute over the validity of the statistics generated by the

Office of Student Research. The disagreement, instead, lies in the interpretation of these statistics" (Wang 1987a). Wang (1987a) suggested three focal areas for the committee investigation: (1) the intentions and rationales that lay behind changes in admissions rules, (2) the decision-making process, and (3) the adequacy of public notification of admissions policy changes.

The Lynn Committee Debacle

The "open dialogue" between the task force and the Lynn committee turned out to be short-lived. In the first week of October 1987, the findings of the not-yet-released draft report of the subcommittee were leaked to the media. Chairperson Lynn, apparently in anticipation of the release of the auditor general's report, concluded that the university was free and clear of discriminatory policies. The draft report stated, "The Subcommittee has found no indication of conscious bias in the admissions policies of the Berkeley campus. Admissions data show that Asian and whites with the same Academic Index score have very nearly the same probability of admission to a given academic program if allowance is made for the protected categories" (Lynn Committee 1987).

But the findings of the Lynn committee were quickly discounted and the report was never publicly released.[1] Task force member Wang immediately denounced the committee for having drafted the report and shared its results with University of California administration officials and legislative leaders *before* the official release of the auditor general's report on October 7. The task force accused the committee of having promised to "refer to the data presented in the auditor general's report" and then reneging on that promise. The task force further charged Lynn with going back on a written promise to meet with the task force "again before our report is released" (Sing and Kawaichi 1987b).

Whatever cooperation existed between the task force and the Lynn committee dissolved in the wake of these charges. In their letter to Professor Lynn, Sing and Kawaichi (1987b) wrote, "If the original intent of the Subcommittee was to conduct an independent investigation and to help restore the credibility of the University in the Asian American community, we now seriously doubt if the original intent can be accomplished in light of what we have outlined."

To make matters even worse, the *Daily Californian* reported that the only Asian member of the Lynn committee, Professor Chang-lin Tien, "said the committee had not met since August 13, and he was unaware until a few days ago that a draft report had been prepared" (Ipson and Tjoa 1987). This latest revelation suggested yet a further impropriety: the draft report had been prepared without the participation of its own committee members.

Amid allegations of procedural violations, Professor Lynn resigned as chair, and shortly thereafter the committee voted to disband. A new committee, chaired by Professor William Shack, was appointed by the faculty academic senate to investigate the allegations of bias against Asian Americans in admissions. The deliberations of this new committee were not without conflict, but the committee managed to fulfill its mission and report findings in early 1989. During the two and a half years that it took the Shack committee to complete its investigation, public debate and speculation about the fairness of Berkeley admissions continued, as did the external reviews.

The Report of the State Auditor General

The findings of the auditor general, published just after the revelations about the Lynn Subcommittee on Asian-American Admissions, provoked new disagreements between the task force and university officials. The report, a hefty two hundred pages, over half of which were tables, was largely descriptive and did not take a clear stand on the issue of discrimination. Looking at white and Asian admission rates for five different colleges at Berkeley over a period of seven years, the auditor general found that in a majority of instances, the admission rate for Asian Americans was lower than the rate for whites. By dividing two colleges into two separate admissions processes, the auditor general analyzed a total of 49 different admission rates for the period 1981–1987. In 37 of the 49 instances, Asians were admitted at lower rates than whites. In 26 of those 37 instances, however, the difference between the white and Asian admission rate was less than 5 percent. Referring to Berkeley's largest college of undergraduate enrollment, Letters and Science, the auditor general concluded, "Using our methodology, we determine 83 fewer Caucasians and 83 more Asians would have been admitted if their admissions rates had been the same at the College of Letters and Science in the fall 1986 semester" (Auditor General 1987).

The task force and the university both had mixed reactions to the report. University officials gleaned what victory they could. That the difference between Asian and white admission rates was less than 5 percent in a majority of instances was heartening to them. Most important, the report failed to indict the university for discrimination in admissions. Chancellor Heyman told the *Daily Californian*, "From the evidence I have seen, I remain firmly convinced that our methods are sound and there is no pattern of unfairness" (Papillon and Kazmin 1987). Other university administrators cited the auditor general's report in their answers to queries about discrimination against Asians. In early 1988, for example, at a presentation on discrimination against Asians at a conference on higher education, Alice Cox, assistant vice president of student academic services for the UC system, was there to defend Berkeley policies. After the speaker's presentation, Cox rose to counter the allegations of discrimination, saying, "the auditor general's report showed absolutely there was no evidence of discrimination."[2]

But not all university officials were satisfied with the report. A few felt compelled to explain further the differences between Asian and white admission rates. Bud Travers told the *Daily Californian*, "The statistics in the report are not complete" (Papillon and Kazmin 1987). According to Travers, the difference between Asian and white admission rates was due to the "admission of 'protected' groups such as handicapped, rural students, and athletes, the members of which are predominantly white" (Papillon and Kazmin 1987). Ray Colvig, university spokesperson, suggested that the auditor general compared "things that aren't totally comparable, and when you do that, you can't drawn inferences. We don't reject the report, we just don't think it answered the questions" (Papillon and Kazmin 1987).

For the task force, the issue was not whether Asian and white admission rates were comparable or not. The real issue, according to task force member Henry Der, was whether competition for admission to Berkeley was fair. For the members of the task force, the auditor general's report confirmed what they had been saying all along—that Berkeley discriminated against Asian applicants. Der told the *Daily Californian*, "I'd like to believe that both white and Asian applicants want a fair competition. But at the University there is an absence of a fair playing field" (Papillon and Kazmin 1987). The student senator Jeff Chang agreed, saying, "This confirms our worst fears. To be admitted to Berkeley as an Asian, you have to have a higher academic index score than if you are a white student" (Papillon and Kazmin 1987). Sumi Cho, chair of the Graduate Assembly at Berkeley, put it this way, "Here at the university it is the survival of the fittest—until it seems that Asians may in fact be the fittest" (Papillon and Kazmin 1987). Cho went on to accuse university officials of laying blame for the discrepancy between white and Asian admission rates at the door of affirmative action. She said, "The most vile thing the university is doing is using affirmative action as a scapegoat. This is just a tactic of divide and conquer. Affirmative action is a protected category that does not affect the number of Asian or white admissions. Asians are competing with whites for spaces, but the competition is not fair." Der agreed with Cho: "Many university official comments have been laced with innuendoes that black, Chicano/Latino and Native American students are taking spaces from Asians. But the fact is that Asian applicants are competing with white applicants" (Papillon and Kazmin 1987).

"Is This the Right Way to Run a Tax-Supported, World-Class University?"

Although the task force used the auditor general's findings to buttress its own position on discrimination, it was not completely satisfied with the report. In a five-page, single-spaced response to the report, the task force (AATF 1987) expressed disappointment that the report failed to "cover the rationales or academic justifications behind the several changes in Berkeley's admission policies and procedures since 1983, nor did it determine whether the decisions to make these policy changes were made with adequate public input and whether the general public was sufficiently informed of these changes." The task force also questioned the auditor general's use of a random study of 100 individuals that showed that Asians scored 4 points higher on the "supplemental criteria" in 1985 and 1986. According to the task force, "several unanswered questions remain unanswered," such as how the 100 students were sampled from 20,000 applicants, and how the personal essay was scored and by whom. The task force maintained that since these and other questions were unanswered, the "audit into the use of the supplementary criteria must be considered inconclusive and inadequate" (AATF 1987:3).

The task force was also concerned with other "unaddressed issues for further consideration." The "foremost" problem was the "poor admission data collection and management at UC Berkeley."

The task force commentary on the audit stated, "Repeatedly, the auditor general complained about the inaccurate and inadequate criteria and data used by the University and his inability to 'fully test the admissions systems at Berkeley's colleges either for compliance with their selection criteria or for the appropriateness of decisions.' Is this the right way to run a tax-supported, world-class University?" (AATF 1987:4).

In addition to its complaint about data management and record keeping at the university, the task force was "appalled" by the auditor general's revelation that Berkeley had engaged in the practice of "rejecting some and admitting other applicants who had not submitted all officially required grades and test scores." And finally, the task force registered "surprise" that there "is no uniform or consistent application of admission policies among the different colleges and some colleges appear to have no policy at all" (AATF 1987:4).

At Berkeley, access to admissions statistics was part of a much broader dispute between university officials and the task force over the public accountability of admissions practices. The nine-campus system of the University of California is a public institution supported by the taxpayers of California. As a state institution, the university is publicly accountable to its constituents, the people of California. The task force, having already accused the university of "violating the public trust" (AATF 1985a), continued to press for an explanation of how and why changes in admission policies were implemented in 1984, 1985, 1986, and 1987.

Criticism by the UC Regents, Fall 1987

Berkeley officials attempted to safeguard the public trust in a formal explanation of admissions policy to the Regents, the governing board of the University of California, in the fall of 1987. The administrators' explanations for Asian American admissions to Berkeley fell apart, however, under sharp questioning at the fall meeting Regents held at the Riverside campus. In a tense session,[3] the Regents queried Berkeley officials about the general problem of Asian American admissions. After reviewing both the auditor general's report and the Travers (1987) memo, several Regents focused the discussion on the specifics of the admissions process. They wanted an explanation of how the "supplemental criteria" were used. But neither of the two Berkeley officials present at the meeting, Vice Chancellor

Park or Assistant Vice Chancellor Travers, was able to answer the questions to the Regents' satisfaction.

Regent Yori Wada opened the discussion, expressing his dismay with Berkeley. He reported that he had defended the university against charges of discrimination in front of Asian American groups but that the findings of the auditor general "caught him off guard." He went on to cite the auditor general's findings on "careless record-keeping" and the "lack of criteria in the selection of tier two applicants" in several of Berkeley's five colleges. He concluded by stating that although he would continue to defend the university to critics, he hoped that the university, in turn, would do "its best to earn that defense" (Regents 1987). From there the discussion went from bad to worse for the Berkeley officials.

Regents Dean A. Watkins and Frank W. Clark, Jr., asked Travers to describe the scoring of an applicant's essay, worth 500 points out of a total of 1,300 supplemental criteria points. Travers offered a general description of the evaluation process. But the Regents were still not satisfied. Regent Watkins pressed on, asking how many points an applicant would receive who, for example, had honors and public service but had written a poor essay. In other words, did the essay stand in and of itself, or did the honors stand by themselves? Travers responded that it would be difficult to say. Several other specific questions on the scoring of the essay followed. Finally, when specifically asked about the methodology for assigning the 500 essay points, Travers said he did not have an answer but promised to investigate and report back to the Regents.

Both Park and Travers remember the meeting as "embarrassing." A remorseful Travers recalled, "And so I feel bad about that Regents meeting, you know. It was a tough one for me 'cause I was put on the spot and one Regent remarked, 'Well if you can't answer it, who can? It was tough on Park'"[4]

Roderic Park was angry as well as embarrassed about the meeting. He recalled, "It was upsetting to me for a lot of reasons. I like to be prepared in meetings, I don't like to get sandbagged that way. I felt that this institution was being let down."[5] Since 1985, when Park had first seen the task force report, he thought that Watson Laetsch and his assistant Travers were "handling" the issue. Park said, "It never came to me. I didn't have anything to do with it, even though Laetsch nominally reported to me, the two of them totally did that by themselves. Then it was a closed game."[6] In the wake of the debacle at Riverside, Park decided that "Travers totally blew it" and concluded that "the fact is they'd [Laetsch and Travers] gotten into the damndest political mess because of their lack of perception and understanding that I've ever seen in my life."[7]

Park returned to Berkeley determined to get the "mess" straightened out. Both Laetsch and Travers were to play lesser roles in the admissions process. Park turned to other university officials, including Patrick Hayashi, an assistant in the chancellor's office, for help with collating data and materials for an upcoming presentation by Berkeley officials on Asian admissions in front of a state legislative committee.

A Chancellor Apology

Asian admissions was the subject of hearings in Sacramento (originally proposed for Los Angeles) before the State Assembly Subcommittee on Higher Education chaired by Assemblyman Tom Hayden in January 1988. The phantom "SAT 400 memo" that had been written by Director of Admissions Robert Bailey and sent to Vice Chancellor Laetsch suddenly appeared at the hearings, produced by an Assembly aide.[8] This time, Berkeley officials moved deftly to recoup their losses. At the subcommittee hearings in Sacramento, Berkeley Chancellor Heyman offered an unprecedented apology to the Asian American community. Heyman said, "I wish we were more sensitive to the underlying concerns. While they did not manifest themselves as neatly as I now see them, Berkeley could have acted more openly and less defensively. I apologize for that" (Chang 1988a). In addition, the Daily Californian reported that the chancellor agreed to "bring more Asians into key positions in his administration" (Chang 1988a). He also announced that a special committee on Asian American concerns at Berkeley, headed by the librarian Janice Koyama and the Nobel laureate Yuan T. Lee (physics), would play an important role in reviewing admissions policies. Finally, the chancellor said that he would establish an Admissions Coordination Board that would give interest groups an opportunity to respond and comment on Berkeley admissions policy (Chang 1988a).

Members of the task force lauded the chancellor's apology, saying, "We are delighted the chancellor has apologized for the mistakes and the lack of sensitivity by his staff" (Gordon 1988). Within the next two weeks, during which the chancellor created the Admissions Coordination Board, the task force again endorsed the chancellor's actions. Professor L. Ling-chi Wang said, "We are certainly pleased that the university has taken steps to make sure the admissions process will be fair and that there will be input from various minority groups" (Chang 1988b).

The chancellor's apology marked an important turning point in relations between the task force and the university. But the inauguration of a new era of cooperation between the Berkeley officials and the task force got off to a shaky start. Though encouraged by Berkeley's new proactive approach to the Asian admissions issue, the task force felt that the chancellor's apology did not make up for the controversial SAT 400 memo. Its mysterious appearance at the Hayden subcommittee hearings in Sacramento reinvigorated task force complaints about the administrators responsible for it. Calling the memo the "smoking gun" of Berkeley's discriminatory policies, task force members accused university officials of "conspiracy," "lies," and a "cover-up.' The task force wanted the guilty parties, Laetsch and Travers, removed from the administration. Professor Wang (1988b) faulted Heyman for an apology that "failed to mention what concrete actions, if any, he plans to take to hold accountable those administrators responsible for the mishandling and for causing the needless anxieties inflicted on countless Asian Americans on and off the campus." In an audacious move, the task force refused to cooperate with the university until Laetsch and Travers were removed from their positions. Task force leaders said that the task force "continues to maintain [its] position, which we made known to you [Chancellor Heyman] in Sacramento on January 26, 1988, that the task force would not attend any meetings wherein Vice Chancellor Laetsch will represent the university" (Sing and Kawaichi 1988a).

Der's claim that the SAT memo was a "smoking gun" elicited a cool response from university officials. Spokesperson Ray Colvig, decided to challenge Der's criticisms. In a letter to the *Hokubei Mainichi*, a Japanese community newspaper that had published Der's comments, he outlined his disagreements. Colvig's position was that Der was exaggerating the significance of the memo. According to Colvig (1988), "The facts of the 1983–84 memo were explained almost three years ago in written correspondence from UC Assistant Vice Chancellor Bud Travers to the Asian American task force on University Admissions." Colvig, recounting Travers's rebuttal, maintained the memo had been rescinded:

> Utilization of minimum scores was discussed for the 1984 redirection cycle. Verbal SAT test score minimums were considered first at 400 or less and then 300 or less. In fact, at one point a minimum of 400 was set, but shortly after the written directive was issued it was withdrawn.

In review, the profile of test scores of students retained on the Berkeley campus shows that the range of test scores does, in fact, reflect
students whose verbal comprehensive test scores are below both the
400 and the 300 point levels. Subsequent discussion about "minimum"
test scores for both 1985 and 1986 have resulted in no setting of minimum test score levels. (Colvig 1988)

Colvig concluded his letter insisting that Laetsch continued to hold
the "full confidence" of the chancellor.

Colvig's defense of Laetsch and Travers on behalf of the chancellor sparked a new round of struggle between the task force and
the Berkeley administration. Sing and Kawaichi addressed the task
force response to Colvig's letter directly to Heyman. They wrote,
"We are most disturbed by this public expression [in] confidence of
those who we feel are directly responsible for the manner in which
the university has handled the issues of concern by the task force"
and urged the chancellor to "fulfill [his] pledge that you made in the
hearing before the Subcommittee on Higher Education that you
would work cooperatively to restore and enhance the confidence of
the Asian Americans in Berkeley's admissions policies and practices" (Sing and Kawaichi 1988a).

Asian Americans as a Political Interest Group
in Higher Education

While top Berkeley officials considered how to respond to this latest
deadlock with the task force, in February 1988 a group of 350 Asian
American students, faculty, administrators, and representatives
from community organizations gathered in neighboring Oakland to
create a statewide lobbying group on issues relating to Asian Americans in higher education (Jaschick 1988). This, the second annual
meeting of Asian Pacific Americans in Higher Education (APAHE),
was as much a meeting to discuss issues relating to Asian Americans
as an opportunity to organize Asian Americans into a political force
in higher education in California.

Present at the meeting were legislative aides, advisors from the
governor's office, the Speaker of the Assembly, and California state
legislators. According to the *Chronicle for Higher Education*, the state's
political dignitaries enthusiastically welcomed Asian American involvement in higher education politics (Jaschik 1988). For example,
Speaker Willie Brown, Jr., who had recently appointed task force

member Henry Der to the California Postsecondary Education Commission, said, "I want my appointees to be offensive. I want the other board members not to want to drink coffee with them. Because I want them to be twisting the tail of the donkey to meet the needs of Asian Americans" (Jaschik 1988). Leading the list of issues that the group identified as important problems for investigation by legislators and state agencies was Asian admissions at Berkeley.[10]

At Berkeley, the threat of increased political pressure from above was accompanied by continuing political pressure from below. The issue of Asian admissions had not waned on campus. The Student Coalition for Fair Admissions (SCFA), a group organized in 1987 and led by Jeff Chang, worried that the chancellor's apology might be mere rhetoric and decided to watch university policy on admissions carefully. In early March, when Assistant Chancellor John Cummins announced that there would not be sufficient time for the newly formed Admissions Coordination Board to review admissions policy for the upcoming fall and that the board would not be operational until the following year, SCFA members fumed. Cummins explained, "the decisions for Fall 1988 have already been made. We cannot make any changes (in policy) until the board has substantial consultation with all interested parties" (Chang 1988d). In response, Chang complained, "the administration decided that for the whole year, for all of 1988, the new board isn't going to have any input" (Chang 1988d). Accusing the administration of "stalling," the SCFA led a small but vocal group of demonstrators who chanted "Actions not words" and "Fair admissions now" during a visit by Chancellor Heyman to a student dormitory.

Within a month of the SCFA demonstration, Jeff Chang was elected student body president of the Berkeley campus. Chang quickly identified minority issues as one of his major concerns. He told the reporter Judith Lyons (1988) of *Asian Week*, "I want to increase the awareness of issues on race, gender and sexual orientation. I want to make it more harmonious for the student body and highlight the diversity of our students by offering symposia and other programs." Not surprisingly, Chang identified Asian admissions as one of several issues facing the Asian American community at Berkeley.

Still, Laetsch and Travers continued to be the official campus representatives on the issue of Asian admissions. Occasionally, when issues of great significance face the Berkeley faculty, such as the institution of new requirements or the opening (or closing) of academic programs, the academic senate convenes a faculty-wide meeting to discuss them. In mid-April, undergraduate admissions was the focus of a specially convened academic senate meeting. There to discuss the formation of the Admissions Coordination Board and the issue of Asian American admissions more generally were Chancellor Heyman, Vice Chancellor Park, Professor Lynn, the associate director of the Office of Admissions and Records, Richard Shaw, and Vice Chancellor Laetsch.

Meanwhile media claims about Asian admissions showed no sign of abating. David Pickell (1988), writing for the *Berkeley Graduate*, noted, "the story is off the front pages, but the smoke hasn't cleared." Drawing extensively from an in-house Berkeley administration document called the "Asian Admissions Briefing Book," Pickell critically assailed university handling of the 1984 SAT memo. Sparing none of the top-ranking university officials, Pickell blasted the Berkeley administration, at one point suggesting that Bailey and Laetsch might be "profoundly stupid men." He concluded, "The documents here, and the BOOK ostensibly apologizing for them, demonstrate that the administrators of this university are capable of an indifferent and reflexive racism, and who then charged with just this, defend themselves with arrogance, lies and a retreat into the thicket of 'criteria,' 'targets,' and acronyms."

In early May, during a signing ceremony for Asian Pacific American Heritage week, President Reagan expressed his concern about Asian admissions. The President said, "I know there is growing concern that some universities may be discriminating against citizens of Asian and Pacific heritage, accepting a lower percentage of these applicants than get admitted from other groups, despite their academic qualifications. Well, to deny any individual access to higher education when it has been won on the basis of merit is a repudiation of everything America stands for" (White House 1988).

Although Reagan did not specifically name Berkeley, others did. A *U.S. News and World Report* article argued that the Asian admissions controversy was characterized by subtle stereotyping and identified Berkeley as being "at the center of the storm" (Levine and Pazner 1988).

In late May, the chancellor's office, in what was seen by many as a capitulation to the task force, announced that Vice Chancellor Laetsch and his assistant Travers were leaving their current posts in the undergraduate academic affairs office to join the Office of Development. Immediately after the announcement, Henry Der asked

Chancellor Heyman to consider appointing an Asian American to his "inner circle." The chancellor's office responded by reorganizing and redistributing the duties of both positions, carving out of the vice chancellor duties a new position devoted exclusively to admissions and enrollment. Chancellor Heyman appointed his special assistant Patrick Hayashi as the new associate vice chancellor of admissions and enrollment.

The task force, pleased with the reorganization of the vice chancellor position, turned their attention to a new policy just adopted by the Regents. In late May the Regents had affirmed what had already been in practice at Berkeley for several years, the use of supplemental criteria in undergraduate admissions. In addition, the policy restated in somewhat looser terms the basic premise of the 1974 legislative resolution on racial representation at the university. The 1988 policy stated, "The University seeks to enroll, on each of its campuses, a student body that, beyond meeting the University's eligibility requirements, demonstrates high academic achievement or exceptional personal talent, and that encompasses the broad diversity of cultural, racial, geographic, and socio-economic backgrounds characteristic of California" (Regents 1988).

The task force was dismayed by the new policy statement. From their perspective, the Regents had just etched in stone the supplemental criteria, the very problem about which the task force had been complaining for years. In a letter to Frank W. Clark, Jr., chairman of the Regents, the task force called the new policy "vague and confusing" and criticized the Regents for including the principle of diversity without specifying its connection to the supplemental criteria (Sing and Kawaichi 1988b). Task force co-chairs Sing and Kawaichi (1988b) argued that though the recently adopted policy added the principle of diversity to admissions criteria, the policy failed to define "the precise relations between the principles of selectivity and diversity for each campus and falls short of making a strong commitment to have fair and open admission policies and practices." According to Sing and Kawaichi, "without additional clarifications and guarantees, the new policy could be used to undermine or abandon the University's commitment to academic excellence on the one hand and to justify an unofficial use of racial quotas on the other hand." Calling "openness the surest guarantee for fairness," the task force requested that it be allowed to take part in a review of the selection criteria drafted by the administration (Sing and Kawaichi 1988b).

Federal Intervention

Questions of discriminatory admissions policies also continued to exist at other schools. In late 1988 the announcement of two federal investigations, one at Harvard, the other at UCLA, suggested that the controversy extended far beyond Berkeley. Capping a year of state-led investigations aimed at Berkeley policies, the U.S. Department of Education announced in late November 1988 that it had been reviewing admissions policy at UCLA and Harvard since July.[11] Both inquiries, conducted by the department's Office of Civil Rights (OCR), were initiated in response to what the spokesperson for the office, Gary Curran, called "a generalized complaint."[12] According to Curran, such reviews were the result of widespread media articles citing evidence about Asian admissions and were not based on specific individual complaints at those particular schools. Curran explained to reporters that the main thrust of the review would be the alleged use of quotas by schools to limit Asian American admissions, saying, "We had gotten indications that there indeed may be a quota system being used" (Vobejda 1988). Describing the investigations as less than full-scale formal inquiries, Curran said, "We're doing what we call compliance reviews—to decide whether the admission procedures at those schools are in compliance with Title VI [of the Civil Rights Act of 1964], which prohibits discrimination on the basis of race, color, or national origin" (Gitell 1988).

Officials from UCLA and Harvard denied the use of quotas. Susie Chao, director of minority recruitment at Harvard, told the *Boston Globe*, "It's against Harvard's best interests to limit the number of Asian American applicants just because of their background. When a certain group is over its national percentage, I don't think we worry" (Gitell 1988). David Eun, a student recruiter in the Harvard admissions office, agreed with Chao. He dismissed the charges of quotas, saying, "We go out of the way to be fair. Everyone's always going to look at Harvard just because it's Harvard" (Gitell 1988). At UCLA, Vice Chancellor Thomas Lifka denied the existence of quotas. He told the *Los Angeles Times* that the administration, "while not alarmed," was "taking it very seriously" (Woo 1988). Asian Americans welcomed the federal probe. At Berkeley Professor Wang, citing a 1985 memo by Director of Admissions Rae Lee Siporin on declining white enrollments, called the evidence against UCLA "compelling." At UCLA Don Nakanishi, said that although the admission rates of Asian Americans there had stabilized since the early 1980s, there were still concerns about possible anti-Asian bias (Woo 1988).

Some individuals, including the OCR spokesperson Gary Curran, felt that Berkeley should have been included in the compliance reviews with Harvard and UCLA. He attributed the omission of Berkeley from OCR reviews in 1988 to a bureaucratic snafu.[13] Curran knew that the Department of Justice had received individual complaints from seven students who were turned away from Berkeley, Yale, and Stanford. But in apparent confusion over which federal department had jurisdiction in the matter, the individual complaints were held for over a year by the Department of Justice (Jaschick 1989b). By the time the specific complaints were turned over to the Department of Education, the individual complainants were no longer interested in pressing their cases. According to Curran, the Justice Department "bungled" the investigation.

Members of the task force, however, believed that bureaucratic snafu or not, there was no reason for OCR to investigate Berkeley in 1988. Wang told the *Daily Californian*, "Berkeley is the wrong place to initiate an investigation. The Asian community is well organized here. There is ongoing communication between Asian Americans and the University. There is no need for the Office of Civil Rights. I oppose [the Department of Education] entering Berkeley and interrupting the dialogue that's been going on" (Chuang 1988b). But while the dialogue between Asian Americans and university officials at Berkeley may have kept federal investigators away, it could not fend off neoconservative entry into the public debate.

The Task Force's Unwanted Allies: Neoconservatives

In late November, less than two weeks after the Office of Civil Rights announced its investigations, Attorney General William B. Reynolds, the head of the Civil Rights Division of the U.S. Department of Justice, introduced the neoconservative solution to the problem of Asian admissions. Speaking before a conference organized by Senator Thomas Daschle (D-S.D.) on discrimination against Asian American students in higher education, Reynolds placed the blame for discrimination against Asians at the door of affirmative action. Citing figures on GPA and SAT scores, Reynolds (1988) argued, "There is substantial statistical evidence that Asian American candidates face higher hurdles than academically less qualified candidates of other races, whether those candidates be minorities (black, Hispanic, Native American) or white." A frequent critic of preferential policies, he traced the problem of discrimination against Asians to affirmative action programs, saying, "In other words, the phenomenon of a 'ceiling' on Asian Americans admissions is the inevitable result of the 'floor' that has been built for a variety of other favored racial groups" (Reynolds 1988).

Reynolds's solution to the Asian admissions problem, the elimination of affirmative action in higher education, provoked immediate controversy. The other panelists at the conference, Asian Americans and university administrators, all disagreed with Reynolds. University officials from Brown and Berkeley defended affirmative action as necessary to achieve diversity. Dean Eric Widmer of Brown said, "It is inconceivable to me that one wouldn't want to take steps to increase opportunities for blacks and Hispanics to enroll and that requires affirmative action—it's not going to happen without it" (Eaton 1988). Similarly, Alice Cox, assistant vice president of student academic services at the University of California, said, "Without affirmative action programs . . . we would lose a tremendous enrichment" (Eaton 1988). Henry Der and a Yale law student, Grace Tsuang, tried to distance themselves from their unwanted ally's critique of affirmative action. Both emphasized that Asians wanted to be treated fairly in the competition with whites and that such goals were entirely compatible with affirmative action programs.

Reynolds's remarks offered a tidy settlement to the years of conflict between university officials and the task force. On the one hand, his claim embraced task force accounts of discrimination against Asian Americans in higher education. In fact, in his talk at the conference, Reynolds recited the arguments and facts originally presented by the Brown AASA and the task force. On the other hand, Reynolds recapitulated administrators' claims of Asian American overrepresentation in his efforts to show that university officials were using preferential categories based on race, a policy outlawed by the *Bakke* decision. In Reynolds's view, diversity and discrimination were two sides of the same bad coin, affirmative action.

Reynolds's speech marked the beginning of a new era in charges by conservatives and neoconservatives concerning Asian admissions. The construction of these claims, the subject of the next chapter, effectively shifted the discourse on Asian admissions once again—this time from diversity to affirmative action. But before turning to an examination of the neoconservative explanation of the problem, it is important to understand how the trajectory of debate over admissions between 1987 and 1988 made this shift in discourse possible.

The Politics of Facts

In Chapter 3 I examined how university officials countered claims of discrimination with claims about diversity in higher education. This chapter has focused on a complementary development, the attempt to resolve the controversy over Asian admissions politically, through external reviews. The campaign for a political resolution of the issue, a strategy adopted by the task force, focused on gathering and analyzing admissions data. In effect the external reviews served two functions: to pressure university officials into a dialogue with Asian Americans and to provide both sides with the same statistics about which they could talk.

That many of the external reviews of Asian admissions—by the auditor general, the State Assembly Subcommittee on Higher Education, and the Office of Civil Rights—chose to use the admission rate (and not parity measures) as the standard measure for discrimination was a partial victory for Asian American critics of university admissions policy.[14] In the battle of rhetoric, defining Asian admissions as a problem of discrimination or diversity hinged on which standard—admission rates or parity—was being used.

Both sides hoped that the external reviews would vindicate their respective positions. The infusion of more statistics into the debate suggested a certain optimism that the debate might be resolved through a better, clearer, technical understanding of the issues. Indeed, early in the debate, one university official praised Asian American critics for their reliance on facts and data. Dean Ann Girgus of Princeton told the *New York Times*, "They [Asian Americans] seem to believe—as I think they should—in the power of analysis, to put data in the properly analyzed form" (Winerip 1985).

As it turned out, putting the data in the right form was not a simple matter. The reviewers of admissions policy, whether they were members of a faculty committee or members of the state legislature, needed specific kinds of data to answer questions never before asked about admissions decisions. At the Berkeley campus, for instance, the Regents wanted to know exactly how the application essay was scored; the auditor general wanted to know the qualifications of those Asian American applicants who were admitted and rejected through Tier 2. In most cases, the information reviewers asked for was either not available or not in the form requested. The result was that university officials were faced with the task of collating and analyzing their admissions data in particular ways to be able to respond to inquiries about admissions.

Both sides at Berkeley say that the external reviews led to positive changes in record keeping at the university. Director of Admissions Robert Bailey recalled that before 1983 the university computerized only demographic information on applicants. According to Bailey, the only way to analyze admission rates by qualification was to read through all of the individual files. He said,

> We had some demographic data on the applicant, but for example a freshman has to have A to F requirements, certain course requirements. Those aren't computerized, so if they had an omission or were missing one course, the only way you could know is to go back and open the file folder and look in. Well, if you get 32,000 applications in a 12–month period, it doesn't lend itself to looking back in each file folder. There's no way of pulling, saying, "Show us all the ones you accepted by appeal," because we don't flag it on the system; you'd have to go back and look at every folder to determine which ones.[15]

The problem with computerizing some but not all information about applicants became especially apparent during the auditor general's review of Berkeley admissions for the period 1981–1987. Given the kinds of records kept by Berkeley it was difficult, and sometimes impossible, to reconstruct past admissions decisions. Consequently, the auditor general's report contains a detailed discussion on the limitations of the study. These problems include possible inaccuracies in the data, incomplete applicant files, and the lack of computerized information essential for completing the investigation. Bailey explained to me, "There was no audit trail, so you couldn't sort of tell what was happening in December, what was happening in January. You could tell that it happened, but there was no snapshot by month, and that causes some difficulties in the statistical analysis."[16]

Although other schools may have had more complete and/or better accounting systems for their admissions processes, they too were faced with the task of finding the proper data and proper statistical analysis to address the question of discrimination against Asians. Without exception, all of the in-house committees focused their investigation on the admission rate of Asian Americans. In cases where it was found that Asians were admitted at a rate lower than that of whites, most of the committees considered two possible explanations for the discrepancy. Asians were either not as well qualified, not members of certain groups given preferential treatment in admission, or both. The Princeton faculty committee, for instance, as well as other faculty committees, found that Asian American applicants were less qualified than whites—or, in other words, that Asian American personal ratings were lower than those of whites. The other common explanation of discrepancies in admission rates offered by Brown, Harvard, and Princeton was that Asians were underrepresented as athletes and children of alumni, two groups afforded preference in admissions. If a committee did not find that Asians were any less qualified than whites, then it was likely to exclude from the analysis certain preferred groups of students—athletes and children of alumni, for example—and reexamine the evidence. If differences between whites and Asians still persisted after eliminating certain students, then some committees, such as those at Stanford and Brown, conceded discrimination. However, other schools, notably Harvard, found at this stage of the analysis that differences in admission rates between whites and Asian disappeared, prompting them to suggest that differential admission rates were an artifact of preference for alumni children or athletes.

Between 1987 and 1988, Asian American critics of the Berkeley administration hoped to move the public debate on admissions away from the issues of diversity and back to what they saw as the "real issue," discrimination. They pursued this objective by seeking state-sponsored reviews of Berkeley admissions policies—hoping that such reviews would vindicate their claims of quotas and ceilings on Asian American applicants. Although the various in-house and external reviews answered the empirical question of discrimination, the question of how best to frame the issue—diversity or discrimination—remained unaddressed.

In the stalemate over how to define the problem, the proliferation of more data and statistics sometimes brought with it a certain cynicism about the numbers. At the same time that the external reviews pumped out more data, many people on both sides of the issue began to place less stock in the value of the statistics. For example, Assistant Chancellor John Cummins told the *Berkeley Graduate*, "We can argue over the statistics forever" (Lye 1986). John Bunzel (1988c) of the Hoover Institution went to the heart of the matter when he noted, "Any thoughtful discussion about college admissions procedures and decisions is likely to turn into a discussion about competing values and their relationship to the hard choices an admission officer faces."

Between 1987 and 1988, the combination of the increased availability of statistics and the clash in values between officials and their Asian American critics over the framing of the problem presented an important transitional moment in claims about Asian admissions.[17] On the one hand, administrators and their critics shared a basic conviction that the facts and statistics of admissions constituted the incontrovertible pieces of evidence to document or dispel claims of discrimination. On the other hand, both sides used the same facts to construct quite different interpretations of the problem as discrimination or diversity. One writer described the conflict between the shared belief in the value of statistics and the conflict in values over Asian admissions as ironic: "The one thing both camps agree on is, ironically, the one thing they have not been able to do—neither seems able to dispel a notion that somewhere, deep down in the reams of data, lurks the truth" (Lye 1987). Neoconservatives were quick to capitalize on the irony of the moment. While Asian Americans and university officials bickered over the "truth," neoconservative intellectuals shifted the debate about truth to a different level.

CHAPTER 5

Affirmative Action and Its Discontents: Asian Victims and Black Villains

Students at highly selective colleges in the United States share a heightened sense of awareness about their educational accomplishments. They worked hard through high school, juggling band practice, after-school clubs, and sports with academic work and advanced placement courses. Earning an admissions spot at a school such as Berkeley, Harvard or Stanford is often viewed as a just reward for years of concentration and hard work.

The competition for admission to the elite colleges has grown keener in the 1980s and early 1990s—at some schools, only one in ten applicants is admitted.[1] Respectable grades and test scores are not enough to gain entrance to the highly selective schools. By the late 1980s admissions officers at elite schools reported that they were turning away students boasting perfect GPAs and test scores in the 98th percentile (Harris 1988).

These days, applicants to the top schools must sharpen every competitive edge. They plan, sometimes years in advance, their regimen of extracurricular activities and academic subjects in high school to achieve a "balanced" program. Applicants take privately run prep courses, hoping to boost their college board scores. And a growing number of applicants now seek the help of private admissions counselors—paying fees up to $2000—to help "package" their applications (Tifft 1988).

In this atmosphere of cutthroat competition for admission,

racial differences in educational achievement became a locus of white grievances in the 1980s. At many colleges and universities white students came to view themselves as "victims," squeezed between Asian American achievement and preferential policies for blacks. Many white students, while insecure about competing against Asian Americans in higher education, were openly angry about what they perceived as underachievement among their black peers. Despite the fact that blacks had always constituted a relatively small proportion of freshman enrollment at the highly selective schools, many whites, and some Asians too, accepted the presence of blacks in higher education only begrudgingly. A complaint often heard was that less qualified blacks were accepted while better-qualified whites were rejected.

Black/white differences in academic achievement became the cornerstone of the belief that white students made it to college on the basis of merit while black students slipped in through the back door of affirmative action and/or racial preferences. The view that affirmative action was synonymous with lower academic "standards" found support in the Protestant work ethic—you should work for what you get. According to many students, blacks didn't deserve to be at the top colleges. Said a white coed from Berkeley, "Everytime I see a black person, not an Asian, but any other person of color walk by, I think, affirmative action. It's like that's your first instinct. It's not, maybe that person was smart; it's gotta be Affirmative Action. They don't even belong here" (Diversity Project 1989).

The Resurgence of Racism in Higher Education

By the mid-1980s white grumbling about black students was punctuated by an alarming "new racism," a wave of harassment, verbal insults, and incidents of outright racial violence.[2] The 1986 World Series brawl between white student Red Sox fans and black student Mets fans at the University of Massachusetts, Amherst, was only the beginning of a disturbing upswing in campus bigotry. During the 1988 academic year, arsonists set the first black fraternity ablaze at the University of Mississippi; a fraternity at the University of Wisconsin, Madison, held a mock "slave auction"; freshman pranksters at Stanford caricatured Beethoven's racial heritage; a swastika along with the words "white power" were found on the door of the Afro-American center at Yale; and a writer for the *Dartmouth Review* described a black professor as a "used brillo pad." At some campuses, the verbal insults were backed by organized white student campaigns against affirmative action. At Florida State and Temple Universities, the establishment of a White Student Union in 1988 and 1989, respectively, suggested that white working-class racism had managed to roost in higher education. Members of the groups liked to differentiate themselves from the white supremacists of earlier eras. The students claimed that they sought racial equality for whites through "proper" institutional channels and that they did not engage in the frightening and hateful violence characteristic of groups such as the Ku Klux Klan. Rather, they said, they focused their attention on what they felt were the inequities of affirmative action. Michael Spletzer, co-founder of the Temple White Student Union, argued against racial preferences, saying, "Individual merit should be the only criterion" (Gibbs 1990).

Affirmative action policies were symbolic of the heightened importance of race identity and racial issues in campus life, or what Michael Omi and Howard Winant (1986) refer to as the process of racialization.[3] Other elements of this trend included the consolidation of ethnic studies programs, the proliferation of student organizations along racial lines, and the faculty/student drive to make the curriculum relevant to the changing racial demographics of the student population.[4]

For many white students of the late 1980s, finding a meaningful place for themselves in the racial terrain of campus life became awkward and frustrating.[5] White students complained that they were tired of hearing about racism. To many of these students, the significance of race in their social and academic world appeared exaggerated. Occasionally students have expressed such feelings in malicious jokes and crude stereotypes. In one instance, a caller to the campus radio station at the University of Michigan, Ann Arbor, took an ugly stab at "black history"—"who are the two most famous black women in history? Aunt Jemima and Mother Fucker" (Wiener 1990).

In contrast to the coarseness of white student resentment, more sophisticated critics began to argue that racialization had torn at the fabric of academic excellence. In particular, some critics denounced certain academic programs—ethnic studies and women's studies—as intellectual shams. Thomas Sowell (1989), a leading black conservative scholar, described black studies as "low quality" and devoid of serious academic content.[6] Although the defenders of ethnic studies countered that such critics failed to appreciate "difference," the conservative view appears to have swayed a small but vocal segment of the academy.

At the core of the new conservative critique was the belief that institutions of higher education had abandoned standards of "academic merit" to accommodate special interest groups such as black student organizations and black faculty. Complaints from both students and the professoriate about "declining standards" were often illustrated with stinging anecdotes of inarticulate and/or near-illiterate students who "cannot make the grade at the university." Although the racial background of these students might go unmentioned, in a majority of instances the references were to minority students, particularly blacks. Feminist intellectuals and women's studies programs too were frequently implicated in what one writer called "minority terrorism" in higher education (Bernstein 1990). A speaker at the inaugural conference of the National Association of Scholars, a five-hundred-member organization dedicated to restoring the academy to its earlier pristine condition, free of "radical egalitarianism," urged his fellow conservatives to "stand up to them. They crumble. Say to the feminists, 'what do you mean by separate course?' You have no methodology" (Mooney 1988).

Liberal university officials and faculty of the late 1980s dismissed the conservative call to "take back" the university, saying that their policies of diversity and multiculturalism were a necessary step in broadening the intellectual and academic landscape of inquiry in higher education. They explained the resurgence in racism as a by-product of a generational transition in American politics from the altruism of the 1960s to the "me" generation politics of the 1980s. The new mood of individualism and narcissism among students in the 1980s was, according to liberal wisdom, cultivated by years of social "meanness" during the Reagan presidency. Some, such as Mary Maples Dunn, president of Smith College in Northhampton, Massachusetts, suggested that the new racism was the result of unfinished business, the failure to complete the political project of transforming race relations in the 1960s. She told *Newsweek*, "We thought we'd done good things in the 1960s, but we rested on our laurels" (Tifft 1989). Albert Camarillo, chair of the Stanford University Committee on Minority Concerns, suggested that the new racism was fueled by a broader politics of discontent with the welfare state. He said, "They [the students] have been raised in an era when equal opportunity has been questioned" (Tifft 1989).

But these liberal explanations of the new racism faltered against various critiques of diversity and affirmative action offered by neoconservatives. Neoconservative intellectuals and politicians folded discrimination against Asians into a trope of broader disaffection for liberalism in higher education. The end product was the most trenchant neoconservative critique of affirmative action yet.

Affirmative Action: Solution or Problem?

Interestingly enough, the neoconservative assault on liberal administrators on the issue of race has been publicly articulated by black intellectuals as well as white. Calling liberal views of affirmative action and diversity the problem, not the solution, Sowell (1989) suggested that "vicious racial incidents have been most prominent where the prevailing liberal (or radical) vision has been most prominent."[7] Similarly Shelby Steele (1989), a black professor of literature at San Jose State University in California, explained the new racial ugliness on college campuses as a product of "racial equality, not inequality."

Asian American achievement and the developing controversy over admissions provided Thomas Sowell and like-minded neoconservatives a crucial vehicle for their offensive against liberal educators. Beginning in late 1988 and continuing through 1989 and 1990, the intellectuals John Bunzel, Frank Gibney, and others along with political figures such as Dana Rohrabacher and William Bradford Reynolds fused elements of the rhetorical arguments from both university officials and Asian American organizations to forge a new interpretation of the facts of Asian admissions. In doing so, they repackaged the problem and simultaneously shifted the discourse from diversity to affirmative action.

In part, the ascendancy of neoconservative thought has been due to the ability of its intellectual leaders to grasp complex, multilayered social problems and recast them as questions of fairness. In addition, neoconservative thinkers have shown themselves to be the ultimate "spinmasters." They were able to tackle a complicated web of related problems and distill the issues, often without loss of subtleties, to a single policy or problem. During the early 1980s, for instance, neoconservatives meshed together the social crises of crime, the decline in family values, and despair among youth into a revisionist view of the causal linkages between welfare spending and poverty (Murray 1984). In the late 1980s they accomplished a similar revision in popular discourse about higher education.

Constructing a Neoconservative Vision of Asian Admissions

The link between affirmative action and Asian admissions eluded many, but not John Bunzel. The president of San Jose State University before his appointment at Hoover, Bunzel approached Asian admissions through the issues of ethnic diversity, academic excellence, and fairness. In 1987, with Jeffrey Au, Bunzel argued that an appropriate methodology for discerning discrimination against Asian Americans in admissions policy should be based on a comparison of Asian and white admission rates. Citing admissions data from Brown, Harvard, Princeton, and Stanford, Bunzel and Au (1987:62) suggested that "Asian American admission rates have been determined more by the policies, preferences, and practices of college admissions officers than by the qualifications of Asian American applicants." Bunzel's first foray into Asian admissions did little to recast the debate already in progress between Asian Americans and university officials. In this instance the two authors took their place alongside the task force in the debate. Bunzel and Au (1987) rejected university claims of Asian overrepresentation, charged officials with "serious ignorance of Asian culture," and hinted that at some private universities, alumni and athletic preferences constituted a weak explanation for admission rate differentials.

In late 1988, however, publishing somewhat different pieces in the *Los Angeles Times* and the *Public Interest*, Bunzel (1988b, c) unveiled a new interpretation of the problem. Although he continued to embrace task force accounts of the problem, Bunzel redirected his sights to focus on the "dilemma" of affirmative action, by which he meant balancing diversity with merit in university admissions. Aiming his criticism at Berkeley's affirmative action policy, Bunzel (1988b) suggested that race-conscious admissions policies there had gone too far. Observing university claims about the need for "diversity" in order to justify its affirmative action policies, Bunzel (1988c:116) wrote, "Yet diversity is open to different meanings and

interpretations. Is ethnic diversity desirable because it benefits society, because it is fair, and there good for society, because it has been
mandated, or because it is popular? How is the goal of ethnic diversity to be balanced against other factors?"

Bunzel (1988c:116) neatly tucked task force claims of discrimination against Asians into his objections to the term "diversity":
"And can 'diversity' also mask some of the criteria that admissions
officers use in making their decisions? Asian American leaders
charged that Berkeley has systematically de-emphasized objective
admissions criteria in the name of achieving diversity, knowing that
the change in policy would harm Asian American applicants with
high academic qualifications." Bunzel's argument was clear: one
consequence of preferential policies at Berkeley, however well intentioned they might originally have been, was that better-qualified
whites and Asian Americans were losing to blacks and Hispanics in
the zero-sum game of admissions.

A small group of neoconservative writers extended Bunzel's
critique of diversity into an all out attack on affirmative action. These
observers believed that discrimination against Asians at the top universities suggested the ultimate coup de grace against affirmative
action policy. Their commentaries all pointed toward the same conclusion: affirmative action inevitably leads to discrimination. In early
1988, James Gibney, writing for the *New Republic*, noted that "racial
re-alignment has brought new racial tension." He emphasized the
zero-sum relation between Asian admissions and affirmative action
(Gibney 1988). In his view, Asians and blacks were each other's
main opponents in the admissions: "If Asians are underrepresented
based on their grades and test scores, it is largely because of affirmative action for other minority groups. And if blacks and Hispanics
are underrepresented based on their fraction of the population, it is
increasingly because of the statistical overachievement of Asians.
Both complaints can't be just, and the blame can no longer be placed
solely on favoritism toward whites" (Gibney 1988).

Taking a somewhat different tack, Daniel Seligman (1989),
writing for *Fortune*, cast Asian admissions as a continuation of reverse discrimination toward whites: "It had to happen, so now it is
happening. Racial preferences in college admissions, legitimized by
the Supreme Court's infamous Bakke decision in 1978, is now being
used against the wrong people [Asian Americans]. Affirmative action logic states firmly that Asian Americans should now suffer

reverse discrimination, just as the whities [*sic*] have suffered it for years. In California, furthermore, the same logic implies even more restrictive policies toward Asian Americans than toward whites."

Although Seligman viewed the *Bakke* decision as legal means of discrimination, others upheld *Bakke* as a legal standard that university officials failed to meet. One individual who upheld *Bakke* as a legal standard was Arthur Hu. In late 1988, Hu, a graduate of the Massachusetts Institute of Technology and a computer programmer by day, began to spend his evenings writing caustic editorials on Asian admissions and affirmative action for *Asian Week*, a California-based Asian community paper. In early 1989, Hu (1989a) blasted both Berkeley and UCLA for admissions policies that resulted in the growth in minority admissions "at the expense of Asians." He accused University of California admissions officials of violating *Bakke*:

> Their [UC] "goals" have become quotas in everything but name. No matter the other complicated objective criterion that are used in the admissions process, the bottom line [is] that the number of accepted minorities was cut off at the goal level. . . . Not only that, but by reserving 20 percent of spots for minorities at UCB, they have created precisely the kind of quota that was struck down by the Bakke decision. (1989a: 4)

Hu, who thinks of himself as a neoconservative and counts John Bunzel along with Thomas Sowell and Nathan Glazer among his ideological heroes, became a regular columnist for *Asian Week* in April 1989. His first column was an unabashed critique of liberalism in higher education. Hu's parody of why Asian students were better prepared than others sarcastically suggested that Asian parents were not corrupted by "progressive theory":

> Asian parents are more likely to believe that a child's success is due more to his or her individual effort than any "aptitude" that was fixed at birth. They still believe the now discredited notion that the best way to get ahead is to obey your elders, stay out of trouble and study hard. They haven't been enlightened with the more progressive theory that minorities are helpless victims of racism, and only political and affirmative action, not individual effort, will make a difference. (Hu 1989b)

Like Seligman and Gibney, Hu worried about the declining white enrollments at UC. He noted, "The most ironic result is that whites are now the only underrepresented minority on campus. Only 38 percent of UCLA freshman are white, even though they are 64 percent of the graduating seniors. Black or Hispanic seniors are nearly twice as likely to be at UCLA as their white counterparts" (Hu 1989a).

In their construction of claims about Asian admissions, Bunzel, Seligman, Gibney, and Hu borrowed from the rhetoric of both liberal and Asian American accounts of the problem of admissions and, at the same time, rejected the conclusions of each. For instance, neoconservatives agreed with university officials that white students were the new underdogs in university admissions but also chastised university officials for continuing to sing the praises of racial diversity.

The neoconservative view borrowed most heavily from the claims of discrimination by the task force, the Brown AASA, and ECASU. Frequently neoconservative claims about Asian admissions mimicked the opening arguments presented by Asian American critics of the university. The neoconservative accounts accepted Asian American claims of quotas and discrimination with little or no criticism. For example, this passage from a *Washington Post* column by the conservative George Will (1989) entitled "Prejudice against Excellence" might well have been written by the task force: "Coinciding with rising academic attainments by Asian Americans has been a suspiciously sudden tendency by colleges across the country to de-emphasize high school academic performance of applicants. Admissions offices place more emphasis on, for example, extracurricular activities."

But though Will freely borrowed factual grist from the task force, he remained critical of the liberal blush of task force politics. Will (1989) called the name of the organization headed by Henry Der, Chinese for Affirmative Action, "unfortunate," saying, "the name Chinese Affirmative Action reflects a felt need to participate in an ethnic spoils system. However, affirmative action discriminated against Asian Americans by restricting the social rewards open to competition on the basis of merit."

What was new and original about the neoconservative construction of the Asian admissions problem was the manner in which claims from both university officials and Asian Americans were pressed into the service of a broader critique of diversity. Neoconservative apportionment of Asian American students as the new victims of affirmative action was a useful way to combine task force accounts of Asians as disadvantaged subjects of discrimination with university administrators' counterclaims about diversity. Groups like the task force charged discrimination but advocated diversity.

University officials invoked diversity as a defense against charges of discrimination. Neoconservatives claimed that diversity policies were the heart of the problem—creating a breeding ground for racism and discrimination.

The Free Market Approach to Admissions

The neoconservative critique of diversity rested on a specific vision of fairness and equity in admissions policy. That vision, shared by Bunzel, Gibney, Sowell, and Hu, was that applicants ought to be evaluated strictly on the basis of individual achievements and not on the basis of race. In other words, competition for admission to the highly selective schools should function much like a free market— individuals should compete against one another on the basis of individual merit. In the ideal world of free markets, those who reap unfair advantages in the market through collusion or control undermine the efficiency of the system. Similarly in admissions policy, preferences for certain groups, undermine the quality of the final product by giving less qualified students an advantage over better-qualified students. That less qualified minority students might gain admission at the expense of better-qualified whites or Asians was a violation of free market principles. Neoconservatives often cited the finding that at some schools the average SAT scores of Asian American applicants were higher than the average SAT scores of the class of admitted students.

Proponents of the free market approach to university admissions took a "get tough" approach to the problem of black and white differences in academic achievement. Neoconservatives argued that differences in achievement between racial groups were the result of differences in policy toward each group.[8] Closing the achievement gap was best accomplished, therefore, by abolishing any preferential policies for the underrepresented. In other words, for neoconservatives, racial preferences were the *sine qua non* of differential achievement. Neoconservative rhetoric suggested that the concern for equality and affirmative action in higher education spawned one of the more disturbing developments of the 1980s, that is, the politics of difference. According to Shelby Steele, such a politics produced a "troubling" and "volatile" atmosphere on college campuses in which both blacks and whites experienced personal and racial anxiety. If black students suffered under the belief that all whites think of them as affirmative action beneficiaries, Steele (1989) said, white students were burdened by the ever-present fear of being labeled a racist. On both sides, anxieties about race often developed into aggressive posturing. On many campuses, black students demanded that the administration support separate facilities—for example, "theme" dorms, black graduation ceremonies, and black studies departments. White students contended that "blacks should complain less, and work harder in school."

In drawing a hard line against diversity policies, neoconservatives claimed to be addressing the problem of racism. But their position was hardly a majority view, and attempts to persuade education officials and the general public that a free market approach was best for everyone proved to be an uphill struggle.

Students and their parents, the faculty, and the administration were all keenly aware that racial balkanization of the type described by neoconservatives was an everyday fact of campus life. But few were willing to attribute such developments to the very policies that were aimed at preventing racism. In addition, public concern over racial differences in academic achievement and the upsurge in racism in higher education were hardly the exclusive political domain of neoconservatives. For many, the neoconservative contention that diversity was the root cause of discrimination and differences in achievement was not compelling. A vocal group of students and faculty argued that the real problem was that diversity policies were at best superficial. Reginald Wilson, a senior scholar at the American Council on Education, told the *Los Angeles Times*, "Some universities have created a [minority affairs] office or program and say they solved the problem. I see on many campuses where the minority affairs officer doesn't have any power. Yet when you ask people who is responsible, they point to that person" (Reichmann 1989).

Neoconservatives found in Asian admissions an excellent opportunity to energize their vision of individual merit and the free market approach to admissions. Issues of diversity, balkanization, and black/white differences in academic achievement were all concentrated in the problem of Asian admissions. Neoconservatives were quick to catalog the particulars of Asian admissions as hard evidence for their critique of diversity, the politics of difference, and affirmative action. They adeptly picked out the meritocratic-sounding arguments of groups like the task force to support their proposal for admissions policies based on individual merit, not race. The qualifications of Asian American students provided neoconservatives with a group of ethnic champions with which to disarm liberalism in higher education.

By bringing Asian *achievement* into the ring of conflict over black and white differences in academic achievement, neoconservatives insisted that their free market vision of admissions was not racially motivated but, rather, inspired by fairness. Still, several neoconservative authors were acutely aware that their struggle to gore affirmative action once and for all was possible because the high achievers were *Asian*, not white. Some drily noted the convergence of logic between the neoconservative attack on affirmative action and the "droolers" over affirmative action. Commenting on an editorial on Asian admissions that had appeared in the *Washington Post*, Seligman (1989) noted, "Proposition: 'The idea that there is anything intrinsically 'wrong' with a student body's being heavily Asian, if those students represent the best and ablest ones available, is . . . pernicious—not to mention bad for the institutions involved.' Could that sentence have appeared in the paper with 'white' substituted for 'Asian'?"

Although neoconservatives advocated a color-blind system of admissions, they did so by first drawing attention to racial differences in academic achievement and admission. Highlighting the achievements of Asians as a racial minority, neoconservatives used Asian American students as an important racial wedge in the debate in order to criticize institutions for favoring blacks at the expense of Asians and whites. For example, Reynolds (1988) argued that although it was unfair that Asians were admitted at lower rates than whites, it was especially reprehensible that both Asians and whites were admitted at lower rates than blacks. The inequality in admission rates between blacks on the one hand and Asians and whites on the other was, according to Reynolds (1988), the product of a real problem—affirmative action. Neoconservatives charged that the "logic" of affirmative action—constructed from racial parity or proportional representation of a racial group relative to its proportion in the population—dictated that whites should replace both blacks and Asians as the new "underrepresented."

From Diversity to Affirmative Action

Neoconservative arguments about Asian admissions, against affirmative action and for a free market admissions policy, began to appear in commentary, articles, and editorials in late 1988 and early 1989. During this period neoconservative interventions in the discourse on Asian admissions were occasional and episodic. Longer articles appeared in outlets for conservative thought such as the *New Republic* or the *Public Interest*; shorter opinion items were published in major newspapers such as the *Los Angeles Times*. In several cases the focus of the articles was not Asian admissions but some other topic, for example, the new racism or affirmative action, and Asian admissions was mentioned only as an afterthought, or perhaps in order to illustrate an assertion about the inequity of affirmative action. In addition, the authors of these articles did not represent a particular interest group or register their opinions on behalf of an organization of neoconservative thought. Some individuals, including John Bunzel and William Bradford Reynolds, held jobs in the field of education. Others, such as Frank Gibney and George Will, were professional journalists. Still others, Arthur Hu, for example, whose work as a computer engineer placed him entirely outside the field of education, wrote articles on admissions as an avocation.

By the end of 1989, public discourse about Asian admissions had shifted decisively from diversity to affirmative action. News coverage of the issue featured fewer incidents of verbal sparring between Asian Americans and university officials and an increasing number of stories about how affirmative action programs or diversity policies might have caused discrimination against Asians (Goode 1989; Hacker 1989; Irving 1989; Jaschik 1989a; Moore 1989). Events during 1989 conspired to produce the shift in discourse. Two events at Berkeley were key: the completion of the faculty committee investigation and a second chancellor apology. These in turn generated renewed commentary and analysis in the national public discussion of Asian admissions. Perhaps the most significant factor in the discourse shift was that the Republican congressman Dana Rohrabacher (Long Beach, Calif.) mounted a legislative initiative to examine discrimination against Asians. His call for hearings on the subject generated new controversy involving university officials, the task force, and neoconservatives.

It is important to note that although the discourse on Asian admissions shifted to focus on how affirmative action programs did or did not cause discrimination, it would be wrong to infer from this development that the neoconservatives had won or were likely to win in the very near future their goal of a free market approach to admissions. On the contrary, media reports suggested that diversity policies were alive and well at most of the top universities, where minority enrollments continue to swell. Neoconservative success in shifting the public discussion to affirmative action, however, while not a guarantee of a strictly merit-based admissions policy, profoundly influenced discursive framing of the Asian admissions problem. First conceived as a straightforward issue of racial discrimination, then as a problem of diversity, Asian admissions, according to the neoconservatives, led inexorably to the inequity of preferential policies.

The Shack Committee: Whitewash or Yellow-wash?

The Berkeley faculty committee charged with a review of Asian admissions at Berkeley took sixteen months to do its job. Mired in controversy from start to finish, the committee, chaired by Professor William Shack, was appointed by the academic senate to recommence a review of Asian admissions in the wake of a controversial and disgraced set of findings of the Lynn committee. Both committees reached the same conclusion. The Shack committee findings, released in February 1989, found no wrongdoing on the part of the university: "In our investigation we have found nothing remotely resembling a 'quota' on the admission of Asian Americans at Berkeley. Nor have we found statistical evidence to support an inference of significant long-term bias against Asian Americans" (Shack 1989). But the committee did find one impropriety, the 1984 minimum verbal SAT directive. Other findings of the committee included a statement urging the university to prod the College Entrance Examination Board to develop Asian-language achievement tests, a mandate for regular review of admissions decisions, and a series of divided committee opinions on the use of supplemental criteria in the admissions process.

The task force summarily denounced the findings of the report. Henry Der told the *Los Angeles Times*, "It's a whitewash. The evidence of anti-Asian sentiment is staring them right in the face. . . . Maybe it's asking too much for a faculty subcommittee to chastise their colleagues or superiors publicly" (Gordon 1989). Ling-chi Wang (1989a) described the report as a "major disappointment" and a "political compromise much like the Bakke decision." The task force (AATF 1989), in a public statement issued by its two co-chairs, criticized the Shack report as a mathematical cover-up of discrimination. The report, charged the task force, "admits and documents significant discrimination in admissions against Asian American applicants in 1984" but then "conceals this discrimination by amortizing the data over a span of seven years and among all five colleges of the campus." According to the task force, the Shack report, despite its final conclusions, thus confirmed a "pattern of discriminatory policy initiatives in 1984 aimed specifically at making Asian American applicants less competitive with white applicants, thereby contributing to the unexpected disproportionate decline of Asian American freshmen in that year" (AATF 1989).

In the view of Professor Wang (1989b), the Shack report disclosed that the extent of discriminatory policies was far worse than originally thought by members of the task force. Although the task force had consistently maintained that university policies regarding Tier 2 (involving the use of supplemental criteria and the exclusion of Asians from EOP) had been detrimental to Asian applicants, the Shack report revealed for the first time a change in policy in Tier 1 between 1981 and 1984 that affected Asian applicants. According to the Shack report, before the university began to use the Academic Index score, applicant files were "retained" for admission on the basis of either grade point average or test scores. The Shack committee found that in 1984, Asian applicants were more likely to be retained on the basis of GPA, while white students were more likely to be retained on the basis of test scores alone. Between 1981 and 1984, however, officials at the College of Letters and Science increased the GPA threshold for retention from 3.75 to 3.9 *without* a corresponding shift in test scores. The Shack report stated, "This incongruence reduced the number of slots filled by GPA alone relative to the number of slots filled by test scores alone. It therefore worked to the disadvantage of Asian Americans, who were more likely than white applicants to be retained on the basis of GPA alone." But the report declined to fault university officials for the GPA policy: "We cannot rule out the possibility that this decision had the purpose, at least in part, of limiting the number of Asian Americans admitted relative to the number of whites. But neither can we confirm that possibility" (Shack 1989).

Professor Wang (1989a) felt that this latest revelation was further proof of the legitimacy of task force charges: "In spite of the white-wash by the Shack committee, the evidence presented in the report is most damaging. I feel most vindicated." At a press conference held March 1, both the task force and the Student Coalition for

Fair Admissions called on the chancellor to apologize and name the names of those administrators involved in the 1984 decline of Asians admitted to Berkeley. Complaints by both groups were underscored by the disgruntled student member of the Shack committee, Regina Acebo, a Filipina, who told the *Daily Californian*, "I think these episodes that our committee had determined cannot be seen as isolated incidents. They, in fact, are concrete examples of the anti-Asian sentiment present on our campus" (Chuang 1989a). Acebo maintained that the committee had dodged the issue of accountability: "Through these investigations, the committee said it was near impossible to determine who exactly instigated these admissions policy changes and why and who actually exercises policy changes. If the University cannot be held accountable for its actions, then who is accountable?" (Chuang 1989a).

Though she signed the Shack report, Acebo was unhappy with its conclusions and decided to draft a separate minority report (Acebo 1989). In it she complained that three issues, the 1984 SAT memo, the 1984 redirection policy affecting Asian Americans, and the change in the GPA threshold, were unsatisfactorily examined by the committee. According to Acebo (1989), "The University's response to the Asian admissions and admissions issue overall has been insensitive at best." Her criticisms, along with those of the task force, were aired at a state legislative hearing two weeks later.

On March 13, 1989, Senator Art Torres, chair of the California Senate Special Committee on UC Admissions, made the Shack report the featured subject of hearings on Asian admissions held on the Berkeley campus. In a highly charged session lasting two and a half hours, Torres's committee heard testimony from Shack, Acebo, members of the task force, the SCFA, and selected university officials, including Chancellor Heyman. During Professor Shack's testimony, Torres frequently interrupted to press Shack on several controversial aspects of the report. Torres asked Shack to explain why the presentation of admissions statistics in the report had been aggregated over a period of seven years; to describe the extent of disagreement between the Asian and other members of the committee; and to explain why the report treated as "impressionistic" information from two Asian administrators on Asian admissions.

Torres clearly disagreed with Shack's explanation of all three issues. For example, one dispute centered on a letter written by Patrick Hayashi, former assistant to the chancellor and member of the Office of Undergraduate Affairs, to Professor Shack on the 1984 decline in Asian enrollment. In the letter, Hayashi recounted a 1983 meeting on admissions at which the proposal to implement a verbal SAT minimum was made. Hayashi (1988) recalled, "I further argued that the proposed policy was discriminatory in intent in that some of the people present seemed to be deliberately searching for a standard which could be used to exclude Asian immigrant applicants. I noted that no other alternative solutions to the anticipated over-enrollment problem were being considered." When Shack defended the committee's interpretation of Hayashi's letter as "impressionistic," Torres countered, "It doesn't take that much to figure out they don't want those people in that situation." But Torres, in what amounted to a public scolding of Berkeley officials, reserved his harshest reproach for the chancellor. When the chancellor described Asian students as "disadvantaged" in the admissions process, Torres interjected, "The word is discrimination. There was a bias on the part of certain employees. Let's call it what it is—not disadvantaged and put rhetorical flourishes on it."[9]

Many administrators and faculty at Berkeley, including some who were sympathetic to the task force, were surprised at the harshness of the criticism Torres leveled at the high administration officials. Torres's verbal lashing of the Berkeley administration suggested that Asian admissions was a clear-cut and simple issue of discrimination. A dispute among the members of the Shack committee, however, which eventually resulted in a confidential minority report not discussed at the Torres hearings, maintained that what constituted a fair admissions policy was far from clear or simple.

The Confidential Minority Report

Although Professor Stephen Barnett, a member of the Shack committee, was in general agreement with the committee's report, he felt that the group had ducked an important and highly relevant aspect of discrimination against Asians American students—affirmative action at Berkeley. Professor Barnett claimed that consideration of affirmative action policy was reasonably within the purview of the committee charge, but the rest of the committee disagreed. The conceptualization of the Asian admissions problem had concrete implications for the work of the committee. If affirmative action was indeed a relevant consideration, Asian admission rates ought to be compared with the admission of both whites and underrepresented minorities. If affirmative action was not relevant to the investigation, then the Asian admission rate should be compared only with white admissions. In choosing the latter interpretation, the committee adopted the same position taken by the task force. But Barnett believed that affirmative action was relevant and felt that the committee had been on the wrong track from the beginning of its sixteen-month investigation. To address what he saw as a void in the final committee report, Barnett issued his own statement on the matter, a thirty-six-page, single-spaced, confidential paper, "Fairness to Asian Americans in Affirmative Action for Other Groups" (Barnett 1989).[10]

In the paper, which he called his "dissenting opinion," Professor Barnett registered strong support for admissions policies favoring underrepresented minorities but questioned whether the "extent" of preferential policies was "appropriate" or "sound." Barnett's controversial conclusion was that Berkeley should drop the principle of parity in the admission of underrepresented minorities through affirmative action. He wrote, "The concept [parity] is inconsistent with principles of individual achievement, intellectual merit, and academic excellence. It could logically lead to imposing a quota on the admission of Asian Americans, and it may already have contributed to efforts to limit the number of Asian Americans admitted to Berkeley" (Barnett 1989).

Task force members privately labeled Barnett a "neoconservative" and an "obstructionist." But Barnett had disagreements with neoconservatives as well. Dropping parity as a principle did not mean, according to Barnett, that the university should be, as some neoconservatives suggested, a pure meritocracy. Barnett claimed that he tried to distance himself from neoconservative attacks on affirmative action by restricting distribution of his paper to the Berkeley campus: "I didn't want to give too much ammunition to opponents of affirmative action. If it [the paper] got out, okay, I was prepared to, and am still prepared to accept that, but if it can be kept within the university and not become ammunition for people who are against the whole idea of affirmative action, I prefer that."[11] Professor Barnett criticized the neoconservative position on affirmative action—evaluation of applications on an individual basis only—as unworkable. He said,

> They say you can just consider people individually and not have any quota. But I think you can't, that that's a euphemism; you may not

call it a quota, but you have to have *some number in mind* in deciding how many people you're going to admit on a preferential basis based on race. . . . Justice Powell [in the *Bakke* case] relied on the Harvard system and said at Harvard they have no quota, they look at each person individually. Well, as I was saying before, I think that's a myth. You can't do that because that's a pretense. You have to have some rough admissions figure in mind when you're comparing the minority applicants with the white and Asian applicants in order to know how much weight to give to an individual's minority status. And so you go through a charade of claiming you have no figure in mind (emphasis added).[12]

In Barnett's view, the meritocratic approach to admissions advocated by neoconservatives—Bunzel and Au, for example—while ideologically comforting, raised a practical problem of how to compare *differently* qualified applicants. In reflecting on his own experiences at Berkeley, Professor Barnett said:

They [Bunzel and Au] say you don't need any targets; you can just look at people individually. In my experience in doing this in the law school and in thinking about it, you simply cannot. You would find good things about a number of minority applicants, looking at them individually. But there's no way to compare these things in individual cases with the higher grades and test scores that the whites and Asians have without having in mind some notion of the number of minority admits you want to end up with.[13]

From Barnett's perspective, neither liberals nor neoconservatives had found a panacea to the problem: "There's really no rational way to do it, and in a sense, the only rational way is parity, and that's worst of all."[14] Admissions, according to Barnett, "is a matter of compromises and political trade-offs and, you know, basically, I would take an approach like Karabel's [a new admissions proposal, discussed in Chapter 6]. I would disagree on the figures, but I think, it's politics and it almost has to be in some sense, arbitrary. It's almost better to pick a figure out of the air than to use parity."[15]

A Second Chancellor Apology

In April 1989, Chancellor Heyman and the task force held a joint press conference to announce the beginning of a new era of understanding and cooperation between them. The chancellor publicly apologized for the second time on the matter of Asian admissions, this time acknowledging that Berkeley's policies "indisputably had a disproportionate impact on Asians" (Chuang 1989b). On behalf of the task force, Lillian Sing said, "We are pleased with the statement that the chancellor [made]. With that statement, we can go forward and work toward correcting what has happened" (Chuang 1989b). The announcement marked a congenial end to five years of rancor and distrust between the two sides.

Not everyone was pleased with the new accord. Among the Berkeley faculty, there were some who privately wondered if the chancellor's apology to Asian Americans might be an Asian American version of a whitewash, that is, a yellow-wash. A few people worried that the chancellor's apology was symbolic of a larger problem affecting Berkeley, what they saw as a conflict between the university's commitment to diversity and the issue of quality in higher education. These concerns, along with others, gathered under the broad umbrella of issues labeled "external environment and internal process," were the focus of an ongoing set of discussions among a small group of faculty at Berkeley in the winter and spring quarters of 1989.[16] In a short précis describing the topics of discussion of the faculty group, the organizers of the colloquia stated, "We must ask whether the political tasks confronting American society are an appropriate part of the University's mission, especially if in increasing ethnic and gender diversity we lower standards of excellence."[17] If this small group of Berkeley faculty worried that the university might be capitulating to the demands of ethnic diversity through a lowering of standards, there were others who stated it even more baldly.

Liberalism as Racism

Neoconservatives such as George Will flinched at the rapprochement between the task force and university officials. Will believed that the apology was misdirected. He wrote, "the chancellor's grudging apology pertains to something recent, something that looks like racism practiced by a bastion of liberalism" (Will 1989). For Will (1989), though the chancellor apologized for "insensitivity," the real problem was that "race conscious policies toward Asian Americans may place ceilings through which they are not allowed to rise." He charged that punishing Asians for excellence signaled the return of the "yellow peril," only "this time dressed in the language of liberalism" (Will 1989).

Arthur Hu was more openly contemptuous of liberals and liberalism. His first columns in *Asian Week* elicited an embarrassed and angry disclaimer from the Asian American Resource Workshop, a community organization in Boston with which Hu had formerly been affiliated. A member of the workshop wrote, "We find most embarrassing the implication that the AARW agrees with the opinions expressed by Mr. Hu. In addition to perpetuating negative stereotypes of African Americans, his column also stereotypes Asian Americans" (S. Pan 1989). The AARW protest did not worry Hu. He lumped all Asian American liberals together, from Berkeley faculty members to his "old buddies" at the Asian American Resource Workshop, and called their brand of politics "left-wing, third world revolution bullshit."[18]

According to Hu, the recent "truce" between Asians and Berkeley officials did not mean that the issue was resolved. Hu suggested that Asian admission rates should have been even higher at Berkeley:

> Does the apparent fall in Asian quotas mean that the fight for equality in education is already over? Not necessarily. Asians may have decided to "bury the hatchet" over the past at Berkeley. But even if admission rates are now comparable or very slightly higher than whites, they could be even higher if justified by qualifications. Policies such as alumni preferences, subjective non-academic ratings, non-Asian foreign language requirements, writing and English requirements, and verbal SAT's still weight heavily against Asians. (Hu 1989f)

In mid-1989, just after the chancellor apologized, Hu argued that the issue of quotas and discrimination against Asians was already passé because university officials at Berkeley and elsewhere had shifted their course and were instead discriminating against whites. To Hu, Chancellor Heyman's apology was consistent with Hu's suspicion that in response to charges of quotas for Asians, many of the top schools had instituted a quota on whites to accommodate increases in Asian admissions. In early June, in the first of a two-part column on discrimination against Asians, Hu (1989e) suggested that while "discriminatory quotas and differential admission rates were probably introduced at Harvard, Stanford, UC Berkeley, and UCLA in the mid 1980s," the quotas appear to have been "quietly dropped" by 1989. Hu (1989e) maintained that lower admission rates and declining enrollments of Asians at UCLA and Berkeley were "the result of quotas designed to hold up white enrollments." Hu charged that this was what UCLA officials had in mind in a 1984 memo that, according to Hu, said, "Whites would not be allowed to fall, while Asians might be expected to complain about their declining numbers."

Hu was especially upset by the use of quotas against whites. He believed that minority complaints had forced university officials to adopt policies that had resulted in white underrepresentation at both Berkeley and UCLA. Hu's (1989f) challenge was provocative: "Whites haven't even noticed, much less cared about it. Maybe it's not a problem yet, but sooner or later, someone else will notice. If our educated leaders don't talk about it soon, some nut with an AK-47 may decide to beat them to it."

The real problem, according to Hu, was that *both* white and Asian enrollments should have been higher than they were in 1989. That whites in the late 1980s inherited the quotas against Asians in the early and middle years of the 1980s was, he said, the legacy of affirmative action. Like many other neoconservatives, Hu believed that affirmative action was the problem, not the solution. He wrote, "The largest problem is an outdated and unchallenged affirmative action system. It may have made sense in the black and white world of the '60s, but simply doesn't work with the large number of Asians now enrolling today in the '80s" (Hu 1989f).

White Quotas

A resolute Hu elected to do something concrete about his views on affirmative action. In the spring of 1989 he gathered his collection of facts and statistics about admissions and wrote a formal complaint about admissions policies at Harvard, Berkeley, and UCLA to the Office of Civil Rights in the Department of Education (Hu 1989d). Based on enrollment statistics and admission rates, Hu charged that Harvard implemented quotas against Asians in 1982, and then, in 1987, in response to the controversy over Asian admissions, quietly dropped the use of Asian quotas. Hu charged that at various times between 1984 and 1988, UCLA and Berkeley implemented quotas against whites, Asians, and underrepresented minorities. According to Hu (1989d), for example, in 1988 the enrollment of blacks and Hispanics at or near parity with the proportions of each group in the population indicated that "these proportions [are] being used as rough quotas . . . [which] hurt both white and Asian American students."

But the decline in Asian admission rates at Berkeley and UCLA in 1984 and 1985, said Hu, suggested the use of quotas to protect whites. Hu wrote, "In the absence of quotas, one would expect changes in one group to be reflected equally in all others. That one group, namely whites, was isolated from these changes is a strong indication of quota[s] setting a floor for white students. Though this floor was evidently dropped in 1985, I ask that this policy be investigated, and fully disclosed [so] that it cannot be repeated" (1989d:9).

Hu's complaint to the Office of Civil Rights about quotas offered not only a diagnosis of the problem but also a prescriptive solution. Hu suggested that the arrival of a large pool of well-qualified minority applicants for admission to the top colleges had thrown a wrench in the works of affirmative action. Therefore the principle of equal representation of minority groups in college admissions must be dropped.

> Ideally, affirmative action aims to achieve full representation for minorities, and equal representation for all. But it is impossible for all groups to be equally represented because there are far too many Asians. So most programs actually entitle only minorities to full representation. The result is that whites will be, and are in fact, the only group that is unfairly underrepresented at UC.
> . . . Consequently, the Office of Civil Rights should rule any affirmative action program which uses strict population proportions as a stated goals to be discriminatory and illegal. Groups such as Asians who exceed their proportions imply because they work harder should not be subject to equal proportions. (Hu 1989d:13)

Although the Department of Education received Hu's complaint in 1989, the Office of Civil Rights did not begin an investigation of his charges until the following year. The office, already involved in a compliance review of discrimination against Asians at UCLA and Harvard, eventually chose to examine Hu's contention about white quotas at Berkeley. In the meantime, while waiting for the federal government to get back to him about his complaint, Hu continued his crusade against equal proportions, parity, and affirmative action in the pages of *Asian Week*.

Title VI and White Quotas

Hu's complaint to the Office of Civil Rights was the neoconservative legal recourse to discrimination in admissions policy. But this was not what Grace Tsuang (1989), a third-year student at Yale Law

School, had in mind in her article on Asian admissions that appeared in the *Yale Law Journal*. A veteran of the Asian admissions controversy—as an undergraduate at Brown she had been a member of the AASA—she applied her knowledge of constitutional law to admissions. Tsuang (1989) outlined how a hypothetical Asian plaintiff, claiming that his or her school's admissions policies violated equal protection (from discrimination on the basis of race, color, or national origin) guaranteed by Title VI, might sue a college or university. But whereas Tsuang was writing about the application of Title VI to Asian Americans, Hu was extending the principles of Title VI to whites.

Despite their different opinions about affirmative action, there were certain points of convergence between their analyses of admissions. Both Tsuang and Hu were critical of the use of alumni preferences in admissions policies at the highly selective private universities. Hu (1989d:7) charged that Harvard's policy of alumni preferences, while accounting for differential admission rates between whites and Asians, was "racially biased in effect, if not intent, and Harvard should be asked if there is any policy that can remedy this disparity." In her article, Tsuang (1989) conceded that although alumni preferences might be justified by the financial concerns of private colleges, such preferences were "shortsighted" because they "did not weigh the future contributions of potential Asian alumni."

Although Tsuang felt that individuals such as William Bradford Reynolds and Arthur Hu were "trying to manipulate the issue and shape it into their own agenda," she suggested that such arguments avoided the real issue, discrimination. She noted:

> Even if it is true that certain portions of the class are set aside for some type of affirmative action consideration—not defining specifically what those considerations may be—there's no reason that in the rest of the applicant pool on the East Coast, 80 percent of the applicant pool, that Asians should not be able to compete equally with Caucasians. I'm not advocating a pure meritocracy where the only things you look at are grade point averages and SAT scores. I'm saying even if you look at extracurricular achievement—selection of majors and however nebulous you want to define this personal rating criteria—there's no basis for that kind of disparity in admit rates.[19]

But Tsuang's arguments about discrimination could not overtake neoconservative momentum on the issue of affirmative action. These neoconservative claims received increasing visibility in 1989. In addition to the neoconservative twist in the debate over Asian admissions spurred by Reynolds, Bunzel, and Hu, Representative Dana Rohrabacher brought Asian admissions into the arena of congressional political debate in late 1989.

Congressional Resolution Number 147

Congressman Dana Rohrabacher (Long Beach, Calif.) does not like to identify his politics as neoconservative.[20] Neoconservatives, he says, are former liberals, a label that he claims has never described his political orientation. Labels aside, Rohrabacher is in broad agreement with neoconservatives on the issue of Asian admissions. In June 1989, the freshman representative introduced a bill condemning the use of illegal quotas and urging universities across the country to scrutinize their admissions policies for possible bias against Asian American applicants.[21] In addition, the bill called on the Department of Education to move expeditiously on the compliance reviews at UCLA and Harvard and asked that the attorney general vigorously investigate any schools that were alleged to have discriminated on the basis of race. Finally, Rohrabacher suggested that Congress hold hearings on discrimination against Asian American students in college admissions and invited prospective individuals to contact his office about testifying.

Although Rohrabacher's bill (HR 147) carried no legal punch or remedy for discrimination, it was a highly symbolic show of Republican party interest in Asian admissions. The issue offered Republicans a unique opportunity to link concerns about racial discrimination with the Republican party. Representative Duncan Hunter (R–San Diego, Calif.), chair of the Republican Research Committee, told the *Press-Telegram*, a Long Beach newspaper, "I think it's important to show that the Republican Party is sensitive to discrimination, and that's what we're doing" (Halpert 1989). Rohrabacher recalled that his decision to sponsor HR 147 was in part a response to the enthusiastic reception to a speech he gave before a group of Asian American Republicans in the first half of 1989. Combining themes of "equal opportunity for all and special privileges for none"—themes that historically have been the domain of the Democratic party— Rohrabacher criticized discrimination against Asians in higher education. The effect, according to Rohrabacher, was immediate: "the whole place lit up."[22]

In June 1989, when his bill was first introduced, Rohrabacher was backed by an unusual combination of liberal and conservative supporters: B'nai Brith, the Heritage Foundation, and the Organization of Chinese Americans. Co-signatories on the bill were twenty-two other members of Congress, including the co-author of the resolution, an Asian American Republican from Hawaii, Patricia Saiki. In addition, several Asian American representatives lent their support for HR 147—including Robert Matsui, a Japanese American Democrat from California. Supporters of Rohrabacher welcomed Democratic and Asian support and hailed the bill as a bipartisan effort to eliminate illegal quotas in higher education.

The main backers of the bill, conservative Republicans, were quick to link the problem of discrimination against Asians with what they saw as a lowering of standards for other students. Republican leaders often cited Chancellor Heyman's recent apology and various enrollment and admission rate statistics culled by Asian American organizations in their support for HR 147. In addition the rhetoric of support for HR 147 often referred to past discrimination against Jewish applicants, as if to justify claims of discrimination against Asians. Frequently this rhetoric was trussed up with claims about less qualified students. Representative Duncan Hunter, for example, in a supporting statement for HR 147, said, "The University of California at Berkeley rarely accepts Asian students with GPAs lower than 3.7 while all other applicants may be admitted with GPAs as low as 2.78. This situation is comparable to Harvard University's discrimination against Jewish students in the mid-1920s, when Jewish admission fell from about 26% to approximately 13%."

Republican claims linking discrimination with lower standards of achievement were interpreted by some as the early warning signs of an imminent attack on affirmative action. In the fall of 1989, bipartisan support for HR 147 soured as some of the initial backers withdrew their support. All of the defectors worried that the bill was a veiled attack on preferential policies for underrepresented minorities. In spite of Rohrabacher's insistence that the bill said "nothing about affirmative action," Representative Matsui and the Organization of Chinese Americans retracted their support for HR 147. So did the Jewish American Committee, an organization that had indicated its intent to support the resolution but later reversed that decision after some members expressed concern about the effect of HR 147 on affirmative action policy. Some additional groups who were asked to support the bill—the Japanese American Citizen's League, for example—declined.

The Republican core of support for the resolution, Representatives Rohrabacher and Hunter, were dismayed by the loss of their left flank. Rohrabacher said, "I have been dumbfounded by the reaction of some members of the civil rights community, the Department of Justice, and some Members of Congress." He accused the Justice Department and civil rights groups of stalling on the issue, saying, "the executive branch enforcement agencies have not taken reports or specific complaints seriously." He also argued that the resolution was a statement that "quotas and other racial discrimination have no place in our Nation's schools or for that matter, anywhere else. Please join me in fighting this discrimination. It is unfair for Asian Americans and unfair for America. . . . Why are civil rights and other ethnic culture groups scared of that?"[23]

Erasing Race from the Rhetoric

Although Republican references to less qualified non-Asian students avoided describing students by their race, the general political discourse about race in the United States, especially with regard to Asian admissions, suggested that the less qualified students were black or Hispanic. Popular interpretations of "less qualified" were nearly always associated with affirmative action and particular races—black, Hispanic, or Native American. In late July 1989, for example, an NBC Nightly News clip on Asian admissions featured an Asian applicant to Berkeley, Hong Jim, a Taiwanese "A" student with extracurricular activities. He told the NBC correspondent that although two of his black friends with lower grades were accepted at Berkeley, he was rejected. Said Hong Jim, "I don't hold it against them, they're my friends. I want to tell them I still love them, but I guess there's no . . . it's not justice for me. I mean, I think I'm more qualified." The NBC correspondent concluded, "Many Asian Americans are beginning to feel that affirmative action, while a worthy goal, is hurting them" (Kur 1989). Thus, even though Republicans formally abstained from linking affirmative action to Asian admissions, many others, including Asian American students, were willing to state the problem more baldly—affirmative action limited Asian American admission to the elite schools.

Unlike the outspoken attack on affirmative action by Arthur Hu, the Republican perspective on HR 147 was that rhetoric on Asian admissions was not explicit about the *racial* implications of the problem. Supporters of HR 147 readily identified quotas against Asians as a racial issue insofar as qualified Asians had been turned away from top colleges because of their race. But they were reluctant to articulate any remedies to the problem of discrimination in *racial* terms. Rohrabacher explained that HR 147 was not a bill about racial quotas or affirmative action, but "just talked about discrimination."[24] Although he believed that discrimination against Asians constituted an "illegal racial quota," he added that such a finding should not be construed as an attack on the concept of affirmative action.[25]

In their rhetoric, the proponents of HR 147 were careful to define the problem of discrimination against Asians without explicitly attacking preferences for other students on the basis of *race*. In other words, Republican support for HR 147 refrained from blaming less qualified blacks or Hispanics for discrimination against Asians. Instead, Republicans preferred to cast racial differences in admissions strictly in terms of academic achievement. Thus the rhetoric of blame attributed discrimination against Asians to preferences for less qualified *students*, not to less qualified *blacks*.

The shift from race to achievement added more weight to Republican denials that they were "out to get" affirmative action. Representative Rohrabacher, unlike Arthur Hu, claimed to be a staunch supporter of affirmative action. Whereas Hu advocated a blanket end to affirmative action, the congressman supported it as "long as it is not setting different standards for different races."[26] He said, "What I believe is affirmative action—and I would be very supportive [of] affirmative action, . . . is a legal affirmative action, which is outreach programs aimed at improving the skill level of underrepresented minorities. That way you're basically improving people's abilities rather than changing the standard for them."[27]

Rohrabacher's support for what he called "legal affirmative action" suggests that claims by neoconservatives were no more consistent with one another than were claims by Asian Americans and university officials. Neoconservative writers, though uniformly critical of affirmative action, wavered on the degree and extent of their criticism. Some individuals, Hu and Reynolds, for example, opposed any form of affirmative action. A few others, including Rohrabacher, supported what they called "legitimate" forms of affirmative action. The rhetoric of claims criticizing affirmative action also varied considerably. Hu defined admissions as a zero-sum game of racial advantage and disadvantage. He believed that the adoption of a strictly free market approach to admissions would correct the inequities of affirmative action. For Hu, discrimination against Asians was the direct result of preferential treatment for blacks. Others, such as John Bunzel, suggested that the question was no longer, "whether there will be affirmative action, but how much is desirable and for what purposes" (Bunzel 1989). Unlike Hu, Bunzel argued that affirmative action debates were as much a discussion of values as of raw numbers and policy.

Asians in the Racial Politics of Higher Education

By the end of 1989 the center of public debate about Asian admissions had shifted once again, from diversity to affirmative action. The neoconservative position on Asian admissions suggested that discrimination against Asian applicants was the logical outcome of affirmative action for blacks and Hispanics. Neoconservatives did not add new facts or statistics to the debate, nor did they challenge the validity of facts and statistics already entered in the debate. Rather, the originality of the neoconservative view lay in their synthesis of claims drawn from university officials and Asian Americans.

At times neoconservative explanations for Asian admissions parroted some highly debatable claims offered by others. All of the neoconservative writers on Asian admissions, for example, agreed with claims by Asian American organizations that Asians were victims of "de facto" discrimination. With few exceptions, neoconservative discussions of the issue *assumed* that Asian applicants had been unfairly turned away from highly selective universities. Bunzel and Au (1987) argued that differential admission rates were a base indicator of racial discrimination.[28] And, from university officials, neoconservatives accepted without question the claim that less qualified blacks and Hispanics were admitted at the expense of better-qualified Asians. Neoconservative writers assumed that any Asian decline could only be measured by black gains in admissions.[29]

Neoconservative claims about Asian admissions were viable, not because they were valid, but because they resonated so well with certain developments in racial politics in the late 1980s. In particular, neoconservative claims linking affirmative action to Asian admissions were articulated during a crucial juncture in the process of racialization. On the one hand, the increasing significance of race in campus life, from race-conscious admissions policies to the organization of student groups along racial or national lines to demands for multicultural curriculum, was a constant reminder of a kind of racial tracking. On the other hand, a heightened racial consciousness was accompanied by an array of new racial problems, such as white student resentment, racial balkanization on campus, a resurgence in racism, and disappointing results in the improvement of the academic achievements of underrepresented minorities, all of which called for a reevaluation of racial politics.

It is important to note the increasing significance of the Asian American student experience, and rhetoric about that experience, in racial politics. In the main, it has been black and white experiences that have defined the poles of racial politics in higher education. During the second half of the 1980s, it was declining black enrollment, concern over black and Hispanic retention, and conflicts between blacks and whites, that were at the core of "racial concerns" in higher education. Even the controversy over curriculum changes tended toward the poles of black and white; the fury about books concerned black writers, Malcolm X and Alice Walker (and not Maxine Hong Kingston and Toshio Mori), versus "dead white men," Shakespeare and Mann. Asian Americans, because they have not been considered "minorities" in admissions or because their academic achievement has placed them apart from the educational experience of blacks and Hispanics, have often found themselves at the periphery of such racial politics in higher education.[30]

Reconstructing Affirmative Action Discourse

Neoconservatives changed the character of racial politics by insisting, through their claims about admissions, that Asian Americans be brought directly into the arena of racial politics in higher education. The result was a transformation in the debate about affirmative action. In particular, the controversy over Asian admissions afforded neoconservative writers a unique and propitious opportunity to reframe their challenge to affirmative action. The "old" complaint about affirmative action, incipient since Bakke, was that preferences for minorities discriminated against whites. In that old scenario, whites were projected as "victims" of preference for blacks. But refurbished neoconservative claims projected Asians as the new "victims" of affirmative action. In the neoconservative view, blacks remained the beneficiaries of racial preferences, but in the late 1980s, the color of the victims changed.

Compared with whites, Asians constituted more sympathetic victims of affirmative action in the public eye. Here the stereotypic notion that Asian Americans constituted a "model minority" contributed to the notion that Asian American students were admirable for their adherence to family values and diligence in school.

Neoconservatives succeeded not only in reinterpreting the debate over affirmative action but in redefining the debate over Asian admissions. Whereas Asian American organizations such as the task force accused university officials of discrimination against Asians in order to protect whites, neoconservatives charged university officials with discrimination against Asians in order to protect blacks. According to neoconservative claims, discrimination was a matter not between blacks and whites (as was suggested by media concerns about declining black enrollments) or between whites and Asians (as was suggested by Asian American critics—the task force, ECASU, and the Brown AASA) but between blacks and Asians.

Between 1989 and 1990, various conservatives and neoconservatives argued that discrimination against Asians was the direct and inevitable result of racial preferences for blacks. In essence, neoconservatives forced Asian Americans and university officials into a reconstructed debate over affirmative action. They were able to accomplish this important change in racial politics by redefining successive disputes within the controversy over Asian admissions. For example, neoconservatives played both sides of the racialization equation, appealing at times to the public disdain for racial discrimination by calling attention to the plight of Asian American students and, at other times, retreating from the issue of race and racial inequity to the color-blind politics of achievement.

But though the neoconservatives "won" a rearticulation of the problem of Asian admissions, a victory that was reflected in the public discourse, it was not yet clear how that triumph would affect the preferences and policies of admissions officers. There is no doubt, however, that the overall shift in discourse had a palpable effect on admissions policy, on the focus of the federal investigations of Asian admissions at Harvard and UCLA, and perhaps most important, on the course of race relations and racial politics in higher education.

CHAPTER 6

The Race for Class: The New Affirmative Action

*T*he shift in the center of the Asian admissions debate from diversity to affirmative action offered the public a provocative shuffle in its understanding of who benefits and who loses from affirmative action. Neoconservative images of Asians as "new victims" and blacks as "old villains" brought together inchoate public disillusionment over black educational achievement and reassuring impressions of Asians as a model minority. According to neoconservatives, Asian Americans were the new political allies of whites. Nathan Glazer, a leading neoconservative, suggested that Asians, like many whites, were not much interested in the causes of liberalism—for example, in revising the Western Civilization canon at Stanford. In a barb directed at blacks and Hispanics, Glazer (1988) doubted that Asian American high achievers "cared much about *what* was in the Western Civilization syllabus," because they were too busy studying and had little interest in such controversy.

Between 1989 and 1990, university officials and Asian American supporters of affirmative action conceded that neoconservatives had gained the upper hand in the controversy over Asian admissions. The neoconservative capture of the discourse forced university officials and Asian Americans to articulate their differences not just with each other but also with these new opponents. Charges of discrimination against Asians became inextricably bound up with conservative challenges to affirmative action at the same schools. Both administrators and Asian Americans contended that Asian admissions and affirmative action were "separate" issues, but such contentions did little to offset increasing public anxieties that affirmative action was "reverse discrimination" (Rodamor 1990; Pear 1990; Roberts 1990; Shogan 1990; Toner 1990; Edsall and Edsall 1991b).

Upset by the ascendancy of neoconservative claims about affirmative action, liberal university officials and Asian Americans held each other responsible for this latest shift in discourse. Some officials from Berkeley, UCLA, and several Ivy League schools privately blamed Asian Americans for the neoconservative backlash. They believed that the stubborn pursuit of claims of discrimination by Asian Americans had found its final mark: affirmative action. Their Asian American critics responded that the university had done "too little, too late" to distinguish discrimination from diversity. However, despite their past differences, other university administrators and Asian Americans, particularly the members of the task force, worked together to reverse the neoconservative tide. The task force and several university officials publicly accused neoconservatives of subterfuge, of using Asian admissions as a ploy to "undo" affirmative action. Ironically, some of the same officials who were pitted against Asian Americans over charges of discrimination in earlier times now allied themselves with their former opponents to defend university admissions policy from Office of Civil Rights investigators. For example, Chancellor Charles Young of UCLA, exasperated, said at a news conference that the OCR investigation at his school was "a politically inspired undertaking" and that it was clear that the investigators were "just going to keep firing shots at us as long as they can in an effort to prove that the efforts we've been engaged in amount to reverse discrimination" (Curtis 1990a).

A few Asian Americans expressed lingering doubts about joining university officials as partners in the battle against neoconservative claims. They hinted that some administrators who harbored private doubts about affirmative action were secretly pleased that federal investigators were critical of the current race-specific policies. But despite these early suspicions, both sides defended university policies of diversity and affirmative action. Between 1989 and 1990 the task force lobbied aggressively against Rohrabacher's congressional resolution while university officials made sure their affirmative action policies were legally and politically defensible. The temporary coalition partners publicly claimed that the federal investigations of discrimination against Asians were tainted by anti–affirmative action partisanship.

A defining feature of the liberal response, which centered on admissions policy at Berkeley and UCLA, was a concerted move away from race-based or race-specific preferences in admissions policy in favor of class or socioeconomic preferences. Paradoxically, the move from race to class, or what I have termed here the race for class, though initiated and nurtured by neoconservatives, was ultimately implemented by liberals who believed that they were salvaging affirmative action. The liberal "rescue" of affirmative action was reinforced by certain other developments, notably, the conclusion of Office of Civil Rights investigations of graduate admissions at UCLA and of undergraduate admissions at Harvard. A cluster of Supreme Court decisions, in cases concerning preferential policies in employment, made liberal proposals to de-racialize affirmative action seem more viable than ever.

In their construction of a new affirmative action policy based on class, liberals were responding, in part, to the hostile political environment generated by the neoconservative backlash. Although it can be said that the new affirmative action is exactly what the neoconservatives ordered, it is also important to point out that the liberal vision of race and racism is significantly different from a neoconservative understanding of race relations. Liberals, unlike neoconservatives, believed that preferences for minorities, whether couched in race-based or class-based policies, were an important principle of fair admissions. Although liberals substantially changed the *rhetoric* of affirmative action, they did not necessarily transform the practice of racial preferences in admissions.

Like all of the ideological positions adopted by participants in the controversy over Asian admissions, liberalism did not represent a unitary doctrine or monolithic belief system about Asian admissions. Most liberal views of contemporary race relations were focused on conflicts between blacks and whites and had little, if anything, to say about Asian Americans. Nor was the controversy over Asian admissions much of an exception. The liberal response was constructed in large part as a response to neoconservative attacks on affirmative action: that is, preferences for blacks, Hispanics, and Native Americans, not Asian Americans, in admissions. But in mounting a political rejoinder to neoconservatives over Asian admissions, liberals were forced, if only for a fleeting moment, to bring Asian Americans from the periphery to the center of their analyses of race relations.

Diversity and Affirmative Action: Now More Than Ever

Neoconservative criticism of diversity, preferential policies, and affirmative action met stiff resistance among students, faculty, and administrators at many of the nation's campuses. Supporters of affirmative action responded insistently that the policy was needed "more than ever" (de Groot 1990). At Harvard, students chanting "Hey, Hey, ho, ho, the old boy network's got to go" staged a one-day boycott of classes in the spring of 1990 to demand more faculty diversity backed by stronger efforts at affirmative action recruitment (Wu 1990; Scheer 1990). Derrick Bell, one of three black faculty members at the Harvard Law School, focused national attention on the lack of faculty diversity there with a dramatic refusal to teach until the school successfully recruited a tenured black woman to the faculty. At Berkeley in 1989, a proposal that students take a one-semester course comparing the experiences of American cultures—Native American, black, Hispanic, Asian, and EuroAmerican—was approved by the faculty after heated debate. A year later, the United Front, a coalition of progressive student organizations at Berkeley, led a two-day strike to publicize demands for faculty diversity and fair admissions policies.

   This passionate call was heard at every other campus between Berkeley and Harvard in the closing years of the 1980s. At UC Santa Cruz a rally in the spring of 1990 against homophobia turned spontaneously into a four-day sit-in for ethnic studies at the vice chancellor's office, when students attending the rally discovered that funds for temporary lecturers in ethnic studies were in danger of being cut. In 1988, Stanford, which enjoys the reputation of being the most elite private university in the western United States, became the center of national attention when students rallied "en masse" to demand greater diversity in their required reading lists for the freshman "core" curriculum. In 1989 a Stanford faculty review committee issued its findings, "Final Report of the University Committee on Minority Issues" (Committee on Minority Issues 1989), which included recommendations for an ethnic studies requirement and continued funding for ethnic "theme" dorms. At other schools, a string of "plans" for greater diversity and affirmative action—for example, *The Madison Plan*—set timetables for increasing minority student admissions, diversifying the faculty, and pumping money into the pipeline of institutional support for minority students and faculty. Andrew Hacker (1990) commented in a review of a collection of books on affirmative action, "Affirmative action may be out of favor at the Supreme Court, but it is becoming a stronger force on the nation's campuses."

A casual browse through college catalogues, admissions brochures, and college viewbooks from all of the top universities, including the most highly selective, confirmed that diversity was "in." College viewbooks, which are used to introduce and attract students to the top universities, stressed diversity in words and in glossy pictures (Mills 1990).[1] "Stanford values a class that is both ethnically and economically diverse," read one; and in the Harvard register we read, "Diversity is the hallmark of the Harvard/Radcliffe experience." In addition, there were the ubiquitous and predictable photos of diversity posing as real life: black students mingling with whites, browns, and Asians, perhaps huddled together over a lab experiment or cavorting in the afternoon sun on campus.

But most of the staunchest advocates of diversity conceded that pro-diversity and pro–affirmative action policies were plagued by such troubling developments as the rise in racist incidents across the nation's campuses and the erosion of popular support for affirmative action. Contrary to neoconservative claims, some pro–affirmative action advocates argued that the increased racism was the consequence of "white ignorance" and unenlightened "distrust" of affirmative action. Accordingly, the solution was more education— in the form of ethnic studies requirements, for example. Another strategy to contain racism, banning racist speech and racist behavior from the university campus, unleashed a furious national debate over who defines racist speech and the constitutional implications of limiting "free speech" in higher education.[2]

At UCLA, for example, *The Daily Bruin* ran a cartoon in which a student stops to ask a rooster on campus how he was admitted to UCLA.[3] The rooster responds, "affirmative action." The editor and art director were each suspended for violating a policy against articles that perpetuate derogatory or cultural stereotypes. Other universities that have implemented policies to punish racist or sexist speech include those schools where the problems have been most explosive, such as the University of Michigan, Ann Arbor, and Berkeley. Even those colleges that by virtue of their size and location are often insulated from the main currents of controversy in higher education, however, have found themselves caught in the debate over free speech and "fighting words." At Colgate University, a 1989 proposal to ban fraternities from the campus set off a local uproar (55 percent of the students belong to Greek houses) and flung the small picturesque college of 1,400 into the national debate.

Balkanization: In Search of a New Language of Race

Still another troubling development recognized by the supporters of affirmative action and diversity has been tenacious racial tracking in campus life. Nearly four decades after the Supreme Court outlawed the "separate but equal" doctrine in its historic decision *Brown v. Board of Education*, racial integration is still a distant ideal on most college campuses. A quick glance at the local eateries on campus is more suggestive of segregation than integration. Blacks sit with blacks, whites sit with whites, Asians sit with Asians, each group clustered at separate tables. The seating arrangements at lunch, of course, offer us but a small window into what ails race relations in higher education. The sociology professor Troy Duster has provided this brief description of racial balkanization at Berkeley: "Whether white or black, Asian, Latino, or Native American, the leitmotif is the same. Students come here expecting to meet people from different backgrounds and have a good experience. What happens is often just the reverse. After their first five or six weeks, what they learn is how to be a member of an ethnic, racial, or political group. For some, this is empowering. But others find that it inhibits their capacity to fully experience other groups" (Rodamor 1990).

Liberal supporters of affirmative action, like their neoconservative opponents, agreed that racial balkanization was upsetting. At the very least, both sides believed that de facto racial segregation in college life indicated the existence of a deeply rooted social problem. Neoconservatives insisted that the source of the problem stemmed from the same policies designed to eliminate segregation, namely, affirmative action and diversity. But although liberal faculty and university officials privately agreed that such accounts were "engaging," they insisted the real story of racial balkanization was far more complex and that the solutions to the problem, correspondingly, were complex as well.

The most thoughtful analysis of racial balkanization from a liberal perspective came from Berkeley, where a team of social scientists led by Professor Duster conducted a two-year study of campus race relations. The findings of the Diversity Project (1990), based on interviews with groups of racially mixed and racially homogeneous students, suggested that the overriding sentiments toward diversity, regardless of the student's racial background, were ambivalence and contradiction: "If there is a single pattern emerging from the study, it is that the students are deeply conflicted, disturbed, divided, and confused about Affirmative Action as a policy, yet support the idea of diversity" (Diversity Project 1990:4).

Not surprisingly, different groups of students experienced conflicts about race in different ways. Minority students complained of
a "subtle racism" and feelings of being "ignored or excluded," particularly in mixed racial settings—the classroom, sporting events,
social gatherings. The racism described by these students did not
just blame whites, but sometimes, as in the following example,
blamed other minorities. One student said, "they [African American
students] talk about racism and then a Chicano/Latino will go, 'Oh
yea, I know what you mean,' and they'll just look at you or you
know, or if you're not dark enough they don't think you've experienced it . . . and I've come out and say, 'Well, Chicanos/Latinos face
racism too'" (Diversity Project 1990:73).

White students related the discomfort of being white in a
highly racialized campus climate. Many expressed fear and dismay
at being labeled "racist" or "oppressor." As one student noted, "It's
Chicano now or Chicana, Mexican, Latina, Hispanic, I mean . . . I
just [laughter] every year it changes. I just . . . I mean I don't know
what to say. I mean if you say the wrong thing you're a racist or
they yell at you. I mean I don't know, it's so frustrating, but we're
always the white honky, y'know we don't, we don't get to change
our name every year" (Diversity Project 1990:60).

As the above quotation suggests, language, in the form of correct label(s) for racial identity, was an important part of racial social-
ization and etiquette for students and a source of frustration as well.
Indeed a defining characteristic of the sentiments expressed by all
students—anger, resentment, alienation, feelings of inadequacy—
was that language about race and racism had not kept pace with the
panoply of their experiences. For example, one subject that generated predictable controversy was affirmative action. The Berkeley
professor Robert Blauner commented, "I'm not saying we should get
rid of it, because I certainly don't have a better answer. I don't know
if the problem is in the way we're applying it, or in how we're getting across the message about why it's needed. But in the context of
today's economic situation, I think we have to start looking for some
new ideas that aren't so divisive" (Walsh 1990).

Similarly, Professor Duster said, "We have one word, *racism*,
that stretches to include everything from lynching to somebody
frowning at you in a restaurant. When I ask black students what
they mean when they say this is a 'racist' place, they often don't
know what to say" (Walsh 1990).

According to the Diversity Project, black students, and presumably by extension other students as well, were inarticulate about what they perceived as racism on campus because of "the very lack of a textured and nuanced language to fit the newer and more subtly perceived forms of discomforting racism [that] make the charge sound hollow in their own ears as they self-censor before they can give language to it" (Diversity Project 1990:27). The problem, said Duster, was that "we need a new language of race" (Walsh 1990). From the liberal perspective, simple solutions to balkanization such as a wholesale end to affirmative action would at best only partially ameliorate student grievances about race and would fail to address the thorny problem of the chasm between racial experience(s) and the language available to capture those experiences. Accordingly, much of the force of the recommendations offered by the Diversity Project centered on promoting interaction and exchange between students through (1) the establishment of small focus groups (10–15 students) for freshmen to facilitate orientation and integration into campus life, (2) institutional support for student groups organized along both ethnic and interethnic lines, (3) clarification of admissions policies, and (4) encouraging faculty to play a greater role in fostering interaction between students over curriculum.

Asian American Students: Ambivalence amid Diversity

Asian Americans and liberals alike suggested that neoconservative characterizations of Asian American students were overgeneralized and too facile. For example, though the Diversity Project found many Asian Americans who were critical of affirmative action, "It would be too simple an account to state that it is simple meritocracy or qualifications that is at issue" (Diversity Project 1990:49). Instead, the Diversity Project described Asian Americans as an internally diverse group (by ethnicity, class, and generation) whose members, in their attempts to locate themselves in the racial politics of the campus, found themselves caught in an array of cross-cutting stereotypes. These ran the gamut from "model minority" to clannish, grade-grubbing foreigners. The result was that Asian Americans voiced a broad range of conflicting sentiments about their achievements.

Neoconservative reconstruction of the Asian admissions discourse added another image to racial politics; Asian American student achievement threatened university preferences for less qualified

minorities. In other words, differences in academic achievement between Asian American students and black students were now translated into competing interests between the two groups in the
admissions process. Black interests were associated with diversity
and affirmative action, nonmeritocratic admissions, anticompetitive-
ness, and equality of outcomes. In contrast, Asian American interests were construed as meritocratic, competitive, and emphasizing
the ideal of individual equal access.

The construction of Asian American students as having interests opposed to those of blacks not so subtly reinforced a particular
conception about the problem of Asian admissions in particular and
racial politics in general. That conception, which linked Asian admissions to affirmative action, emphasized competition between differently qualified racial groups for limited resources. But such a
conception failed to acknowledge how racial resentment and competition are, in turn, fueled by the lack of a textured language to describe and confront the racial differences that divide us.

The Task Force Goes to Washington

Having reached a satisfying accord with Berkeley officials in 1989,
the task force poised itself to derail neoconservative attacks on affirmative action in the Congress. Ironically, while the task force solved
the local problem of Asian admissions at Berkeley, a menacing discourse had developed at the national level. Task force members L.
Ling-chi Wang and Henry Der were alarmed at the rise in neoconservative claims linking Asian admissions to affirmative action. They
were especially upset by Congressman Rohrabacher's crusade on behalf of Asian American victims of discrimination and "against" affirmative action. Der said, "He's using our issue to try to undo
affirmative action for all minority groups, and we can't go along
with that" (Jaschik 1989a). Wang and Der decided to travel to Washington, D.C., to brief federal officials and congressional representatives personally on what they called an "Asian American national
agenda on college admissions."

Joining them were Paul Igasaki, chair of the Japanese American
Citizen's League, Dale Shimasaki, chair of Asian Americans in
Higher Education, Professor Don Nakanishi of UCLA, and Melinda
Yee, president of the Organization of Chinese Americans. The
group met with officials from the Department of Justice and the De-

partment of Education, numerous congressional representatives, and officials from major civil rights organizations.

In their meetings, the group sought to disentangle Asian American concerns in higher education from attacks on affirmative action. For example, after an initial investigation into Asian admissions at UCLA, the Office of Civil Rights had recently returned to the campus to gather more information on affirmative action. In addition, just before the group of Asian American lobbyists headed for Washington, the Office of Civil Rights had announced that it would investigate charges of discrimination against whites at Berkeley. Concerned that neoconservative claims were influencing the course of federal investigations of Asian admissions, Wang and Der had hoped to gather signatures for a bipartisan letter to President George Bush opposing the direction of OCR's reviews at Harvard and UCLA. The group also alerted its audiences to other Asian American concerns in higher education, for example, faculty diversity and the lack of Asian-language achievement tests.[4]

Many of the civil rights organizations and congressional representatives, however, while very sympathetic to the group's concerns, were preoccupied with drafting a national civil rights bill in anticipation of the upcoming debate in congress. Although the group fell short of its ultimate goal of shifting the focus of the OCR-investigation away from affirmative action, it was satisfied to have at least balanced neoconservative claims with Asian American concerns. Wang commented, "The reason I thought it was important for us to go to Washington was to apply counterpressure [to OCR]. Otherwise they'd only be getting pressure from one side."[5]

New Admissions Policy at Berkeley: The Karabel Report

At Berkeley, officials were keenly aware that their admissions policies were once again under fire. After reaching a "truce" with the task force in 1989 following five years of disagreement, university administrators turned to face mounting neoconservative criticism of affirmative action in admissions. Many Berkeley officials felt that these new complaints, which often singled out Berkeley's affirmative action policy, were hurting the public image of the school. An opinion piece appearing in the *New York Times*, for example, complained specifically about Berkeley: "Two students from Westminster, an elite college-prepatory high school, apply to Berkeley.

Student A with SAT scores totaling 1290 is denied admission while Student B with SAT scores of 890 and who according to the school counselor is 'less qualified' is accepted. Student A is white and Student B is black" (Werner 1988).

Berkeley officials were understandably skittish and defensive about their affirmative action policies. Some breathed sighs of relief when the school was considered but passed over for an investigation of discrimination against Asians in 1988 by the Office of Education. Publicly, university administrators continued to defend their admissions policies, but privately they were concerned over an increase in negative public opinion toward affirmative action. Many lamented that affirmative action was "out." That Berkeley was often the focal point for neoconservative attacks prompted officials there to keep a vigilant eye on their policies to ensure that they were publicly defensible and legally sound.

In early 1990 Berkeley officials received bad news. The federal Department of Education announced that the Office of Civil Rights would investigate Arthur Hu's complaint that Berkeley admissions policies were discriminatory against *whites*. Unlike the OCR investigations at Harvard and UCLA, which focused on discrimination against Asians, this investigation would by the very nature of the complaint entail a review of all affirmative action practices at Berkeley. Although the announcement of an investigation did not constitute a guilty finding, it added to a nagging stack of claims that Berkeley's affirmative action policies were unfair and possibly illegal as well.

The announcement of the OCR investigation of reverse discrimination at Berkeley affirmed what the faculty committee at Berkeley in charge of reviewing admissions policy, the Admissions and Enrollment Committee, had been discussing all year long: it was time for a change in admissions policy. Actually, admissions policy had changed slightly every year since the task force had first raised its claims of discrimination, but the kind and degree of changes that were under consideration in 1989 went far beyond any changes in previous years. Typically, modifications in admissions policy were filtered to the public through memoranda that passed between the administration, admissions officials, and faculty. At the end of spring semester 1989, however, the Admissions and Enrollment Committee unveiled its proposal for a new admissions policy in a professionally bound booklet, *Freshman Admissions at Berkeley: A Proposal for the 1990s and Beyond* (Admissions and Enrollment Committee 1989).

The new policy, dubbed the Karabel report after the committee's chair, Professor Jerome Karabel, featured the end of guaranteed admission for UC-eligible racial minorities (and athletes and disabled students) and the introduction of new categories of secondary review—socioeconomic status, reentry candidates, and students who barely missed being admitted under strict meritocratic criteria. In addition, the new admissions proposal affirmed excellence and diversity as basic principles of admissions policy and, in doing so, sought to regain the public trust eroded by years of political struggle between university officials, Asian Americans, and neoconservatives.

The two highlights of the Karabel report, the end of race-based guaranteed admissions and the establishment of a review category based on socioeconomic status, were part of a larger shift and realignment of the tier system that had been in effect since 1985. Under the Karabel proposal, the former two-tier and complemental category system was to be reorganized. In the new system, the percentages of students admitted through each tier were slightly altered and the criteria for admission through Tier 2 were radically changed. In the first tier, which remained essentially the same as before, the proportion of students admitted (strictly on the basis of the Academic Index score) would climb from 40 percent to 50 percent.

The major changes concerned Tier 2. Forty-five percent of the entering class would be admitted through a new and revamped Tier 2. This "new" Tier 2 would be created by combining the old Tier 2 admissions (Academic Index score plus supplemental criteria) with the former complemental category admissions (UC-eligible but not competitive students: athletes, affirmative action students, special talent students, disabled students, rural students, and Filipinos). Under the new Tier 2, students from socioeconomically disadvantaged backgrounds were to be a new and explicit target group added to the list of complemental categories. Also under the new system, members of those groups who in the past had been automatically admitted if they were UC-eligible—athletes, disabled students, and affirmative action students—would no longer enjoy "total protection." Rather, admission to Berkeley for every student through Tier 2 would be governed by a combination of factors, strict academic criteria, secondary review (formerly complemental categories), and supplemental criteria. Finally, as with the old system of admissions, some spaces in the freshman class, 5 percent under the new system, were reserved for special action admissions to accommodate those student who, while not UC-eligible, displayed exceptional promise or talent (see Table 6.1).

Table 6.1. The Old Tier System Compared with the Karabel Proposal

	% of total admitted	Criteria for admission
Tier 1		
1984–1990 system	40–60%	Academic Index scores
Karabel 1991	50	Academic Index scores
Tier 2		
1984–1990 criteria	60–40	AIS + supplemental criteria + complemental categories
Karabel 1991	45	AIS + supplemental criteria + secondary review categories
Special Action		
1984–1990	6	Not UC-eligible but displaying talent and/or overcoming substantial odds in educational attainment
Karabel 1991	5	Not UC-eligible but displaying talent and/or overcoming substantial odds in educational attainment

Although the Karabel proposal was not yet official policy and was not even scheduled for debate on the floor of the faculty academic senate until the fall of 1989, the admissions office quietly implemented one of its main features before the fall debate—dropping guaranteed admission of UC-eligible minorities for students admitted to the entering class of fall 1990.

The End of Race-based Guarantees at UCLA

At UCLA in 1989, admissions officers dropped guaranteed admission for UC-eligible blacks and Hispanics. The UCLA officials echoed Berkeley officials' justification for the change, saying the practice of affirmative action admissions—in the form of "total protection"—was no longer viable.

The end of "automatic admission" of minorities at UCLA in 1989 was part of a larger package of changes in admissions policy. With considerably less fanfare than at Berkeley, UCLA officials, citing enrollment pressures, proposed a new admissions policy in 1989 that took effect in the fall of 1990. The new admissions policy differed from the old system in two ways. First, under the new system, affirmative action was no longer race-specific, and correspondingly, set-asides or separate tracks of admission for particular groups were abandoned. Second, the new system of admissions at UCLA featured a selection model whereby every applicant would be ranked (and selected) on the basis of academic and supplemental criteria.

Officials at both Berkeley and UCLA publicly dismissed the idea that the new admissions policies were a response to the investigation or threat of investigation by the Office of Civil Rights. The new admissions proposals were viewed by officials at both schools as a liberal defense of diversity and affirmative action from neoconservative encroachments into admissions policy. The Karabel report cited "erosion of public trust" and Winston Doby, vice chancellor for student affairs, cited "enrollment pressures" as the primary motivation for drafting new policies. The new policies provided officials with an opportunity to inscribe university commitment to diversity within a set of formal principles governing admissions. But perhaps most important, the new policies provided a chance to "save" affirmative action by de-racializing preferential policies.

At Berkeley, Professor Karabel was explicit about ensuring that the cancellation of total protection at Berkeley did not result in the wholesale loss of affirmative action as well. He recalled,

> And so, after much, much discussion, and, actually a lot of, I think, attempts on my part to convince people that this was really something that had to be done but with a recognition that their concerns were legitimate, that taking away total protection opened the door some years down the road to a big rollback in affirmative action, that was a very legitimate concerns, and that our job was to set up safeguards so as to prevent that from happening.[6]

At Berkeley, administrators and Asian Americans alike were pleased with the new admissions proposal. From the perspective of the task force, the establishment of a secondary review category based on socioeconomic disadvantage meant that Asian American applicants from low-income backgrounds would be eligible for secondary review under the Karabel proposal, whereas these same applicants were ineligible for consideration under EOP supplemental criteria in the old system of admissions. University officials welcomed the new proposal because of its commitment to diversity, merit, and affirmative action in admissions and the absence of race-based guarantees in admissions policy. Chancellor Heyman praised the Karabel report for its "impressive research and consensus" and suggested it was "a blueprint for selecting top scholars who reflect the diversity of this state" (*Berkeleyan* 1989).[7]

White Discontent with Diversity

A small number of Berkeley faculty were highly skeptical of the new admissions proposal. They viewed the chancellor's claims of diversity *and* excellence in the new admissions policy as hollow campaign promises. Some felt that the new proposal, while promising, had not fully addressed several serious questions. Professor Barnett, a former member of the Shack committee and author of the committee's confidential minority report on Asian admissions, felt the Karabel proposal had failed to receive a serious and thorough review at the September 1989 meeting of the Berkeley academic senate. During the meeting, he raised a number of objections to the proposal, including a suggestion that the size of the secondary review category—socioeconomic disadvantage—ought to be severely limited until the effects of the policy were clear. But his objections barely slowed the approval of the new admissions policy. The academic senate overwhelmingly accepted the Karabel proposal without modification.

Over the next six months, after the fall admissions data were released, it became clear that the elimination of guaranteed admissions for underrepresented minorities in the new admissions proposal was enhancing, not inhibiting, racial diversity in admissions. The loss of "total protection" for UC-eligible underrepresented minorities in 1989 produced a more racially diverse freshman class in the fall of 1990 than ever before. The percentage of blacks admitted to the fall 1990 freshman class was 11.4 percent, Asians constituted 27.8 percent, and Hispanics, 21.4 percent. Together these three minority groups filled 60 percent of the spaces in the entering class.

White enrollment, at an all-time low, sank to 32 percent of the class.[8] Similarly, the end of guaranteed admission of UC-eligible minorities at UCLA resulted in a no less diverse freshman class than in the previous year. In fall 1990, the Asian share of UCLA admissions was 34 percent, up from 27 percent in 1989; black admissions declined slightly from 8 percent in 1989 to 7 percent in 1990; Hispanic admissions stayed even at 19 percent in 1989 and 1990; and white admissions declined from 41 percent in 1989 to 34 percent in 1990.

For some white conservative faculty, the decline in white enrollment was nothing short of an outrage. Some professors, spurred by the belief that the administration was "giving away" the university to minority concerns and hence turning its back on white interests, registered strong discontent with the new policies. At Berkeley one individual particularly upset was Professor Vincent Sarich, who accused the administration of "systematically discriminating against white students" (Sarich 1990a). Arguing that Berkeley had substituted race for achievement, Sarich (1990b) lamented the costs of diversity: "What our recent admissions policies really have done is given us two student populations whose academic levels barely overlap." In a letter of complaint to UC Regent William French Smith, Professor Sarich called Berkeley admissions policies "immoral" for ensuring that "academic performance and achievement at Berkeley will be strongly correlated with race and ethnicity" (Sarich 1990a). In addition, Professor Sarich publicly circulated his complaints about admissions policies to the Berkeley faculty in an essay, "The Institutionalization of Racism at the University of California, Berkeley." Chancellor Heyman, in turn, circulated a reply to Sarich's complaints and renewed his support for the Karabel proposal (Heyman 1990a).

Professor Sarich was not alone in his criticism of the administration. While Sarich framed his attack on the Berkeley administration with transparent anxiety about white representation at Berkeley, other opponents of the administration were more careful to argue that the real issue was one of academic standards. In early 1990 a group of twenty-nine members of the faculty—twenty-seven white men and two white women—privately complained to President Gardner about the loss of academic standards in faculty hiring at Berkeley. Apparently concerned about Berkeley's reputation as the top university in the nation (ahead of Stanford and Harvard in 1983 ratings) and the plight of minority faculty who allegedly struggled to keep up with the group of world-class scholars at

Berkeley, the twenty-nine faculty members affirmed their support of affirmative action at the same time that they suggested that academic appointments sacrificed competitive, traditional, and widely accepted criteria for racial and gender preferences.

The suggestion that the university had replaced standards of "excellence" with preferences based on nonacademic criteria was a familiar one; it had often been raised by neoconservative opponents of affirmative action. But not all of the white critics of the Berkeley administration agreed that excellence ought to be equated with academic criteria. Professor Barnett, in a lengthy letter to Regent Smith on the exchange between Professor Sarich and Chancellor Heyman, strongly disagreed with Sarich's position. He wrote, "I do not share his apparent view that Berkeley should not be granting any preferential admissions based on race. I agree with Chancellor Heyman that it would be 'absolutely unacceptable' for Berkeley to base its admissions solely on grades and test scores and thus to reduce the percentage of underrepresented minority students in its freshman class to something like 3 percent" (Barnett 1990).

Barnett's criticisms of Sarich, which mirrored the arguments of pro-diversity forces on campus, were balanced by his biting criticisms of the Karabel proposal. Barnett's objections to the Karabel proposal centered on the number of slots that should be allotted to the secondary review category "socioeconomic disadvantage," and he challenged whether such a category was significantly different from university attempts to meet affirmative action goals.

Black Discontent with the New Admissions Policy

Some critics felt the new admissions proposal was anti-white; others felt it was anti-black. Many black faculty, staff members, and students at Berkeley were highly critical of the Karabel proposal for reasons very different from those offered by white faculty. The Black Faculty and Staff Organization at Berkeley offered a detailed critique of the new admissions policy, arguing that the wording of the Karabel report was vague and that "little is said about the logic and procedure for assigning weights to the various categories in tier II" (BFSO 1990). According to the BFSO (1990), "it was obvious" from the Karabel report that the percentage of "UC-eligible blacks in the freshman class will decline, barring some dramatic increase in the number of UC-eligible blacks who apply and enroll."

The Afro-American Studies faculty at Berkeley, miffed at not being consulted about the changes, gloomily predicted that the new policy would reduce black enrollment. In particular, the black faculty were furious that the policy of total protection for underrepresented minorities had already been withdrawn in a December 1989 decision by the Admissions Coordination Board (Wilkerson et al. 1990). Because the Admissions Coordination Board had been established in the heat of the crisis over Asian admissions, some black faculty wondered whether black interests were adequately represented in admissions decisions. In an irate letter to the chancellor, the faculty of the Afro-American Studies Program complained, "Insofar as we are able to determine, the Chancellor and Faculty Assistant Ling-chi Wang's promise of consultation and dialogue [about admissions] applies only to the Asian American community" (Wilkerson et al. 1990). From the perspective of many blacks on campus, Asians enjoyed a greater degree of institutional participation in making major decisions than any other racial group.

Asian Americans were indeed gaining important and visible positions in the university administration. By early 1990, just when black complaints about the Karabel report surfaced, there had been a spate of Asian American appointments in the top administration at Berkeley. Professor Wang headed the Admissions Coordination Board; Patrick Hayashi was associate vice chancellor for admissions and enrollment; and Professor Chang-lin Tien had recently been chosen to become the highest-ranking official at Berkeley, replacing retiring chancellor Ira Michael Heyman. Even in student government, there had been an impressive show of Asian American political clout. Within a month of the black faculty protest of admissions policy, an Asian American candidate, Bonaparte Liu, would be elected student body president to replace outgoing president Tisa Poe (who in 1989 had replaced President Jeffrey Chang).

Many students, particularly blacks, were also unhappy with the decision to end race-based guarantees and preferences in admissions policy. At UCLA minority students claimed that there had been a 35 percent drop in black enrollment between 1989 and 1990.[9] An advertisement for a rally against undergraduate admissions policy in the spring of 1990 warned other students: "Yo People! Wake Up! [to the threat of the new admissions policy] Exterminating our people from campus." At Berkeley, Lance Johnson, co-chair of the African Student Association, told the *Daily Californian* that he did not support the end of race-based affirmative action and promised that his organization would attempt to remove that clause from the Karabel report.

The issue of affirmative action in admissions was a potentially divisive one among leftists, particularly blacks and Asians, on campus. Because Asian Americans were not considered an "under-represented minority" at Berkeley, a popular view held that Asian Americans did not "need" affirmative action to gain admission or to succeed in school. In a show of solidarity with blacks and other un-derrepresented minorities, left-minded Asian American students at Berkeley insisted that Asian Americans *needed* and supported affirm-ative action. Erich Nakano (1990), in a lengthy editorial in the *Daily Californian*, claimed that "right-wing" arguments against affirm-ative action also hurt Asian American applicants to college. Accus-ing the right wing of equating "academic excellence" with standardized test scores and grade point averages, Nakano (1990) wrote:

> The double-edged sword of SATs and GPAs can work against us as well. Because of stereotypes about Asians being good at math but basically "passive" and non-verbal, countless Asian students suffer from lower grades based on lower expectations[,] especially in Eng-lish, social science and humanities courses in public schools. Further, since both American and foreign-born Asians do not do as well on the verbal SAT, would it then be right to forbid Asians from entering fields such as law, business, the arts, and social sciences, which re-quire verbal skills?

Nakano and other Asian American leftists accused the "right wing," namely Congressman Dana Rohrabacher and Arthur Hu, of using affirmative action to "divide and conquer" racial minorities. Nakano adamantly resisted any attempts to splinter Asian American inter-ests from those of other minorities. He believed that Asians had "historically faced racism and injustice at the hands of others" and that their "future is ultimately linked with other people of color" (Nakano 1990).

Aside from their general exhortations of support for affirmative action, some leftist students offered cautious support for the Karabel proposal. Phil Ting, co-chair of the Asian American Political Alliance at Berkeley, balanced his doubts about the policy—"I thought it was a dangerous step. If they are going to take affirmative action away, what next?"—with a more pragmatic view that taking away race-specific policies might be a necessary protective step to safeguard affirmative action in the midst of a "dangerous political situation" (Robertson 1990).

The Liberal Choice: Class-based Affirmative Action or None at All

The dangerous political situation cited by Nakano referred to the conservative rollbacks in affirmative action manifested in a series of Supreme Court decisions in the late 1980s. Pro–affirmative action advocates usually date the beginning of the rollbacks to the 1978 *Bakke* decision, which outlawed minority set-asides in university admissions (*Regents of the University of California* 1978). But the *Bakke* decision has been subject to different interpretations. Supporters of affirmative action breathed a sigh of relief that the court's ruling on *Bakke* positively affirmed race as one of several factors allowable in admissions criteria. But critics of affirmative action maintained that the decision sustained a focus on race instead of highlighting individual merit and achievement in admissions criteria. After a decade of anti-quota and anti–affirmative action rhetoric, the rollbacks continued. In 1989, in another legal blow to affirmative action, the Supreme Court ruled against state- and local government–sponsored set-aside programs for minority business enterprises in *City of Richmond v. J. A. Croson Co.* (1989). Also in 1989, in a move that made it more difficult for plaintiffs to launch discrimination complaints, the Court ruled that statistical disparities that showed a high proportion of nonwhite workers in unskilled jobs and a low percentage of such workers in skilled jobs were not sufficient to establish a prima facie case of discriminatory intent, a violation of Title VII of the Civil Rights Act of 1964 (*Wards Cove* 1989). Less than a year later, in January 1990, the Supreme Court agreed to hear an appeal from a white businessman who charged that the Federal Communications Commission unfairly denied him a license to operate a television station in Connecticut. The FCC had given the license, instead, to a Hispanic-owned company (*Metro Broadcasting* 1990).

Yet there were some indicators that the Court might look favorably at some aspects of affirmative action. In 1990, for example, embracing the principle of equal access for all, the Court ordered the Virginia Military Institute, long an all-male academy, to admit women. Then, in June 1990, the Court affirmed the power of Congress to establish programs aimed at increasing the numbers of minority broadcast licenses—explicitly supporting affirmative action or racial preferences—at the federal level. In spite of these two cases, most views of legal trends in Court views toward affirmative action conceded that the mood was decidely "anti–affirmative action."

In early 1990 Gary Morrison, chief deputy counsel for the University of California, in a confidential memo, advised Chancellor Heyman of the dire legal consequences of Berkeley's affirmative action policy in admissions. Morrison's conclusion was, "I think there is now the greatest likelihood of legal action against the university in this area since *Bakke*." He noted, "The federal government, including especially the Office of Civil Rights of the Department of Education (OCR), has become increasingly aggressive in questioning whether our affirmative action admissions efforts are lawful. There are still many judges who may simply refuse to accept the idea of affirmative action programs and may reach out to enjoin affirmative action programs across the system while any particular case is making its way through the judicial process" (Morrison 1990).

Morrison's warning was compelling to the university administration, the admissions office, and the Admissions Coordination Board. Patrick Hayashi, associate vice chancellor for admissions and enrollment, citing Morrison's legal advice, told the discontented black faculty, "Given the hostile legal climate in which we now operate, continuing to offer guaranteed admission to any group solely on the basis of race or ethnicity would be to invite a lawsuit under the Bakke decision that the University would almost certainly lose. Loss of such a suit could substantially narrow the scope of our affirmative action policy." The grim alternative, he said, was, "If the courts were to order the university to base admissions exclusively on grades and test scores, for example, the result would be a freshman class composed of about 5 percent underrepresented minority students compared to 37 percent in the fall 1989 freshman class" (Hayashi 1990). When framed in this way, the choices for left-minded political groups were stark. Either they agreed to the change in affirmative action or risked losing it altogether. Many leftist students and black faculty admitted that abandoning total protection was a calculated loss against the possibility of complete forfeiture of minority enrollment at the university.

In their discussions with faculty and administrators, members of the pro-diversity student coalition at Berkeley came to understand that admissions was a complicated issue. Their initial conviction that the university should restore "guaranteed admission" for UC-eligible underrepresented waned with the realization that their demand for "guaranteed admissions" might actually be bad for affirmative action. When in the spring of 1990, after two days of protests resulting in 101 arrests, the chancellor agreed to discuss their demands, the students were quick to negotiate on the admissions issue.[10] Afraid of doing the wrong thing out of principle, the students abandoned their demand for total protection. Instead they settled for promises of student representation and participation in interviews with affirmative action student applicants to Berkeley.

In contrast with their willingness to negotiate on admissions, students' discussions with the chancellor of other demands, such as overturning negative tenure decisions on two minority faculty, implementation of a lesbian/gay and bisexual studies program, separate meetings with Native American students on admissions policy, and the designation of the university administration building as a multicultural center, continued over the next several weeks with no success. A month later, the pro-diversity coalition, calling itself the United Front, emerged from failed negotiations with the chancellor and announced plans to organize a two-day strike for faculty diversity. Noticeably absent from the students' demands and slogans was the topic of university admissions policy.

Federal Investigations at Harvard and UCLA

The Office of Civil Rights of the Department of Education in Washington, D.C., coordinates the investigative activities of nine regional offices across the country. One of the main functions of the office is to safeguard equal opportunity in educational institutions receiving federal financial assistance, a guarantee of Title VI of the 1964 Civil Rights Act. Routine tasks of the regional offices include conducting local reviews of individual complaints of discrimination and local compliance reviews to ensure that the practices of educational institutions do not violate civil rights statutes.

The reviews of Harvard and UCLA begun in 1988 and of Berkeley in 1989 were anything but routine. Education officials from around the country, mindful that the results were likely to carry implications for their own policies, kept a watchful eye on these activities. But OCR kept a tight rein on what it was doing and why. The office was willing to say that the purpose of its investigations was to ensure that schools were in compliance with Title VI, which forbids discrimination on the basis of race, but remained mute about just about everything else. Questions from university officials, Asian Americans, and neoconservatives about the progress of the investigations or what measures were being used to ascertain discrimination, for example, went unanswered. Top OCR officials allowed only that there were two salient issues in their reviews: access and outcomes in admissions. Equipped with little official information, university administrators, along with Asian Americans and neoconservatives, watched carefully for any tell-tale developments.

An important sign came in 1989, when OCR officials returned to UCLA to widen the scope of the investigation from discrimination against Asian Americans to a review of affirmative action. This news cheered the neoconservatives, who had maintained all along that Asian admissions was inextricably tied to affirmative action, but was viewed as a major setback by others. University officials and Asian Americans, both of whom initially welcomed the OCR reviews, now spoke out against this shift in focus. High administration officials from the chancellor to the director of admissions suggested that OCR's intentions were politically motivated by a desire to dismantle affirmative action, and they described the investigation as harassment. Task force members agreed with the university and argued that OCR was being "politically pressured" by anti–affirmative action officials from the Justice Department.

The scale of the reviews at UCLA and Harvard was enormous. The Boston regional office assigned two to three full-time staff to the Harvard inquiry, and the San Francisco office allocated between four and five full-time staff to the review of UCLA. Office of Civil Rights officials examined computer records spanning ten years of admissions at Harvard and three years of admissions at UCLA. In addition to the computerized analysis of admissions, OCR officials read and re-read hundreds of individual applicant files. In the case of UCLA, investigators decided to examine both graduate and undergraduate admissions. Because graduate admissions at UCLA, as everywhere, are conducted by individual departments, OCR officials conducted separate reviews of admissions in eighty-four different graduate programs.

In August 1990, after two years of work, the OCR investigations appeared to be stalled. Those awaiting the results were impatient and growing increasingly suspicious about why the reviews were taking so long. Gary Curran, who had been a member of the OCR staff before becoming chief of staff for Congressman Rohrabacher, complained that his former colleagues were dragging their heels on the compliance reviews because "They don't want to use Title VI against affirmative action."[11] In an effort to expedite the compliance reviews, Rohrabacher lobbied the Senate Education Appropriations Subcommittee in August 1990, complaining of delays in the OCR investigations and requesting federal monies to ensure a speedy resolution.

OCR officials in Washington maintained that the issues were "complicated" and that compliance reviews "take time." One official there held that delays in the review were the fault of UCLA officials who had "stalled" in providing requested information.[12] But sources close to the regional OCR office located in San Francisco suggested that from the beginning of the investigations it was unclear who was in charge of the investigation—Washington, D.C., or San Francisco.[13] Although the regional office was technically responsible for conducting the reviews, there were numerous alleged incursions from the national office. For example, on a site visit to UCLA in 1989, the San Francisco regional office staff assured Chancellor Young, Director of Admissions Rae Lee Siporin, and a host of deans and chairs from various departments that the OCR review would focus *only* on Asian admissions and not on affirmative action. Later that year, however, with strong encouragement from the Washington office, the San Francisco staff returned to UCLA to widen the scope of their review to include an analysis of affirmative action.

The question of who determines policy at the Office of Civil Rights, which in turn dictates the course of compliance reviews, was and still is a matter of differing opinion. When asked directly who is responsible for making policy at OCR, some officials say they are not sure or don't know; others hastily retreat under the cloak of bureaucratic and legal jargon. On the record, OCR officials say that policy is determined not by individuals in the office but by directives set in legal standards, for example, Title VI of the Civil Rights Act. Who sets such standards, and more important, who interprets their applicability to review situations and who adjudicates when there are differences of opinion or conflicts in interpretation, is unclear. Officials at the national level offer only vague descriptions of the chain of command. For example, Kathy Lewis, an attorney in the Washington office who advises OCR about its official policy, claimed that the national office offers a "supporting role" to the regional offices and helps them to "think through issues."[14] But the shift in focus of the UCLA investigation suggested that in some instances policy directives may come directly and forcibly from the D.C. office.

Harvard Cleared, UCLA Guilty

In October 1990, after a full two years of tight-lipped answers to questions about its reviews, the Office of Civil Rights announced that it had completed two of four reviews of college admissions, Harvard undergraduate admissions and graduate admissions at UCLA. In the case of Harvard, OCR concluded, "Over the last ten years, Asian American applicants have been admitted at a significantly lower rate than white applicants. However, we have concluded that this disparity is not the result of discriminatory policies or procedures" (Hibino 1990). OCR's rationale for the Harvard decision was that in spite of statistical disparities, Asians and whites were treated the same in the admissions process. At UCLA, however, OCR found "noncompliance" with Title VI in graduate admissions to the math department and "insufficient data" in an additional eight graduate programs (Palomino 1990). Similar to their findings at Harvard, OCR found that white applicants to UCLA's math department were admitted at higher rates than Asian applicants were in 1987 and 1988. But unlike the findings at Harvard, at UCLA, "OCR could not discern a consistent basis for the admissions decision nor could it conclude that the Department adhered to its stated admissions policies, practices and criteria in making its admissions decisions" (Palomino 1990).

According to the Office of Civil Rights, in 1987 there were three Asian applicants rejected for admissions with academic records comparable to those of three white students who were accepted for admission. In 1988, there were two Asian applicants that, OCR said, should have been admitted because they had qualifications similar to those of a group of admitted white applicants. OCR ordered UCLA to make belated admissions offers to the five Asian applicants (Hibino 1990).

Thus admissions data at both schools revealed that Asian applicants had a consistent and statistically significant lower rate of admission than white applicants. However, while Harvard could justify such disparities based on preferences for athletes and legacies, UCLA could not, according to OCR officials.

Republican critics of affirmative action were quick to take some of the credit for pressuring the Office of Civil Rights to complete its investigation of UCLA. Though the Republican party has never been known as the political ally of racial minorities, the issue of discrimination against Asian Americans turned out to be politically profitable in 1990. Congressman Rohrabacher was pleased with the OCR verdict at UCLA, because it lent some political credence to his own claims about discrimination. He told the *Washington Post*, "[it] marks a turning point in efforts to stop discrimination against Asian American students by colleges and universities" (J. Mathews 1990).

Chancellor Young of UCLA immediately denounced the OCR findings as "faulty reasoning and political pressure" (Gordon 1990). Young claimed that federal investigators relied too much on grades and test scores and failed to take into account the extent to which graduate programs also emphasize personal recommendations and the quality of the applicant's undergraduate school. Young said that UCLA would appeal the findings because "we believe the study and the results are in error. We believe there is no basis for the findings they have reached" (Gordon 1990). He further dismissed the findings as bureaucratic office politics, saying, "It is very clear that OCR reviewers were under deadline by their superiors . . . I believe they were under pressure to reach the conclusion they reached. A conclusion reached beyond Oct. 1 was unacceptable, as well as a conclusion that there was no violation" (Dinh 1990).

Asian American critics of UCLA admissions policy were disappointed with the university's stubborn refusal to accept the OCR findings. Many suggested that rather than appeal the findings, the time and energy of the UCLA administration would be better spent on a closer examination of the issues. Asian Americans were deeply concerned about the seriousness of the findings. L. Ling-chi Wang noted that the findings "highlight the absence of standardized procedures" (Ossias and Packer 1990). Henry Der said, "It [the finding] goes to the core of the autonomy and subjectivity granted to departments in selecting graduate students in a highly decentralized fashion" (Ossias and Packer 1990). Stewart Kwoh, executive director of the Asian Pacific American Legal Center in Los Angeles and president of the Asian alumni group at UCLA, said, "We are hoping that UCLA will conduct a more in-depth review to come up with more systematic admissions guidelines" (Gordon 1990:3).

Asian Americans were not the only ones who disagreed with the administration's decision to challenge the OCR findings. The editors of the *Daily Bruin* admonished the administration for "disputing" diversity rather than promoting it: "We think this is a situation where the university should, in effect, say nolo contendere, we're not going to fight it, and turn its attention where it's sorely needed: the disastrously revised admissions policy, the strengthening of the ethnic studies centers, the ethnic and gender studies requirements, and the hiring of faculty of color" (*Daily Bruin* 1990).

Members of the task force were disappointed but not surprised by OCR's findings at Harvard. Calling preferential policies for legacies "affirmative action for the white privileged class," Professor Wang noted that Asians were the only group that did not receive any special consideration in the Harvard admissions process, given that white students benefited from alumni preferences and black and Hispanic students benefited from affirmative action (Jaschik 1990). According to OCR, although all applicants qualify for consideration under affirmative action, as a general rule Asian Americans did not benefit from the program. Wang, joined by a chorus of other Asian American faculty and community leaders, called for further inquiries into policies that they said were facially neutral but whose outcomes were discriminatory.

Wang's criticisms of the OCR investigation at Harvard were echoed by two sociologists, Professor David Karen of Bryn Mawr and Professor Jerome Karabel, author of the 1990 admissions proposal at Berkeley. In an opinion piece in the *New York Times*, Karabel and Karen (1990) criticized the OCR decision at Harvard as an example of the "hypocrisy of today's politics of affirmative action." Questioning OCR's acceptance of Harvard's legacy explanation for differential Asian and white admission rates, Karabel and Karen (1990) suggested, "The truth is that the elite private colleges have never selected their students on academic criteria alone. The real question, therefore, is which qualities of applicants will receive preferential treatment and whose interest will be served by such programs?"

Liberal Claims about Race

The liberal rebuttals to neoconservative attacks on affirmative action ranged from the complex to the simple. A simplistic liberal position insisted that racism was on the rise across college campuses because universities had relaxed their commitment to diversity and affirmative action. This slump in university commitment to liberal policies, in turn, was the product of a national mood of conservatism that had begun with the Reagan presidency and continued with the election of George Bush. By the late 1980s, angry students and frustrated education officials sought to reverse the twin trends of conservatism and racism by demanding that their educational institutions redouble their commitment to diversity and affirmative action.

These simple liberal explanations were vulnerable to conservative and neoconservative arguments that liberal policies themselves were the problem, not the solution. Conservatives pointed out that if liberal policies were the solution, then one would expect that schools that had adopted liberal policies would be the least likely places for incidents of racial conflict. But to these observers the evidence suggested the opposite conclusion, that racial conflict occurred at those schools with strong liberal pro-diversity and pro–affirmative action policies (Sowell 1989; D'Souza 1991a,b). In addition, said conservatives, many schools that had not pursued strong diversification policies reported few or no incidents of racial conflict.

Many liberal educators privately conceded that conservative criticism of liberalism and its politics had been trenchant and often persuasive. But many of these analysts, while they remained dissatisfied with simple liberal prescriptions for more diversity, insisted that conservative directives to abolish racial preferences in every corner of higher education were doomed to failure. The problem, according to some, was that racial conflict is rooted less in the actual policies than in the patterns and dynamics of interethnic relations, which are governed by language, rhetoric, and the availability of institutional support to bridge differences in values and experiences among different racial groups. Arguing that race relations had become "complex," these analysts retained the liberal commitment to diversity and affirmative action but maintained that the essence of race relations lies beneath the surface of specific policies.

The "complex" liberal perspective, perhaps best exemplified by the pioneering work of Professor Duster and his colleagues at Berkeley, suggested that neoconservative prescriptions to end racism were superficial and facile. The Diversity Project's account of race relations at Berkeley emphasized the lack of language and symbols with which students could articulate their feelings of alienation and isolation in the highly racialized atmosphere of the campus. The problem, according to the Diversity Project, was not that there was a heightened awareness of race, as neoconservatives would have it, but rather that students lacked both the language and the institutional structures to grapple with their experiences and feelings within the highly charged racial atmosphere. A more complete solution of the problem called for nothing short of a new language about race and racism. Toward that end, the Diversity Project suggested strategies to foster both integration of and discussion among different racial groups about their experiences at Berkeley. Berkeley is not unlike many other universities that are committed to multicultural education, diversity, and affirmative action and at which similar strategies for confronting racial conflict might also be effectively deployed. Thus although the conservative author Dinesh D'Souza (1991b) suggested that universities get rid of all race-based programs, the Diversity Project's findings maintained that universities ought to start thinking of ways to help students cope with their racial experiences.

Compared with the conservative solution to racial conflict at the university, such liberal accounts were unwieldy and politically unsexy. To say that racism and race relations had become more "complex," more "subtle," or more "indirect" sounded vague and indeterminate. Moreover, complex arguments and analyses were difficult to translate into clear-cut simple policies. When set next to conservatives' advocacy of an end to racial preferences in college admissions as a means to combat racial balkanization on campus, liberal analyses about the lack of a more sophisticated language of race and racism, however thoughtful, appeared abstract and unfocused. That conservative claims about racism were more viable in the late 1980s, however, does not in any way mean that liberal accounts provided less accurate or less efficacious solutions.

Liberalism against Itself

Paradoxically, conservative calls to take back the university were weakened by a contradictory set of tenets contained within liberalism. A major hallmark of liberal thinking about race relations and racism has been that in spite of different historical experiences, different minority groups share a common experience of individual and institutional racism. But liberal policies designed to address racial discrimination moved in two somewhat different and conflicting directions.

One tenet of liberal policy thinking has emphasized one of the most fundamental values of liberal democracy, the notion of equality of individual opportunity. In practice, this principle meant that individual candidates for school or jobs were judged on the basis of individual and meritocratic criteria, standards that were universally applicable to all individuals without regard to race or ethnicity. For example, separate educational facilities for blacks and whites were considered unconstitutional because such a plan violated an individual's constitutional right to make a free choice about schooling.

A second tenet encoded in liberal policies has emphasized the importance of a "level playing field" on which individuals from different racial groups are equally matched for competition. The basic logic underlying this tenet is that differences among racial groups ought not to disadvantage an individual's participation in competition. This principle, equality of group opportunity, was designed to balance differences among groups in advance of any fair competition between individuals. In practice, equality of group opportunity manifested itself in preferential policies for racial minorities, affirmative action, to ensure that minority individuals would be adequately represented in public and private spheres of economic, social, and political life. In 1987, for example, a decade after a judicial finding of discrimination, there were no black paratroopers above the rank of corporal in the state of Alabama. The Supreme Court upheld a federal court decision to order the state to promote one black paratrooper for every white trooper promoted, provided that there was an available pool of black candidates (*Pardise* 1987).

The development of claims and counterclaims about Asian admissions brought liberalism's tenets to a crucial juncture. The emergence of a highly competitive pool of Asian American applicants confronted liberalism with the difficult task of reconciling equality of individual opportunity with equality of group opportunity in the zero-sum game of admissions. In admissions, equality of individual opportunity corresponds to the competition among individual applicants on the basis of academic standards indexed by grades, test scores, and supplemental/personal qualities; equality of group opportunity corresponds to campus affirmative action programs for the purposes of either recruitment or enrollment and is based on either race or class. At all of the top universities in the United States, individual merit and affirmative action were intended to be complementary, not contradictory, principles governing access to social goods. All of the top universities prided themselves on high standards of academic excellence and also boasted affirmative action programs to recruit students from diverse racial backgrounds.

In their rebuttals to Asian American claims of discrimination,

university officials judged Asian American applicants as typically ineligible for equality of group opportunity programs and "competitive, but not qualified" under the criteria of equality of individual
opportunity. Asian American complaints of discrimination revealed
a gaping hole in university admissions policies—the so-called standards of academic excellence might systematically disadvantage
non-underrepresented minorities such as Asian Americans. University officials, in their rush to defend their policies, frequently interpreted Asian American complaints as a threat to affirmative action
and not as a challenge to the use of selective or supplemental criteria
in judging academic excellence. In doing so, administrators set the
stage for a clear conflict between individual merit and affirmative
action. Their claims about Asian American applicants spelled out
what conservatives had feared most, that universities were compro-
mising excellence by abandoning standards of individual merit in
admissions.

Officials, faculty, and students at the highly selective universities were sensitive about charges of a decline in standards and loss
of excellence. Any decline in standards was interpreted as a direct
reflection of the quality of individual achievement by students and
faculty at the university. Accusations by conservatives that the top
universities were trading excellence for color—for example, discrimination against Asians amid preference for blacks—placed liberal university officials, faculty, and students on the defensive. At pains to
reassure their public that conservative claims about declining standards were not true, the proponents of liberalism zealously reiter-
ated their commitment to individualism and merit.

Officials from Berkeley and UCLA fixed their commitment to
academic excellence in part through repackaging affirmative action
into universalistic criteria based on socioeconomic status or class.
Citing a wave of anti–affirmative action resentment, these administrators did not attempt, either legally or politically, to defend race-
based affirmative action programs.

Do the Liberal Thing: Asian Admissions
and Affirmative Action

From the liberal perspective, doing the right thing about affirmative
action meant salvaging affirmative action from the hostile environs
of rising anti–affirmative action sentiment. As noted earlier, the

basic choice facing liberal officials was to change affirmative action or risk losing the program altogether. Under the circumstances, many liberals felt that they had successfully transformed affirmative action into a "progressive" policy based on more universalistic criteria—class or socioeconomic status.

For the most part, the affirmative action policies in place in the early 1990s at elite universities from the University of California to Harvard, met with conservative and neoconservative approval.[15] Many conservative commentators on higher education, including Allan Bloom, John Bunzel, Dinesh D'Souza, Richard Ramirez, Thomas Sowell, and Shelby Steele have argued that class-based affirmative action is fairer social policy than race-based affirmative action. Ironically, the liberal "rescue" of affirmative action represented a convergence toward more conservative ideology about higher education.

CHAPTER 7

The Retreat from Race

*I*n December 1990, the U.S. Department of Education issued a startling announcement. Michael Williams, assistant secretary of the Office of Civil Rights and one of the nation's highest-ranking black officials, declared that "race-exclusive" scholarships were discriminatory and, therefore, illegal. According to Williams, universities offering such scholarships were in violation of federal civil rights law and risked losing their federal aid.

Williams's announcement was the result of a federal review of an unusual offer by the organizers of the Fiesta Bowl, an annual New Year's Day college football game. The organizers, in an effort to blunt criticism that the 1991 game was to be played in Arizona—the only state in the nation that had not recognized Martin Luther King's birthday as a public holiday—planned to establish a $100,000 minority scholarship fund for the two teams slated to play in the game. Williams's office decided that the proposed scholarship fund violated Title VI of the 1964 Civil Rights Act because whites would not be eligible to apply. As an alternative, Williams suggested that the scholarship money could be used to benefit "economically disadvantaged students, educationally disadvantaged students, or those from single-parent families" (Marriot 1990b). According to Williams, the shift from race to class in minority scholarships was mandated by a straightforward reading of the law.[1]

Williams's decision was met by a torrent of furious opposition from university administrators, education officials, and civil rights organizations. University officials and civil rights organizations called the announcement "outrageous," saying it would severely hamper their efforts to attract and recruit minority students to college. Even President Bush, a contributor to the United Negro College fund, was reportedly "surprised," "embarrassed," and "disturbed" by the announcement (Rosenthal 1990b). President Bush and White House officials remained uneasy about the awkwardness of the situation—they did not wish to criticize Williams publicly, but at the same time they were displeased that he had failed to consult with them about the ruling.

The President, in an attempt to distance himself from the far right in the Republican party, pressured Williams to retract the decision. Following a week of strife within the Bush administration over Williams's decree, John H. Sununu, White House chief of staff, ordered the Department of Education to make a half-way reversal of the ruling. Race-exclusive scholarships would be permitted only if funds for such scholarships were drawn from private donations earmarked for such purposes and not from a university's general operating fund.

The partial reversal, intended to appease liberal supporters of racial preferences without alienating conservative critics of affirmative action, failed on both counts. Among liberals, the revised policy was seen as no better than the original. Robert Atwell, president of the American Council on Education, told the *New York Times*, "The situation was only made worse by the clarification. This is not a retraction, it's confusion" (DePalma 1990).

Conservatives who praised Williams's original decision were also dismayed by the revision. John Scully, counsel for the Washington Legal Foundation—a conservative think-tank accused by some liberals of being the real architect of Williams's scholarship policy—said, "There is no question this is not over. They [White House officials] realized that the law was clearly as Mr. Williams originally interpreted it, and they wanted, for political reasons, to backtrack from that" (*San Francisco Chronicle* 1990).

Williams's blundered solo attempt to nix race-exclusive scholarships was a stunning example of a broader trend in American politics and policy—what I call the retreat from race. In terms of social policy, the defining characteristic of this trend has been an increasing reluctance—by both liberals and conservatives—to address contemporary racial problems with explicitly racial solutions. Frequently the withdrawal of racial preferences has been accomplished, at least in part, through the substitution of class-based preferences. In the public debates prompted by the minority scholarship issue and Asian admissions, for example, rhetorical arguments against race-based preferences extolled class or socioeconomic criteria as more universalistic and hence more fair preferences. A similar shift has occurred in political discussions of welfare and civil rights policy. Liberals and conservatives alike propose that race-based policies be abandoned in favor of class-based or race-neutral policies. Ronald Brownstein (1991) of the *Los Angeles Times* observed in 1991, "A new generation of scholars is stressing class, not race, in an effort to break the civil rights impasse." Similarly, Steven A. Holmes (1991b) of the *New York Times* noted, "As the nation struggles to come to grips with issues of race and how to rectify past discrimination, a thought-provoking notion is beginning to be voiced: shift the emphasis of affirmative action programs from race to class."

By "retreat from race," I am also referring to a shift in American race relations manifested in how we construct and talk about race and racism. It is now a given that race has become central to political discourse about contemporary social problems. But as the minority scholarship controversy suggests, racial politics became enormously complex during the 1980s. Issues of race and racism, once the near-exclusive political domain of liberal Democrats, have been smartly eased into conservative attacks on the liberal state. In addition, race became a subterranean yet pervasive element of domestic party politics and political discussions of contemporary social problems. Thomas and Mary Edsall (1991a:53) point out that race has become an essential component of American politics:

> Race helps define liberal and conservative ideologies, shapes the presidential coalitions of the Democratic and Republican parties, provides a harsh new dimension to concern over taxes and crime, drives a wedge through alliances of the working classes and the poor, and gives both momentum and vitality to the drive to establish a national majority inclined by income and demography to support policies benefitting the affluent and the upper-middle class.

As Edsall and Edsall suggest, the retreat from race is not simply a question of policy but is also a discursive practice—in which American political discourse has become thoroughly imbued with racial meanings. For example, recent debates in higher education widely publicized by the national media—definitions of the canon, political correctness, minority scholarships, and student-athletes—were all heavily lined with racial imagery although such meanings were not articulated in explicitly *racial* terms. Similarly, in American politics, social problems such as "drugs" and "crime," and terms such as "inner city" and "urban crisis" have become code words for "black."

The retreat from race is a historical development in higher education and American politics that is still in the making. In most arenas of social policy, the retreat from race is an *idea* that has not been fully detailed in concrete policy proposals. With the exception of admissions policy at Berkeley and UCLA, there are no policy proposals to replace racial preferences with class preferences in, for example, employment. Though it is early for full-blown predictions, it is crucial, I think, to begin to anticipate the effects of the retreat from race on future racial politics and racial dynamics in the United States.

The Legacy of Asian American Admissions

At the beginning of the 1980s, issues of race and racism at the university were relatively straightforward matters—minorities were underrepresented in the student body, in the faculty, and in the curriculum. Addressing racial problems in higher education typically meant recruiting, admitting, hiring, and promoting more minorities. Accordingly, through much of the decade, racial progress in higher education was measured by increases in the numbers of minority students and faculty and in curriculum examining minority experiences.

But as the controversy over Asian admissions suggests, racial progress has gone beyond the "numbers game." Racial politics has become more than a "black" and "white" or "us" versus "them" conflict. Increasingly, race and racism have become a politics of competing interpretations—mired in arguments over what policies and which visions are fair and equitable. At the core of competing interpretations of racial progress are racial differences. The liberal vision assumed that racial differences—for example, in academic achievement or in skills preparedness for jobs—could be eliminated through the application of racial preferences aimed at repairing the effects of past discrimination. Conservatives argued just the opposite, that racial differences were the consequence, not the cause, of racial preferences. What changed during the 1980s was that many liberals moved toward, and in some cases completely over to, the conservative point of view.

Discourse about the Asian American student—the model minority image, for example—was an important part of the reason many liberals ultimately moved to get rid of racial preferences or, at best, offered only qualified support for affirmative action. Between 1989 and 1990, old debates about affirmative action, which had until then largely ignored the Asian American, were reconstituted—this time with Asian Americans included as part of the debate. In earlier debate about affirmative action, conservatives argued that racial preferences victimized whites. In the reconstructed debate, Asian Americans replaced whites as more sympathetic "victims" of racial preferences. The emergence of a "good" minority—Asians—suffering discrimination as a result of preferences for "underrepresented minorities"—that is, blacks and Hispanics—offered liberals a difficult choice: scrap affirmative action or change it.

Claims and counterclaims about Asian admissions opened a political Pandora's box—conservatives sounded like Asians, liberals sounded like conservatives, and increasingly conservatives were beginning to sound like liberals. For example, claims that Asian American students were as well qualified but less likely than whites to gain entry to the elite schools set in motion a tedious debate over the definition of "excellence," "merit," and "diversity." Groups such as the task force argued that Asian American students were both "excellent" and "diverse"; university officials contended that Asian American students, while perhaps "excellent," were not "diverse"; and neoconservatives argued that Asian American students were simply "excellent," that the notion of "diversity" was irrelevant, and that whites were the new "victims."

Asian admissions also dramatized other important changes in racial politics: changing coalitions in ethnic politics, liberal and black rethinking of the civil rights agenda first established in the 1960s and 1970s, and last but not least, a reframing and rearticulation of affirmative action debates by conservatives and neoconservatives. The move toward class-based preferences presented a tough dilemma for the political coalition of minorities established during the 1960s and 1970s—blacks, Asians, Chicanos/Latinos, and Native Americans. A major rupture in the coalition occurred between Asians and blacks. Racial tension between blacks and Asians was suggested by the fact that while a majority of blacks supported affirmative action, a majority of Asians did not. Among blacks and other "underrepresented" minorities, the loss of race-based preferences was viewed as a direct attack on their *group* interests. As the case of Berkeley admissions illustrated, some blacks were reluctant to publicly oppose their historically liberal "friends" in higher education politically. Many blacks were privately angry, however, with liberals for what they felt was a capitulation to Asian American interests in admissions policy.

Others at Berkeley, including some blacks and many Asians, welcomed the advent of class-based preferences in admissions, because they felt such a policy saved affirmative action from the clutches of neoconservatives. In addition, many hoped that class-based preferences offered a way to mend the fractured relations among racial minorities, particularly blacks and Asians, that seemed to be inherent in race-based affirmative action debates.

Although Asian admissions per se faded from public attention at the end of the 1980s, "diversity," "discrimination," and "affirmative action"—the interpretive cornerstones for the Asian admissions debate—resurfaced in fresh controversies at the university.

Political Correctness and Student-Athletes

What is most interesting about the entrenchment of racial politics in higher education is the way race has been embedded in disputes not explicitly about race. During the 1990–1991 academic year, the issues of political correctness and of student-athletes' graduation rates were two controversies that dramatized the inscription of race in political discourse and that also generated considerable public debate about the university. Political correctness "started as a joke," according to media accounts from progressives and leftists inside the university. Supposedly political correctness was a facetious holdover from left-wing politics in which ideas and behavior were evaluated in terms of absolutes—right and wrong. But the joke went sour when conservatives appropriated the term "PC" to describe a Kafkaesque world of academics where one of this nation's most cherished values—freedom of speech—was on the chopping block. Explicit dialogue about political correctness has focused on whether universities have the right to limit what the University of California termed, "fighting words"—verbal harassment, racial epithets, or derogatory statements about a person's race, class, gender, or sexual orientation. The debate over political correctness generated widespread interest—in one *New York Times* debate featured on the editorial page,

Miss Manners squared off against a senior from Sarah Lawrence College who likened political correctness to her father's blacklisting during the 1950s—in what has become a raging battle between conservatives and liberals about the state of higher education.

Even President Bush became involved in the issue. In his remarks at the University of Michigan graduation in 1991, the President, lining up behind other conservative critics, warned that political correctness had led to an atmosphere of "inquisition," "censorship," and "bullying" in higher education (Dowd 1991). Conservative complaints about free speech at the university such as those articulated by Bush carry a distinctly racial edge. Laying bare the racial undertones of arguments over political correctness, conservative writers insist that liberal pandering to racial minorities has been the root cause of the "new orthodoxy" and "left-wing McCarthyism."

Consider also the 1991 National Collegiate Athletic Association's championship basketball game between Duke University and the University of Nevada, Las Vegas (UNLV). This college sports ritual erupted in controversy when the NCAA disclosed dramatic differences in graduation rates between the two schools' athletes. At Duke, where the starting line-up was predominantly white, athletes graduated at a rate of 96.1 percent. At UNLV, where the starting line-up was predominantly black, athletes graduated at a rate of only 14.3 percent. Glenn Dickey, the *San Francisco Chronicle*'s sports columnist-turned-critic of the university, characterized Duke's victory over UNLV's Runnin' Rebels as the revenge of "student-athletes" over mere "athletes" (1991:C-5).

The publication of a survey of special admissions considerations given to college athletes just prior to the Duke-UNLV championship game sparked a storm of criticism and controversy over academic standards and college athletics (Eskanazi 1991). A major finding of the survey was that college athletes were on average between four and six times as likely as regular students to be admitted through special admissions. A special admit is a student whose academic profile is typically outside the normal range of most regularly admitted students but who is admitted because of a special talent, for example, in sports, music, or art. According to the survey, even among those schools that do not have a special admission policy for athletes—the University of Michigan, for example— athletes tend to have slightly lower academic profiles than the rest of the student body. Said James Duderstadt, president of the University of Michigan, "My own sense is that whether it's a Michigan or a U.S.C. or

Notre Dame or Harvard or Yale, if you were to look at the average quantitative statistics—SAT, ACT, class ranks—you would find those probably on the average somewhat lower than the mean characterizing the institution" (Rhoden 1991).

Controversy over special admissions for college athletes, many of whom are black, replayed familiar themes from the Asian admissions debate. In the debate over Asian admissions, conservatives accused university officials of softening academic standards for black students through racial preferences. In the student-athletes debate, the criticisms were more generalized: academic standards were still the central problem, but this time athletes, nonspecific racial subjects, were the beneficiaries. In this controversy, the terms of discourse might have been easily translated so that "college athlete" meant "black" and "special admissions" meant "racial preferences."

The Presidents' Commission of the NCAA reacted to swirling debate around the Duke-UNLV game with a proposal to toughen academic standards for student-athletes.[2] In responding to the proposal, which set higher minimum standards for NCAA eligibility, NCAA officials anticipated complaints about the disproportionate impact of tougher standards on minority athletes. Although the controversy did not explicitly pit *black* athletes against *white* athletes, racial politics remained a strong undercurrent of debate. Lorna P. Straus, chair of the Academic Requirement Committee of the NCAA, reassuringly predicted that newly ineligible black athletes would be replaced by other better-qualified black athletes: "I don't think its going to change the percentage of black athletes. What you're going to see are better prepared student-athletes, white or black" (Lederman 1991).

I am not reducing the question of academic standards and student-athletes to a simple racial issue. Rather, my point is that the student-athlete issue, like the debate over political correctness, represented the maturation of a racial discourse and racial politics at the university originally seeded in eight years of controversy about Asian admissions. Those eight years of debate offered conservatives a forum to blast racial preferences/affirmative action and, more important, provided a catalyst for altering the ways in which we discuss contemporary racial issues. A cornerstone of the alteration of racial discourse is that explicit discussions of race have been superseded by symbolic metaphor and allusion to racial difference.

Underlying the shift in the ideology of affirmative action wrought by Asian admissions was a deeper shift in political and ideological understandings of race. In a double-edged movement, race became increasingly significant in the social, political, and academic life of the nation's campuses at the same time that the ways conservatives and liberals talked about racial issues became more diffused and coded. For example, while the university curriculum became more concerned than ever before with themes of race and racism, conservatives sought to contextualize those concerns in an attack on liberal reforms—multiculturalism, diversity, and affirmative action—in higher education. As a result, and as the controversy over Asian admissions demonstrated, it became increasingly difficult to distinguish liberal politics from conservative politics. In the case of Asian admissions, conservatives proposed, and liberals concurred on, a retreat from race in admission policy. Liberals embraced the use of class-based preferences in admissions policy as "saving" affirmative action while conservatives claimed the action a victory over liberalism.

The Asian admissions controversy is exemplary of how discourses of race—what Goldberg (1990a) describes as "racialized and racist ways of seeing the world and representing it"—are more than simply forms of "talk" or "language." The course of the shifting debate in which minorities, university officials, and neoconservatives sought to define the central focus of Asian admissions suggests the importance of viewing discursive practices as contingent on struggles between competing political visions. Although both Asian Americans and neoconservatives claimed that Asian American students were the victims of quotas at the elite universities, for example, their respective claims were driven by entirely different political perspectives. In other words, while 'the shifting discourse helped accomplish the retreat from race in policy terms, it also revealed how discursive struggles are fundamentally steeped in political conflicts.

To put the matter in historical perspective, Asian admissions was the beginning of a chain of political controversies in which neoconservatism became firmly entrenched in popular ideology about higher education. A core element of the neoconservative (and conservative) critique of the university is clearly racial. Conservatives decry falling academic standards, political correctness, and the canon debates as liberal capitulation to the special interest demands of racial minorities and women.

Thus the retreat from race, though not explicitly about the Asian American experience, took shape in the period of controversy and debate over the admission of Asian American students to the elite universities in this country. The history of that debate both reflected and contributed to a significant turning point in racial politics on and off the nation's campuses. Debate over Asian admissions culminated in a set of inaugural institutional policies that retreated from race and advanced toward class. The withdrawal of racial preferences at Berkeley in 1990, the removal of "total protection" for minorities at UCLA in 1989, and the increasing significance of class in the evaluation of Asian American applicants at the elite private schools all established the beginnings of a pattern of university admissions practices emphasizing class, not race.

Race Talk: Code Words, Racial Imagery, and Political Discourse

What goes on inside the hallowed halls of education is often not typical of what happens outside them. But when it comes to racial politics, the university is as much a bellwether of contemporary trends as it is a crucible for them. From the late 1980s through the early 1990s the national media presented a relentless stream of reports on political issues and social problems concerning race. Between 1988 and 1990, for example, violence, crime, and drugs in the inner city became almost synonymous with images of alienated black youth, ruthless black gangs, and single black mothers. A catalogue of incidents in New York City—Tawana Brawley, the Central Park jogger, Bensonhurst, the boycott of Korean grocers by black residents in Brooklyn—epitomized racial violence and images of uncontrollable black youth gone wild. Elsewhere in the country, race was an inescapable part of the national politic. In the first six months of 1991, several issues of national scope were heavily dosed with racial interests and racial politics: the beating of Rodney King by Los Angeles police officers, the controversy over the confirmation of Supreme Court Justice Clarence Thomas, battles in many states over apportionment and redistricting following the 1990 Census, and renewed debate over a Democrat-backed civil rights bill.

As racial issues have become increasingly significant in American politics, they have also become more embedded in our political discourse. Edsall and Edsall (1991) have chronicled in their book *Chain Reaction: The Impact of Race, Rights, and Taxes on American Politics*, how thoroughly the language of race, or what might be called "race talk"—which includes the use of racial code words and images—is diffused in political discourse on social issues. According to Edsall and Edsall (1991), race and taxes became the principal organizing issues behind a sustained effort by Republicans not only to retake the presidency after Lyndon Johnson but to reshape the very terrain upon which American politics are founded.

A central piece of conservatives' re-mapping of political discourse has been their ability to link the Democrats with racial codes. Edsall and Edsall (1991:214) note, "The word 'group' in Republican rhetoric came to signify all Democratic claimants for special preference: those who—in this view—sought to enlarge their share of the pie by taking portions of what others had earned through hard work, diligence, and self-denial."

Several of the most pressing social problems of the 1980s and 1990s on America's domestic front—drugs, housing, education, the decline of the nuclear family—connote racial images. The term "drug problem" conjures up black youth gangs, crack houses in ghetto (read black) neighborhoods, ruthless Colombian drug cartels (see R. Harris 1991). In higher education, phrases such as "academic standards" (or "academic excellence") and the "canon" have become code words for what are widely recognized as racial disputes.

The use of racial imagery and racial code words conceals rather than discloses the racial underpinnings of contemporary social problems. Race and racism are pervasive though often implicit in discussions of American politics. We regularly talk about racial issues or racial conflicts in nonracial terms. In the fall of 1990, "job quotas" emerged as a major issue in American politics during election campaigns. In California and North Carolina Republican candidates accused Democratic rivals of supporting job quotas, which, according to Republicans, unfairly set aside a certain proportion of jobs for women and minorities.[3] Democrats denied the charges and blamed Republicans for stirring up racial resentment in pursuit of political gains. Republicans insisted that the issue was not racial. Charles Black, a chief spokesperson for the Republican National Committee, said, "The thing about quotas is that it reminds people that Democrats are elitist social engineers" (Toner 1990). But a television commercial for the Republican Jesse Helms of North Carolina was explicitly racial. While white hands crumpled a rejection letter, an announcer said, "You needed that job, and you were the best qualified. But it had to go to a minority because of a racial quota" (Applebome 1990). Helms defeated his challenger Harvey Gantt, a black

Democrat who had been even in the polls with Helms until the commercials were aired. Had he won, Gantt, who campaigned as a liberal, would have been the nation's first black Democratic senator since Reconstruction.

The issue of quotas was also the centerpiece of Republican opposition to the 1990 civil rights bill. Backed by a chorus of Republican supporters, President Bush vetoed the bill, saying it would "lead to quotas." The Democrat-sponsored bill was designed to challenge several Supreme Court decisions on employment discrimination cases that had the net effect of shifting the burden of proof of discrimination from employer to employee.[4]

The heart of the conflict over the 1990 civil rights bill, as well as in recent Supreme Court decisions on employment discrimination, was the question of who must prove discrimination on the job: the employer or the employee. In 1971 the Supreme Court, in *Griggs v. Duke Power*, prohibited the use of facially neutral policies that had racially discriminatory outcomes. The *Griggs* decision found that two requirements of the Duke Power Company for employment—a high school diploma and standardized tests—differentially impacted whites and blacks and had no demonstrable relation to job performance.[5] The decision thus defined the legal standard in employment discrimination cases as falling on the shoulders of the employer—to justify job requirements as necessary for job performance. According to the Court, "the touchstone is business necessity" (Vieira 1990: 239). Businesses may use employment standards that have discriminatory outcomes, but the employer has "the burden of showing that any given requirement [has] a manifest relationship to the employment question" (Vieira 1990:239).

Seventeen years later, in 1989, the Court changed the legal framework set by *Griggs* and shifted the burden of proof of discrimination back to the employee. The Court ruled in *Wards Cove Packing Co. v. Antonio* that after demonstrating disparate impact, *employees* must "show that other [practices], without a similarly undesirable racial effect, would also serve the employer's interest in 'efficient and trustworthy workmanship'" (Vieira 1990:240). Liberals complained that the decision in *Wards Cove* turned back the clock on civil rights. Civil rights organizations argued that requiring employees to be unduly knowledgeable about business practices made it harder for them to file discrimination lawsuits.

The 1990 civil rights bill challenged the Court's decision in *Wards Cove* and sought to restore the burden of proof to the employer.

Adopting the legal framework set in *Griggs*, the proposed bill required that in cases where disparate impact had been established, employers, not employees, would be required to show how the disputed practice—tests or other requirements—were related to actual job performance. The underlying controversy concerned race. Linda Greenhouse (1990) noted in 1990, "Although it has not been acknowledged as such, the conflict over the civil rights bill is the latest chapter in the much more diffuse and lasting debate over the extent to which the country—including employers, politicians, and judges—can or must, in the words of Justice Harry A. Blackmun's opinion in the Supreme Court's *Bakke* reverse-discrimination decision, 'take into account of race.'"

In 1991, the lead-in to a feature article about race in the *Atlantic* stated: "When the official subject is presidential politics, taxes, welfare, crime, rights, or values . . . the real subject is race" (Edsall and Edsall 1991:53). As I noted earlier in the case of Asian admissions, that conservatives *and* liberals have inserted racial imagery and code words into their political agendas has made it difficult to differentiate a liberal politics of race from a conservative politics of race. *Both* conservatives and liberals support equal opportunity and abhor discrimination—but they disagree over how to achieve the former and how to discourage the latter. In the battleground over policy, the two leading strategies for achieving equal opportunity—racial preferences and color-blind policies—do not neatly correspond to conservative or liberal politics.

Liberals and conservatives share keywords about race but assign conflicting definitions to such terms. "Equal opportunity" encompasses different and opposing notions of *who*, the group or the individual, is competing for *what*, equal access or equal outcomes. As Omi and Winant (1986) suggest, conservatives rearticulated the notion of equal opportunity—which in the liberal democratic politics of the 1960s and 1970s was based on the principle of *group rights* for different races—to mean the right of different racial groups to compete *as individuals*. As William J. Wilson (1987) points out, these different visions of equal opportunity translate into distinct policy initiatives. Liberal adherence to what Wilson calls "equality of group opportunity" is associated with preferential policies for minorities; conservative proposals for "equality of individual opportunity" tend to emphasize color-blind policies that protect the rights of minorities as individuals to have equal access to (not equal results) free market competition for jobs and education. Thus, though policy initiatives

loosely associated with liberals and conservatives are radically different, the rhetoric of racial equality, or race talk, features a sometimes
bewildering juxtaposition of liberal and conservative racial codes
and symbols.

For example, returning to the minority scholarship issue, the
emergence of a small but vocal group of black conservatives—one of
whom is Michael Williams—throws into question the old standard
and accepted supposition that affirmative action and racial preferences can be defined as a "black" (or minority) political cause. That
Williams is black revealed an additional layer of irony in racial politics: the position on affirmative action taken by some black conservatives makes some white Republicans appear liberal. President Bush,
whose controversial 1988 campaign advertisements featuring Willie
Horton capitalized on racial resentment between whites and blacks,
emerges as a racial liberal when compared with the strict anti–affirmative action politics of Williams. The scholarship controversy exemplified yet another twist in racial politics: there are increasing
numbers of self-identified liberals—several of whom are black—
whose political position on affirmative action is virtually indis-
tinguishable from that of many conservatives.

Liberals and Racial Politics

Affirmative action based on class, not race, has garnered support
from both blacks and whites. Probably the leading proponent of
class-based affirmative action is William J. Wilson, a sociologist at
the University of Chicago. Wilson's (1987) argument, outlined in *The
Truly Disadvantaged*, is that the plight of the underclass has been
determined more by changes in the economy—manufacturing decline, capital flight, and the replacement of unskilled labor by technological innovation—than by racism. Affirmative action, a program
that has historically helped middle-class blacks, has had little or no
impact on the mobility of the black masses. According to Wilson, the
vast majority of blacks—both the working class and the impov-
erished—can best be helped through a racially neutral set of *economic* reforms—at work and at school. Similarly, Jim Sleeper, author
of *The Closest of Strangers: Liberalism and the Politics of Race in New
York*, suggests that in New York City, "the real issue is not racism,
but economic decay" (Brownstein 1991). Sleeper (1990), like Wilson,
locates the crisis in the realm of the economy, not race relations, and

argues that government policies should be focused on issues of economic justice, not race.

Ronald Brownstein (1991), a political correspondent for the *Los Angeles Times*, calls advocates of class-based affirmative action the new "synthesis school of race relations." According to Brownstein, the synthesis school is composed of both liberals and conservatives attempting to forge new and sane political territory somewhere between the "old liberal politics of blame" and the "conservative politics of resentment." The new synthesizers include prominent black intellectuals and writers—including Wilson, Cornel West, William Raspberry, and Shelby Steele—who are joined by a circle of notable white intellectuals and policy analysts—for example, the sociologist Jonathan Rieder and Robert Greenstein, director of the Center on Budget and Policy Priorities in Washington.

The advocates of class-based affirmative action and, more generally, race-neutral social policies make two broad arguments. One argument is that economic dislocations, not racism, are the root cause of most problems experienced by blacks and other minorities. Based on this assumption, the new synthesizers—whose policy arguments are a juxtaposition of liberal and conservative claims—argue that legal efforts to address racial discrimination—that is, racial preferences—have not been successful. Indeed, few would argue that the condition of the majority of blacks has substantially improved over the past twenty years.

A second argument, driven in large measure by political expediency, is that the abandonment of race preferences is good for liberalism. Here the synthesizers suggest that racial preferences were a decisive factor in the defection of the white working class from the Democratic party in the 1984 and 1988 presidential elections. By reconstructing affirmative action in nonracial terms, the synthesizers hope to reestablish a liberal coalition of blacks and whites and thereby push more effectively for broad social reforms.

The emergence of liberals who advocate class-based affirmative action has been a telling development in racial politics. The decline in popularity, even in public acceptance, of race-specific or race-based policies has been underscored by a profound uncertainty about the nature of race and racism in our daily lives and how best to address society's racial problems. That uncertainty has been especially acute among liberals and moderate conservatives—a majority of whom were past supporters of affirmative action and racial preferences in education and employment. During the 1980s, liberal support for affirmative action and racial preferences dwindled in the face of an avalanche of conservative attacks on the role of "big government" in social problems—welfare, drugs, crime, and education. Many liberals, softening their support for racial preferences, now speak about affirmative action in tones of qualified support, saying, "it was a good idea in principle that did not work out in practice" or "I support affirmative action, but not quotas."

It remains to be seen how potent the new synthesizers will be in their efforts to revive liberalism and address the social problems of minorities. It is clear from the outset, however, that their efforts to do both depend on their ability to persuade the American people that class, not race, is the critical axis of inequality.

The Left and Racial Politics

Part of the liberal dilemma has been the lack of a clear leftist position toward which liberals might move. As much as the retreat from race is a triumph of conservatism, it has also been a failure of liberal and left visions of racial politics. Admittedly, it is difficult to characterize or to generalize about the "left"—which might be loosely construed as a conglomeration of labor and new social movements—racial minorities, feminists, gays and lesbians, Greens. But over the past twenty years, the constituent parts of the left have often been more preoccupied with single issues and/or with defending their group interests from political attacks by the right than with tracking racial politics. Salim Muwakkil (1991), writing for *In These Times*, has noted that members of "the left, having allowed conservatives to frame the important domestic issues—'crime,' 'welfare,' and 'quota,' now find themselves on the sidelines of mainstream political discourse."

In part the problem is that there has not been enough sustained *dialogue* on issues of race and justice among the different parts of the intellectual left, especially between whites and minorities. Cornel West (1992), commenting on the virtual *de facto* segregation of intellectual life in the United States, put it this way: "Prince's band is more interracial than most of the intellectual dialogue that goes on in America." As public discourse on social problems became more racialized and coded during the 1980s, it became more difficult for progressives to find a forum in which to talk frankly with one another about issues of race. Discussions of race, however lively they might be initially, often end in silence. This is what Michelle Wallace (1991) was referring to in her comments on black rage: "I think 'race' is an embarrassment to everybody. But by ignoring it, we are all conspiring to make it tick."

Among left intellectuals, there has never been a unified or co-
herent view of racial politics that might serve as a strong opposition
to the conservative view. Besides the lack of a global view of racial
politics, the left has been woefully absent from policy discussions
about race—particularly on affirmative action and racial preferences.
Certainly there are a few individuals who remain staunch supporters of racial preferences. Roger Wilkins (1991), for example, former
head of the NAACP, has insistently argued that racial preferences
are necessary to address the effects of past discrimination. A 1991
Newsweek poll (cited in Muwakkil 1991) in which a majority of blacks
supported racial preferences while whites overwhelmingly did not
suggests that Wilkins's position is hardly an isolated political stance.
But the white male left has not rallied behind racial preferences—or,
for that matter, affirmative action—except on occasion to lend limited auxiliary support to racial minorities.

The response by radical intellectuals and social democrats,
many of whom are white, to conservative and neoconservative critiques of affirmative action runs in two main currents. In one current, leftist intellectuals are as opposed to affirmative action as
conservatives. The rationale for leftist dissatisfaction is somewhat
different, however. Whereas conservatives decry affirmative action
as reverse discrimination against whites, critical theorists argue that
affirmative action is a type of bureaucratic bungling that threatens
intellectual autonomy at the university. For example, in a debate
that appeared in *Telos* in early 1991, Frank Adler counterposed affirmative action to excellence: "Affirmative action is committed to the
bureaucratic enforcement of social equality which, however com-
mendable as a political goal, is strikingly at odds with a collegial
institution whose goals, inner-logic and recruitment procedures are
intrinsically related to the commitment to excellence" (Adler 1991:
106). In the same issue, *Telos* editor Paul Piccone (1991:129), agreed
with Adler and added a Frankfurt school tangle of his own: affirmative action exemplifies *artificial negativity* as a government-imposed
creation of a bureaucratic system that "extends rather than challenges the logic of the system." In Piccone's view, artificial negativity—or in this case, affirmative action—is doomed to failure
because racial problems are an artifact of class. He says that racial
problems are increasingly "ideological fig leaves for more pervasive
problems resulting from class domination, social inequality, and traditional capitalist relations" (Piccone 1991:133). Commentary by Emery Roe (1991) on Piccone and Adler mustered only qualified
support for affirmative action. According to Roe, both Piccone and

Adler overlooked the possibility that under certain conditions, administrative and bureaucratic management of affirmative action might lead to greater tolerance of racial preferences at the university.

The debate in *Telos* illustrates how left-leaning theoretical discussions of affirmative action miss an essential point: affirmative action practices are quite separate from ideology and rhetoric about race. The commentators in *Telos* located their analysis of affirmative action practices within debates about postmodern bureaucracies, but never treated ideology about race as worthy of investigation. Indeed, for Piccone, race was reducible to class, and affirmative action (practices) was summarily dismissed as another ideological cover-up for late capitalism.

The failure of Piccone and others to define race as a socially constructed set of relations within a historical context is a commentary on left-inspired critical analyses of race. For many left intellectuals, class is assumed to be multidimensional—defined by different moments or aspects—as structural position and as historical consciousness.[6] Race, however, is often viewed as unidimensional, the effects of which are measurable by income differences, levels of educational attainment, and so on. As a result, when critical theorists tackle a racial issue such as affirmative action they do not bring to it the same analytic rigor afforded to the category of class. Indeed, in their examination of race, writers like Piccone miss that which is so clear about class: race, like class, is not just structural effect but is constituted in the ideological and discursive realm as well.

In contrast with the *Telos* forum, a second group of leftist writers on education focuses on discourse rather than on practices.[7] The focus on discourse is a significant improvement over the approach by Piccone and others, though not without its shortcomings. The analysis of discursive practices rightly problematizes how grand narratives frame or posit social problems in education. But a major weakness is that such analyses are often strong on problematizing and weak on the politics of problem solving, especially when such politics involve the new social movements or issues of race. For example, Stanley Aronowitz and Henry Giroux (1991:188) plead for "constructing a critical discourse to both constitute and reorder the ideological and institutional conditions for radical democracy." The task of critical postmodernism in education, they say, is to challenge the "power of the dominant narratives to frame the questions, issues, and problems of the day in ways that exclude oppositional and radical discourses and movements" (1991:189).

The Aronowitz and Giroux recommendation is a battle cry to

the left to "take back the discourse." But when compared with political slogans in minority communities for "Community Control," or
feminist antirape demonstrations to "Take Back the Night," the Aronowitz and Giroux proposal seems vague and abstract. Challenging state policies on redevelopment, affirmative action, and housing
seems to involve relatively straightforward political matters when
compared with contesting discursive practices. How exactly does
one challenge the dominant narrative? What political project offers
such a challenge?[8]

Aronowitz and Giroux fall short in defining the political proj-
ect(s)—in the form of policy or rough guidelines for radical social
movements. Having laid out the political challenge in the last five
pages of their book, they relapse into sketchy descriptions and critiques of possible radical oppositions—in particular, technological
utopianism and the politics of difference. They discount the politics
of difference, for example, cultural feminism, as "separatism" or as
"community-building without public politics." Their quick dismissal
of feminist, ecological, animal rights, and gay/lesbian politics as anti-
white male intellectualism reads more like ad hominem commentary
than considered analysis of leftist politics.

Aronowitz and Giroux do not go far enough in their discussion
of politics. They take us to the edge of how to challenge the grand
narrative, and then leave us on our own to puzzle out which politics
are key for waging discursive struggle. Aronowitz and Giroux cannot offer a persuasive scholarly critique of the new social movements because they do not fully appreciate how the call to reclaim
discourse from conservatives involves an expressly political project.
They fail to understand how conservative hegemony in political discourse was obtained through political struggle over concrete policy
issues—abortion, welfare, housing, civil rights, and education. The
result of this failure is that Aronowitz and Giroux cannot change the
discourse, although they exhort us to do so, because they completely sever the prospect of discursive change from political
struggles at the university.

Deepening Racial Conflict

The move away from racial preferences in policy and the increasing
use of code words and imagery that disguise race in contemporary
discursive practices are significant and disturbing developments in

American politics. The movement away from the explicit identification of racial issues at the same time that race is an increasingly pervasive and ubiquitous dimension of social problems is likely to increase rather than ease racial tension between those groups directly competing for resources. In addition to racial conflict between blacks and whites, tensions are also escalating among different racial groups—in particular, between blacks and Hispanics, whites and Asians, and Asians and blacks.

In the late 1980s and early 1990s, for example, black-Asian conflict over racial preferences in higher education was fueled by burgeoning black-Asian confrontation in cities such as New York, Chicago, and Los Angeles. There, the disputes were cultural and economic. In New York City the proliferation of Korean-run corner grocery stores generated anger and resentment among black patrons in the Flatbush section of Brooklyn. Members of the black community complained that Korean small business owners were arrogant toward their black customers and viewed all blacks as potential thieves. Korean store owners suggested that black complaints of Korean hostility were exaggerated and misinterpreted. Business exchanges and business culture in Korea, say many Korean businessmen, tend to be abrupt and aloof.

Code words and racial imagery exacerbate rather than heal the deep cultural and economic differences that typify inter-racial and intra-racial conflict. Conservative and liberal arguments that the real problem is class and not race misunderstand how conflicts about class are often experienced and fought on strictly racial grounds.

The elimination of racial preferences—the hallmark policy of the retreat from race, despite warm reassurances from new synthesizers—is not going to deliver on its promises. According to D'Souza (1991b), the end of racial preferences is a step toward racial harmony and racial equality. That mistaken view, now widely echoed by a chorus of conservatives and liberals, is based on the assumption that racial differences are the product of racial preferences. Nothing could be further from the truth.

In the debate over university admissions, for example, neoconservatives and conservatives argue that racial conflict at the university will recede with the substitution of class-based preferences for race in affirmative action. If there were any truth to this claim, we would expect that those universities that do not use race-based affirmative action would be less likely than schools that do employ such admission practices to be racially harmonious places. Berkeley,

Harvard, and Stanford provide an interesting comparison. At Berkeley, between 1985 and 1989, black and Hispanic students who met the minimum academic eligibility requirements were guaranteed admission. There have been no comparable explicit racial guarantees at Harvard. At Stanford, similarly, there have been no racial set-asides or guarantees of admission for minorities. Yet both Harvard and Stanford have been at the center of racial controversy as often as has Berkeley.

In 1989 Stanford became the focus of national attention in its debate over a university "core curriculum." Over the next two years, as debates about the "Great Books" and the required freshman curriculum flourished at other elite institutions—including Berkeley and Harvard—Stanford was often cited as a pioneering example of change in the liberals arts curriculum.

In the spring of 1990, a group of minority students boycotted classes to protest the lack of faculty diversity at Harvard. In the fall of that year Professor Derrick Bell, one of three black faculty at Harvard Law School, refused to teach to protest the school's failure to retain a black woman faculty member. In the 1980s, although several black women had been offered visiting appointments at the law school, none was retained with tenure. Harvard's failure to tenure a black woman law professor was made more glaring in 1991 when Columbia Law School successfully recruited two black women law professors for visiting appointments—Patricia Williams and Kim Crenshaw. Professor Williams, a professor at the University of Wisconsin Law School with a joint appointment in Women's Studies, specializes in commercial, contract, and constitutional law. She had received queries from top law schools across the country about visiting appointments, but not from Harvard Law School. Both Afro-American Studies and Women's Studies at Harvard University, however, were interested in Williams's work, and in the spring of 1992, in addition to teaching at Columbia, she taught a class, "Women and Notions of Property" through the Women's Studies Program at Harvard.

Thus both Harvard and Stanford have had their share of local campus controversies about racial issues. Although Berkeley is often portrayed as the institutional vortex of racial diversity problems and prospects, other top schools that do not have explicit race-based admissions procedures—including Brown, Harvard, Princeton, Stanford, and Yale—have also been plagued by racial incidents and racial conflicts.

The retreat from race is buttressed by other erroneous assumptions. Another often-heard conservative argument is that racial preferences aren't doing blacks and Hispanics any favors because these same students are more likely to drop out or flunk out of the university than are better-qualified whites and Asians. The problem, say conservatives, is that admissions officers, driven by a desire to increase minority enrollments at their school, eagerly admit blacks and Hispanics who are "less qualifed." From there the vicious circle begins, or so goes the conservative argument. Students who are less well prepared to enter the university face an uphill struggle to complete their undergraduate degree because they are forced to compete with better-qualified peers. In addition, many minority students from disadvantaged backgrounds feel "out of place" and face a difficult period of emotional and intellectual adjustment to their new environment.

Although it is true that blacks and Hispanics have lower graduation rates than whites and Asians, it is unreasonable to assume that such differences are the inevitable result of racial preferences. Approximately four years pass between the time a student is admitted to the university and his or her graduation. Why do some students succeed in completing their coursework while others fail or drop out? Obviously, students arrive with different levels of preparedness for university work. A white student with a GPA of 3.9 who attended a prep school in Connecticut is "different" from a black student with a GPA of 3.3 who attended public high school in south central Los Angeles.

Differences between these students—of which GPA is but the tip of the iceberg—pose one of the greatest challenges to highly selective universities in the late twentieth century. They are at a crossroads, and there are two clearly marked paths before them. One path is marked "admissions" and the other is marked "teaching." Either they can refuse to admit the "qualified but less competitive," or they can admit qualified students who bring to the university a diversity of experience and knowledge. The former path, well traveled by conservatives, directs admissions officers to engineer "differences" out of the entering class by selecting only the most competitive applicants. In other words, the conservative plan calls for eliminating differences in graduation rates by not admitting students who are "qualified but not competitive." The second and alternative path, along which many liberals journey, contends that "difference" among students—academic and nonacademic—enriches and enhances learning in higher education. In the liberal vision, admitting different kinds of students forces the institution to meet the challenges of diversity through teaching and advising students from different backgrounds.

Which path universities choose depends in large part on what they think are the minimum qualifications or requirements for work at their institution. Any discussion of qualifications should be related to the different types and ranks of colleges and universities in this country. It is a given that community colleges, state schools, and the elite private and public universities have varying requirements—and that the more selective schools will have tougher admission requirements. But as every admissions officer, particularly those at the more selective colleges, knows, qualifications for college go beyond grades and test scores. The quantitative measures of academic preparedness for college—grades and test scores—are in almost every instance supplemented by consideration of other criteria—leadership qualities, evidence of individual creativity, motivation, and special talents.

Minimum Standards for Admission

The choice of paths is prejudiced by the fact that "less competitive" students, in part through rhetoric and debate steeped in the Asian admissions controversy, have become synonymous with "unqualified" students. This assumption is both insidious and misleading. At the highly selective schools, an overwhelming majority of the applicants are capable of successfully completing the undergraduate work. Because of the limited number of slots available, some highly qualified applicants are rejected. This is the unavoidable consequence of a highly competitive admissions process—competency is no guarantee of admission. With such a large pool of competent applicants to choose from, admissions officers are able to select the best from a diverse range of qualified applicants. At Harvard, admissions officers suggested to Office of Civil Rights investigators that "between 80 percent and 90 percent of [Harvard's] 11,000 plus applicants could probably do the academic work and 50%–60% could do superb work" (U.S. Department of Education 1990:10).

The current wave of popular discontent with racial preferences thus concerns qualified students, not unqualified students. In part, the translation of "less competitive" to "unqualified" has been a legacy of the Asian admissions controversy. Charges of discrimination against Asian American applicants initially focused on grade point averages, test scores, and extracurriculars among the most competitive applicants—whites and Asians. Although there was a great deal of discussion about the top end of the applicant pool, there was virtually no discussion of the minimum criteria for admission.

At Berkeley, the minimum criteria for admission include a 3.3 GPA and satisfactory completion of a series of courses in science, math, and English, otherwise known as the "a–f" requirements. At the elite private schools, there are no comparable minimum requirements. Their admissions officers enjoy a tremendous amount of discretion, which they say allows them to select the best and brightest for admission. Despite the lack of minimum requirements, the vast majority of students admitted to Harvard, Stanford, Yale, and many other selective institutions possess impressive grade point averages, high test scores, and a dazzling array of extracurricular activities as well.

It is important that admissions officers at both private and public elite universities be able to exercise some latitude in their decision making. But the fluidity of the admissions process is both an asset and a liability. Wide latitude in the selection process affords admissions officers the opportunity to admit a freshman class representing a broad mix of talents and interests. Criteria other than test scores and grades—for example, leadership skills, special talents, athletics—allow admissions officers to admit students with nonstandard educational backgrounds who exhibit unusual promise for academic study. Most universities want to admit some nontraditional students—reentry students, exceptionally gifted musicians, athletes, students with high SATs but low GPAs, students from poor families, students from disadvantaged racial backgrounds. These students, who also meet minimum requirements for admission, represent a diverse range of talents and interests in the freshman class.[9]

Yet the looseness of admissions standards reflected in terms such as "excellence," "merit," and "diversity" begs the question of minimum standards for admission and competency for undergraduate work. We all recognize academic excellence at the top end—students who have outstanding grades, spectacular test scores, and who display unusual leadership, athletic, or musical skills. But while students who are accomplished at everything are easily recognizable in the admissions process, what about the majority of applicants, who are promising in many ways but not in every way? How should we compare a white male with rugby talent, a 3.6 GPA, and above-average SAT scores who attended private school in Maine with a second-generation Korean-American woman with a 3.9 GPA and above-average SAT scores who attended public high school in California? Most admissions officers would say that although both students are qualified to do successful work at an elite college, the admission of either would depend in part on how each individual contributed to the overall make-up of the freshman class. The rugby player could be just the running back needed for the college team, or he could be considered athletic but academically average when compared with other sports stars being considered for admission. Similarly, the Korean student might be viewed as an outstanding candidate for academic success or a good but not exceptional Asian American from California. What makes these students extraordinary or ordinary depends on how their records stack up with the rest of the applicant pool and, most important, on what values are defining admissions selection decisions.

To date, any discussion among higher education officials of what values define minimum standards for successful completion of an undergraduate career has been implicit and elliptic, not specific and certainly not broadly based. Such a discussion ought to be a far-reaching dialogue involving different segments of the university—admissions officers, faculty, students, administrators, and higher education officials. A number of general questions should guide the discussion:

1. What kinds of knowledge are important for all entering undergraduates?
2. How should we balance objective 'indicators of academic achievement—test scores and grades—with other indicators of intellect and creativity—leadership, individual motivation, special talents?
3. How and why should racial or class background of an applicant act as "plus" factors in admissions?
4. Given racial differences in academic achievement measured by standardized test scores, how will the university confront such differences in pedagogy, curriculum, advising, and in the social and political life of the campus?

Without discussion of these fundamental questions, which in turn hinge on definitions of minimum requirements, there can be little doubt that the fluidity of university admissions processes will

fall prey to conservative claims about falling standards and the decline of excellence.

The Real Truth about Class-based Affirmative Action

If the retreat from race allows us to suspend thoughtful consideration of minimum standards—a discussion that has potentially far-
reaching implications for teaching and curriculum at the university
—it also misrepresents the real truth about class-based affirmative
action. First, a caveat. My criticisms of class-based affirmative action
are a critique of neoconservative and conservative arguments about
class. I believe that class preferences are a vital and a just element of
university admissions. Like racial preferences, class-based affirmative action is a means of ensuring that our universities seek a broad
range of intellectual interests and talents. But in my view, class preferences and racial preferences are *not* interchangeable—they address
distinct forms of disadvantage. Both are necessary and valid forms
of preference.

Conservatives think that racial disadvantage can be subsumed
under class disadvantage. By conflating race with class, conservatives dismiss the significance of racial disadvantage in college admissions while simultaneously appearing to advance a progressive
agenda in university admissions. My critique is aimed at the assumption that class preferences should substitute for race preferences, and is not a rejection of the use of class preferences per se in
university admissions.

Conservatives argue that class preferences drop the stigma of
racial preferences while still benefiting minorities. Their ultimate
promise is that under class-based affirmative action, racial conflict
will wither and minority graduation rates will rise. D'Souza (1991b:
252) says, "black and Hispanic graduation rates are likely to increase, because only students whose potential is hidden due to previous disadvantage [class] would enjoy preferential treatment, in the
reasonable expectation that they will be able to realize their capa-
bilities and compete effectively with other students."

According to the American Council on Education (1990), however, social class is not always the great equalizer when it comes to
college persistence and college completion rates. The National Center for Education Statistics tracked 1980 and 1982 high school graduates through college and found that although some differences in

persistence and degree attainment among racial groups declined when controlling for socioeconomic status (SES), other differences were magnified. Thirty-two percent of Hispanics who entered four-year colleges attained a college degree, compared with 55.5 percent of whites. But the American Council on Education (1990:8) found that "after matching the two groups by SES quartiles, only 30.1 percent of high SES Hispanic students received four-year degrees, compared with 62.1 percent of whites students in the high SES quartile. The difference in degree attainment between Hispanics and whites in the high SES groups is larger than for the two groups as a whole." At least in some instances, class exaggerated, not reduced, racial differences in graduation rates.

A major myth about class-based affirmative action is that such preferences are good for minority enrollment and good for minority self-esteem because they lack the stigma and conflict associated with racial preferences. I argue that the real problem with class-based preferences is they ignore the problem of racial differences in academic achievement. The rhetoric of class preference suggests that middle-class blacks have unfairly benefited from affirmative action preferences based on race. According to Wilson (1987), the black middle class has risen up with the help of affirmative action on the backs of the "truly disadvantaged," the black working-class poor. In addition, the costs of affirmative action for middle-class blacks have included nagging insecurity—emotional and intellectual—about their ability and qualification for university work. Steele (1990:16) believes that "one of the most troubling effects of racial preferences for blacks is a kind of demoralization, or put another way, an enlargement of self-doubt."

But conservative arguments about the benefits of class preferences for blacks—from the working or middle classes—are at best speculative. Conservatives have been long on promises but short on real empirical evidence showing that class-preferences will not dramatically reduce black enrollment in higher education. In the idealized conservative scheme, middle-class blacks compete with middle-class whites and Asians in the free market approach to admissions. Giving preference to lower-class students rather than to middle-class blacks may seem fair at first glance, but it does not change the fact that middle-class blacks may be more academically disadvantaged than lower-class whites. In particular, the conservative vision of a free market approach to admissions is ignorant, perhaps intentionally, of the enormous differences in the mean SAT scores of

Table 7.1. Mean SAT Scores by Race and by Class, 1976

	High Income		Middle Income		Low Income	
Race	Verbal	Math	Verbal	Math	Verbal	Math
Black	392	406	347	368	311	336
White	467	511	442	485	430	462
Asian	448	537	412	513	365	502

Source: Ramist (1976).
Note: Figures are based on a 10 percent sample of whites and all Asian American and black SAT test-takers in 1976. $N = 147,000$. High income = more than $20,000 per year; middle income = $9,000–$20,000 per year; low income = less than $3,000 per year.

blacks and whites. Neither conservatives nor their liberal followers seem to be able to face reality: class cannot be the panacea for racial preferences, because racial differences in academic achievement exist within classes.

John Bunzel, a vocal critic of race-based preferences, put the matter this way: "What's the real difference between a middle-class black student and a middle-class white student? Or a middle-class white and a middle-class Asian?" (L. Mathews 1987). The answer is: between 60 and 100 SAT points. A study by Leonard Ramist, director of the Admissions Testing Program at the Educational Testing Service, drives home the blunt reality of racial differences in achievement within classes. His 1976 study, "A Review of Admissions Testing Program Ethnic Group Data," examined mean SAT math and verbal scores for 147,000 high school seniors. Ramist found dramatic differences in black, white, and Asian SAT scores by class (see Table 7.1). Middle-income blacks have a mean SAT verbal score 65 points below middle-income Asians and 95 points below middle-income whites. The differences are even more pronounced with respect to math scores. The mean SAT math score for middle-income blacks is 117 points below that of middle-income whites, and 145 points below that of middle-income Asians.

What is particularly striking is that the mean SAT math score for high-income blacks (406) is substantially below that of both low-income whites (462) and low-income Asians (502). The mean SAT verbal score for high-income blacks (392) is substantially below that of low-income whites (430) although higher than that of low-income

Asians (365)—a finding that is not surprising, given that the low-income Asian population contains many non-native English speakers. In other words, on the verbal section of the SAT, regardless of class, blacks are more disadvantaged than every group except low-income Asians.

More formal and systematic studies of race and class differences in SAT scores have not been published by the Educational Testing Service. Ramist, after years of watching trends in SAT scores by ethnicity, says that he doubts that racial differences have disappeared within classes.[10] Mean SAT scores for middle-class blacks are, in all likelihood, different from mean SAT scores for middle-class whites and Asians.

The 1991 profile of college-bound seniors, a descriptive compendium of SAT test-takers, verifies Ramist's hunch. Although the Educational Testing Service profile report is not set up to highlight racial differences within classes, such comparisons are available after reordering the data. The same trends observed by Ramist in 1976 are present in 1991. Blacks continue to have lower SAT scores than whites and Asians who come from similar socioeconomic backgrounds. There is a stubborn persistence of racial differences within socioeconomic groups (see Table 7.2). Obviously more research needs to be undertaken in this area—but we can safely conclude that racial differences in academic achievement persist within and between social classes. Race is independent of class when it comes to academic achievement.

Conservative and liberal supporters of class-based preferences

Table 7.2. Mean SAT Scores by Race and by Class, 1991

| | Black | | Asian | | White | |
Income	Verbal	Math	Verbal	Math	Verbal	Math
Less than $10,000	321	358	340	485	407	452
$10,000—$20,000	334	370	353	499	416	457
$20,000—$30,000	348	381	393	512	423	466
$30,000—$40,000	361	392	414	523	429	474
$40,000—$50,000	371	403	435	535	437	484
$50,000—$60,000	376	408	449	546	445	494
$60,000—$70,000	386	417	456	556	454	502
$70,000 or more	413	447	482	590	471	526

Source: College Entrance Examination Board (1991).

often lace their arguments with rhetoric about the need to "speak frankly" about racial conflict in the United States. The gist of their argument is that "race has become an inflated and exaggerated dimension of social and political life in the United States—so let's stop talking, thinking about, and defining reality in terms of racial difference." But the irony is that the substitution of class for race in affirmative action preferences does not address in a frank or honest way the stubborn problem of racial differences in academic achievement.

Instead, the retreat from race cheats us of a language with which to talk about racial conflict and racial differences. Not talking about racial differences will not make them go away. Rather, the retreat from race reflects a broad crisis in popular and scholarly understanding of racial dynamics in the United States. Both liberals and conservatives are responsible for constructing this crisis, and endless finger pointing between these two political sides over who is "racist" only underscores the inability of both sides to grasp fully the dynamic construction of contemporary racial politics. Eliminating racial preferences abandons the only social policy that acknowledges and addresses racial differences in academic achievement.

Addressing Racial Problems Head On

What would it mean to address racial problems more explicitly, for example, in university admissions? There are three problem areas in admissions at the highly selective universities—minimum qualifications, racial differences in academic achievement, and race relations in campus academic, social, and political life. University administrators, faculty, students, and education officials need to explore and discuss these three areas in order both to assess conservative and liberal moves away from race-based policies and to ensure that admissions policies are socially just and equitable.

Minimum Qualifications

The debate over Asian admissions focused on the qualifications of the most competitive applicants to the highly selective universities, but never undertook a full discussion of the minimum criteria for admission to these same schools. Although Berkeley and UCLA have defined minimum standards for admission, there are no comparable standards at the elite private schools—Brown, Harvard,

Princeton, Stanford, and Yale. Admissions officers at these schools say that minimum standards are not "clear-cut" and depend on a variety of criteria. A student with relatively low SAT scores might be admitted if he or she displays academic promise in other areas. Admission to the selective universities should not be mysterious—rather, the process and the kinds of factors that are crucial ought to be explicit. A discussion of minimum standards is important because it reveals basic assumptions and values about what constitutes academic preparedness for university work.

Various factors clearly contribute to a student's ability to undertake university level work—basic coursework, motivation, and ability to convey and grasp concepts and ideas. If there exist minimum qualifications for doing undergraduate work at the highly selective universities—and all admissions officers contend that such standards do exist—why are selection decisions shrouded in fictions of "building a class" and "creating a diverse mix"? A freshman class that is representative of the pool of qualified applicants could be selected by a process as simple as a lottery. Above and beyond minimum standards, what else is crucial or important in admissions decisions?

Universities will want their admissions standards to allow them to recruit and admit specially talented students—athletes, musicians, and artists, for example. There is no reason that the most selective schools cannot use additional criteria to select students. A discussion of minimum standards, however, would at least make explicit the kinds of priorities (and values) in the use of additional criteria above and beyond minimum requirements. It is a given at many schools—including the most selective universities—that the admissions process includes some form of athletic preference. How should athletic preferences—or legacy preferences—be balanced with racial or class preferences?

At many schools, athletes are a crucial part of the business of the university. If alumni are the "bread"—hence legacies—then athletes are the "butter" of university "development." It is important to keep athletes academically eligible for play to meet NCAA requirements. Several schools, including Berkeley and Duke, have institutionalized academic advising and academic help for student-athletes. Athletes may receive fellowships that cover tuition and living expenses and in addition are eligible for extensive academic help and counseling. In contrast, academic services for racial minorities (who are not also athletes) are negligible. At Berkeley, for example, an athlete can receive several hours of academic tutoring a day for the better part of the year; only limited opportunities are available for minority students seeking academic help.

I am not suggesting that universities should not go to great lengths to ensure that student-athletes have a rich academic as well as athletic life in college but, rather, that universities at least discuss whether other groups—in particular, minorities—might benefit from a similar array of services. It is a basic question of priorities and values—why are we more willing to help athletes than minorities?

Racial Differences in Achievement

Notions of universal standards of excellence and achievement completely ignore the existence of racial differences in achievement among college applicants. College administrators, admissions officials, faculty, and education policy research analysts need to sit down and discuss the long-term implications of racial differences in academic preparedness for college, racial differences in academic achievement, and racial differences in graduation rates. How should admissions officers evaluate an Asian American with a below-average SAT verbal score, an above-average SAT math score, outstanding grades, and strong extracurriculars against others? Because grade point average is a better predictor of Asian American undergraduate grades than test scores, should the admissions officer weigh the high school grade point averages of Asian Americans more heavily than those of whites? The important issue underlying racial differences in academic achievement is whether selection decisions are based on a universal set of criteria or are keyed to the indicators of success for different racial groups.

Conservatives argue for universal criteria—a Social Darwinist approach to admissions—in which differently qualified minority students have only the right to compete with whites based on a universal set of academic standards. Such a process, though appealingly simple, is based on an inaccurate picture of reality. The reality is that racial differences do exist—and that the indicators for black, Asian, and Hispanic achievement are quite different from each other and from the indicators for white achievement as well. For example, Stanley Sue and Jennifer Abe (1988) determined that in contrast to white students, grade point average was a better indicator of Asian American performance in college than standardized test scores. Ignoring these differences is no solution to racial conflict. Confronting these differences through social policy—of which racial preference is but one example—is at least a first step in the right direction.

Race Relations in Higher Education

The balkanization, or self-segregation by race, of social, political, and academic life in higher education is a troubling development. But the retreat from race in admissions policy, even in concert with other neoconservative and liberal policies designed to promote equality in higher education, will not dissolve what are deeply entrenched value differences and value conflicts among different minority groups as well as between minorities and whites. Neoconservative rhetoric has been unforgiving of value differences among different racial groups. It is unclear that such differences, however, which sometimes result in the formation of groups or organizations along racial lines, are always bad for society.[11] Prohibiting the organization of student groups along ethnic lines is as unwise as outlawing student groups organized around academic interests.

Racial balkanization is symptomatic of a problem that runs deeper than the organization of student groups along racial lines. Racial issues—from differences in academic achievement to racial preferences—have come to signify insurmountable inequalities between the different racial groups: whites, blacks, Hispanics, and Asians. The rhetoric of conservative complaints about the university have thoroughly "hidden and anchored" race, to use Goldberg's (1990a) description, in discourse about social problems so that it is easier not to say anything about racial issues rather than to confront them. Although conservatives see separate lunch tables of blacks, whites, and Asians as symbolic of resentment between different racial groups, I think it more likely that such scenes represent the loss of language and hope necessary to talk and act on racial differences. The retreat from race, though well intentioned, only exacerbates that loss and does nothing to bridge the differences that separate society by race. Balkanization—at every level of the academy—is the result of a transitory racial discourse that has become marked by racial codes, racial imagery, and most important, the failure of the effort to analyze and then to respond to the reality of racial differences.

My outline of three areas in which education officials might directly address racial problems rather than retreat from them is necessarily preliminary and incomplete. The prospects and possibilities for opening such a discussion are contingent on both the candor of the dialogue and the participation of many different sectors of the university. Without a doubt, the discussion will be fraught with conflict—as are all political contestations over visions of fairness, justice, and equality. In examining how discourse about Asian students ushered in a new era of racial politics—in which affirmative action preferences have shifted from race to class—we are moved toward that discussion of racial problems.

We should look forward to, rather than shy away from, the conflicts at hand—between conservatives and liberals, between whites and minorities, and between different minority groups. The Asian admissions controversy is a dramatic demonstration of how political struggles change the discourse in ways that arguments about changing the discourse never do. The retreat from race in affirmative action policy and in race talk has been the accomplishment of political struggle between conservatives and liberals. The pivotal center of this struggle has been focused on undermining racial preferences and affirmative action. Won through political struggle, the retreat from race can hardly be expected to wither without additional political conflict over basic issues—qualifications, racial differences in academic achievement, and race relations—that remain at the center of racial politics in higher education. Which interest groups will take up the arduous political task of raising these issues and organizing others to open a discussion about them is a matter of political practice whose outcome remains uncertain.

Notes

1. Asian Americans and Racial Politics

1. See the relevant critique of nativism by Trinh T. Minh-ha (1989: 67–68) in which she notes, "A conversation of 'us' with 'us' about 'them' is a conversation in which 'them' is silenced. . . . Anthropology is finally better defined as 'gossip' (we speak together about others) than as 'conversation' (we discuss a question), a definition that dates back to Aristotle."

2. See Bloom (1987); Sowell (1990b); Steele (1990); and D'Souza (1991b). In addition, a spate of articles in the popular press have issued similar warnings. See Heller (1989); Bernstein (1990); Morganthau et al. (1991); and Adler et al. (1991). Such alerts have also been extended to society in general. See, for example, J. Taylor (1991).

3. According to the American Council on Education (1991), for the decade 1978–1988, total minority enrollment in four-year institutions was approximately 13.5 percent. Whites constituted 84 percent of enrollment, and nonresident aliens made up the remaining 2.6 percent of enrollments.

4. De-racializing means adopting color-blind policies in admissions, academic support services, and other arenas of campus intellectual and social life that may be organized along racial lines. In their call for color-blind policies, conservatives have constructed a new vocabulary about race in higher education. Terms such as "racialization" and "racination" connote the sprawling effects of race on the academy; terms such as "racial fatigue" suggest that racial awareness has gone too far—that we are all now "tired" of hearing about race.

5. Berkeley and UCLA are the leading schools of the nine campuses that make up the University of California system. From 1981 to 1985 applicants who were not accepted at the UC campus of their choice were redirected to other campuses in the UC system. In 1986 the university implemented "multiple filing," through which applicants may apply to more than one UC campus on one application. Students' admission to each campus is governed by their competitiveness in the applicant pool at that particular campus. The University of California was mandated by the state

legislature–approved Master Plan for Higher Education to draw its students from the top 12.5 percent of high school graduates (defined by high school coursework and high school grades). In 1986, 32.8 percent of Asian and 15.8 percent of white high school graduates were UC-eligible. The proportion of black and Hispanic UC-eligible students was under the 12.5 percent goal. For blacks and Hispanics, approximately 5 percent of each group were UC-eligible. Several campuses, therefore, in an effort to construct a class of diverse interests, talents, and races, automatically admitted eligible black and Hispanic applicants. In other words, the demand for admission slots by Asian and whites exceeded supply, while among blacks and Hispanics, the reverse was true.

6. Interview with Susie Chao, director of minority recruitment, Harvard University, April 1989.

7. Cornell was not one of the main sites of the Asian admissions debate. That the administration there conducted a self-study of its own policies suggests that the widespread and well-publicized nature of the debate led many schools to investigate their own admissions policies with respect to Asians.

8. See Willie (1978); Puddington (1979); Pettigrew (1979); Marret (1980); and Pinkney (1984).

9. Some writers on ethnicity have also adopted a constructionist perspective. See, for example, Gans (1979) and Waters (1990).

10. Two exceptions, the first of which focuses on race as ideology in American history and the second on racial theory in anthropology, are Gosset (1965) and Harris (1968).

11. See, for example, the collection of essays in *The Empire Strikes Back*, edited by the Centre for Contemporary Cultural Studies (1982).

12. The role of conditions in constructionist accounts is an issue that has received a good deal of discussion in the field of social problems theory in sociology. The seminal argument for a constructionist approach to social problems was given in Spector and Kitsuse (1977, 1987). See also the criticisms of the practice of constructionism in Woolgar and Pawluch (1985) and Hazelrigg (1986).

13. In 1991, an official from the U.S. Commission on Civil Rights joked with me about this book, "What's to study? You guys are taking over the University. . . ."

14. More than a few people gave me encouraging pats on the back, saying, "Go get 'em!"

15. At some schools, I also spoke to university officials who were important figures in the debate but who were not part of the admissions office. At Berkeley, for example, I interviewed a number of officials who were responsible for admissions policy but who did not work in that office.

16. I selected my sample of universities by choosing those schools that were deemed the most selective by over-the-counter guides to colleges such as *Petersen's Guide*. The initial list included approximately fifteen colleges. I also selected an additional fifteen public and private universities that

were less selective than the most elite colleges but that I thought would have substantial Asian applicant pools. In addition, I sent similar queries to forty-five tenured or tenure-track faculty members of the Association of Asian American Studies.

17. One admissions official from a small northeastern private school explained that Asian admissions was not an issue at her university because there were so few Asian students enrolled there. She went on to explain that the school had a reputation for highly individualized majors that emphasized autonomy and independence in undergraduate research. This official told me she counseled many prospective Asian American students to apply to other universities that had a more standardized curriculum.

2. Clamor at the Gates

1. Between 1970 and 1980, the Asian American population grew 128 percent, from 1,538,721 to 3,500,636. A good portion of the growth was fueled by changes in immigration law in 1965; in 1980, foreign-born Asians made up 62 percent of the total Asian American population.

2. The white population in the United States grew by 6 percent between 1970 and 1980. In the same period, the black population gained 17 percent, and Asians rose by 130 percent (U.S. Bureau of the Census, PC80-S1-3). Such changes continued through the next decade as well. In California, for example, the white population grew 13.8 percent in the decade between 1980 and 1990, while blacks gained 21.4 percent, Hispanics rose 69.2 percent, and Asian Americans gained a dramatic 127 percent (Stevenson 1991). The nationwide picture also shows dramatic differences in growth by race (Barringer 1991a). Asians gained 107.8 percent—compared with a 6 percent growth in the white population, a 13.2 percent black increase, and a 53 percent rise in the Hispanic population.

3. Data are for four-year institutions only. Growth rates are calculated from table 97, "Total enrollment in institutions of higher education, by type of institution and by race/ethnicity of student: United States, fall 1976 to fall 1982," in National Center for Education Statistics (1986), p. 109.

4. In the following year, 1986, Asian enrollment jumped dramatically to 16 percent of the freshman class.

5. For further documentation of the decline in black enrollment, see Allen, Epps, and Haniff (1991).

6. The 1979 "Long Range Development Plan" projected that Asian American enrollment at Berkeley would steadily rise through the 1980s.

7. Interview with L. Ling-chi Wang.

8. Interview with L. Ling-chi Wang.

9. Interview with L. Ling-chi Wang.

10. Interview with Margaret M. Chin.

11. Media reports often mentioned Harvard. See, for example, Winerip (1985).

12. Bock's (1981) analysis of admissions was based on fall admissions to Harvard for 1976, 1977, and 1980. She obtained access to the data through David Karen, then a graduate student in sociology. Karen's (1985) Ph.D. thesis and Bock's (1981) senior thesis are to date the most thorough studies of Harvard admissions after World War II. See also Karen's forthcoming book (Yale University Press) on Harvard admissions.

13. Interview with Margaret M. Chin.

14. Margaret M. Chin reports that coordinators in the early 1980s were paid approximately $5 an hour.

15. Interview with Margaret M. Chin.

16. EOP at Berkeley is a recruitment, admission, and student services program. Applicants who are members of underrepresented minorities are eligible for special consideration in the admissions process. In addition, following admission to the university, EOP student services include tutoring and counseling support.

17. UC eligibility refers to the minimum admission requirements, which are a combination of the type of courses taken in high school (subject), scholarship (GPA), and examination requirements (SAT, achievement tests).

18. According to Au, the 30 percent figure is the subject of some controversy. Admissions officers deny that 30 percent of the applicant pool was Asian American.

19. In 1983, Asian freshman made up 7 percent of the entering class at Stanford.

20. Interview with Elsa Tsutaoka.

21. Interview with Uwe Reinhardt.

22. Interview with L. Ling-chi Wang.

23. The other members of the task force attending the meeting were Professor Paul Takagi, Judge Lillian Sing, Judge Ken Kawaichi, Henry Der, Professor Elaine Kim, and Karen Kai.

24. Interview with L. Ling-chi Wang.

25. Interview with L. Ling-chi Wang.

26. Interview with Patrick Hayashi.

27. Interview with Roderic Park.

28. Interview with L. Ling-chi Wang.

29. Interview with L. Ling-chi Wang.

30. For example, a parity figure would divide the number of Asian Americans admitted or enrolled by the number of Asian Americans in the nation, state, region, and/or the UC-eligible portion of high school graduates. Note that there are several combinations of figures that might be appropriate in the denominator. The denominator could be the number of Asian Americans in the state population, the number of Asian American high school graduates in the state population, or the number of UC-eligible Asian American high school graduates in the state population. Given the variety of combinations, there are a total of 12 possible figures in the de-

nominator. With two possible figures in the numerator (those admitted or those enrolled), the possible number of parity measures is 24.

3. Diversity, Merit, and the Model Minority

1. See, for example, Takagi (1973); Takaki (1984); Osajima (1988).

2. According to 1983 estimates by the California Postsecondary Education Commission, proportionately more Asian high school graduates meet University of California minimum eligibility requirements than any other racial group, including whites. Some 26 percent of Asian high school graduates met the requirements, compared with 15 percent for whites, 4.9 percent for Hispanics, 3.6 percent for blacks, and 13.2 percent overall (Hickey 1986).

3. The Brown Asian American Student Association (AASA 1983:6–7) reported that the Asian applicant pool increased 750 percent between 1975 and 1983. Although they did not present comparable figures for whites, they claim that Asians represent over one-half of Brown's overall growth in applications, while nonminorities (presumably whites) constitute 26.5 percent of the increase.

4. A comparison of average SAT (math and verbal) scores indicates that Asians have the highest scores of all of nonwhite groups, and that relative to whites, Asians score higher on math and lower on verbal. In 1983–1984, for example, the average SAT verbal score for whites was 445, for Asians, 398, and for blacks, 342. By 1987–1988, the gap between white and minority scores had closed slightly. The average verbal score for whites was 445, for Asians, 408, and for blacks, 353. By contrast, in 1983–1984, the average SAT math score for Asians was 519, higher than for whites, 487, and blacks, 373. Approximately the same distribution, with slightly higher scores, held in 1987–1988. The average Asian score was 522, for whites, 490, and for blacks, who made the biggest gain, 384. See National Center for Education Statistics (1989).

5. See Salholz (1987) and Osajima (1988).

6. This bit of college folk wisdom seems to have transcended racial lines. I have had several Asian American students tell me that they dropped out of their science courses because of all those "other Asians."

7. Mitsubishi acquired a 51 percent interest in Rockefeller Center for $846 million in late 1989.

8. Interview with Bob Lee.

9. See Synott (1979) and Karabel (1984).

10. The 1974 Buckley amendment guarantees an applicant's right to privacy covering his or her personal essay and letters of recommendation.

11. Interview with Grace Tsuang.

12. Interview with Grace Tsuang.

13. Interview with Jean Fetter.

14. Interview with Harumi Befu.

15. Interview with Harumi Befu.

16. Interview with Harumi Befu.

17. Interview with Uwe Reinhardt.

18. Harvard officials explain that detailing admissions statistics by race might jeopardize the confidentiality of admitted applicants, particularly when the numbers are very small. There have been instances in which the admissions office has made available admissions data to researchers. See for example, detailed admissions data was used in two theses, one graduate, one undergraduate (Karen 1985; Bock 1981). See also Bunzel and Au (1987).

19. Interview with B. Thomas Travers.

20. Assembly Concurrent Resolution no. 74 (ACR74) was interpreted by university officials as a mandate for parity between enrollment and high school graduates. In 1988–1989, some critics suggested that the university overstated the meaning of ACR74.

21. Interestingly enough, between 1983 and 1987, the proportion of Asian applicants to the College of Letters and Science at Berkeley stayed roughly the same, around 24 percent. White applications to the same college declined from 75.9 percent in 1983 to 68 percent in 1987. Figures computed from the report of the Auditor General (Auditor General 1987: 54–55).

22. Here, the task force argued that equivalent admission rates cited by Travers by themselves were an inadequate measure of fairness. The task force criticized as vague the university's methodology for applying the supplemental criteria (listed in Travers 1987:9):

Supplemental Criteria for Tier Two Admissions, UC Berkeley

1. California residence	200 points
2. Educational Opportunity Program	200 points
3. Four years of Mathematics or three years of Laboratory Science	100 points
4. Four year of one foreign language or two years of two languages	100 points
5. Exemption from Subject A	100 points
6. High school does not offer honors course in the junior year	100 points
7. Essay/honors/special circumstances/public service/ activities	500 points

23. The Lynn Committee (1987) draft report was never released to the public. I am grateful to an anonymous source close to the university who passed a copy of it to me so that I might "get the whole picture."

24. This comment came from Yale dean of admissions, Worth David, but was echoed by every other private school admissions officer I interviewed.

25. I find Habermas's distinction between theoretical and practical discourse to be a useful way to grasp the debate over admissions. Practical discourse consists of the speech acts and claims to validity that can be hypothetically tested. Theoretical discourse refers to the type of argumentation in which claims to truth can be contested. See Habermas (1984).

4. The Tyranny of Facts

1. As noted in Chapter 3, the Lynn report was never publicly released and remains confidential to this day.

2. Personal notes and observation at the Asian Pacific Americans in Higher Education Annual Conference, Oakland, Calif., February 1988.

3. The meeting took place at the University of California, Riverside, on November 20, 1987. I have reconstructed events based on interviews with Wang, Park, Travers, Hayashi. See also Regents (1987).

4. Interview with Bud Travers.

5. Interview with Roderic Park.

6. Interview with Roderic Park.

7. Interview with Roderic Park.

8. The existence of this memo was the subject of much speculation and controversy from 1985 to its "discovery" in early 1988. University officials claimed first that it did not exist, and then later, said the memo had been rescinded. Berkeley officials were unable to ever produce a copy of the memo saying it had been "lost" or "misplaced." At least one admissions officer I interviewed for this study claimed to have been at the meeting in which the memo was discussed, had a copy of the memo "in hand" in 1986 and 1987, and does not remember ever being asked by high administration officials during the Asian admissions controversy to verify the existence of the memo.

9. Interviews with L. Ling-chi Wang and Henry Der.

10. "Summary of Concerns Expressed in the Conference on Asian Americans in Higher Education," February 28, 1988, mimeo, 1 page.

11. Berkeley was not originally named as a site of investigation—in part owing to the ongoing "dialogue" between the administration and the task force.

12. Interview with Gary Curran.

13. Interview with Gary Curran, 1990. See also Jaschik's (1989) description of the "lost" complaints.

14. One of the strongest arguments for using admission rates rather than parity to assess discrimination against Asian American applicants appeared in Bunzel and Au (1987).

15. Interview with Robert Bailey.

16. Interview with Robert Bailey.

17. Baudrillard (Poster 1985:210), in an essay on the media, makes a provocative suggestion: an excess of information in the media—for example, public opinion polls—constitutes "statistical pornography," which has produced a silence and uncertainty in the masses, a lack of political will. His argument is that conflict between two systems—values about statistics and a traditional values system—have generated a "radical uncertainty as to our own desire, our own choice, our own opinion, our own will." Baudrillard's comments on public opinion polls may be extended to the proliferation of statistical information in the Asian admissions controversy. In this case, optimistic values about the possibility of resolving the controversy through statistics clashed with fundamental value differences (between Asians and university officials, for example) about merit and diversity. The stalemate in claims over admissions between those who defined the problem as discrimination and those who defined the problem as one of diversity might also be read as a moment of "radical uncertainty" produced by a glut of statistics.

5. Affirmative Action and Its Discontents

1. For example, the Office of Civil Rights' "Statement of Findings" on Harvard reports that approximately 11,000 applicants vie for 1,600 admission slots there (U.S. Department of Education 1990). Legislative guidelines for the University of California mandate that the university system accommodate the top 12.5 percent of the state's high school graduates.

2. The "new racism" is part of a wider "bigotry" on campuses that has affected Jews, gays, and others. At Cornell, for example, Jewish American women were targeted by campus t-shirts emblazoned with "Slap a Jap" and "I'm a JAP buster." See Williams (1986); Daniels (1988); Yardley (1988); Cutler (1989); Los Angeles Times (1989); Reichmann (1989); Tifft (1989); Wooldridge (1989); Gibbs (1990).

3. The term "racialization" first appeared in Michael Omi and Howard Winant's Racial Formation in the United States (1986), a critical analysis of race relations from the 1960s to the 1980s. They use the term to refer to "the extension of racial meaning to a previously racially unclassified relationship, social practice, or group" (p. 64). Members of the Institute of Social Change, authors of the Diversity Project report (1989) at Berkeley, use the term to connote a pervasiveness of racial awareness in campus intellectual, social, and political life. Even conservative and neoconservative scholars occasionally use the term to describe what they feel has been an undue emphasis on race in policy, curriculum, and admissions in higher education.

4. The significance of racial issues and racial identity in our everyday lives cannot be underscored enough. Perhaps one indicator of the increase

in awareness has been the introduction of courses in "diversity" and "intercultural exchange" in the corporate world. Some writers (e.g., Omi and Winant [1986] and Njeri [1989] speak of racial "etiquette." According to Jacquelyn Mitchell, the director of Afro-American Center at UC Davis, for example, Japanese American students resent it when non-Japanese wear kimonos just as black students view Bo Derek's hair in the film "10" an offensive appropriation of their culture (Njeri 1989).

5. One Berkeley student quoted by the Diversity Project noted, "We are either oppressors or outsiders" (Diversity Project 1990).

6. In addition to Thomas Sowell, Allan Bloom and William Bennett, have also been critical of the academic content of the discipline of ethnic studies. In an incident at Stanford University in 1990, a prospective faculty member, a senior-level Chinese American sociologist, angrily withdrew his application when he discovered he was expected to teach Asian American history as well as sociology. The *Stanford Daily* reported that the candidate called institutionalized ethnic studies "backward" (Phung 1990).

7. This logic is similar to that of Charles Murray (1984), who provided the blueprint for neoconservative critiques of liberal social policies. According to Murray, liberal policies are the problem, not the solution. Thus whereas that poverty caused welfare was the prevailing wisdom, Murray hypothesized the opposite relationship, that welfare caused poverty.

8. Murray (1984) makes this same argument about welfare policy. In higher education, compare Sowell (1989) and Steele (1989).

9. Transcription of tape recording of hearings, March 13, 1989.

10. The paper (Barnett 1989), though widely circulated, was never published. I am grateful to Professor Barnett for sharing a copy with me.

11. Interview with Stephen Barnett.

12. Interview with Stephen Barnett.

13. Interview with Stephen Barnett.

14. Interview with Stephen Barnett.

15. Interview with Stephen Barnett.

16. The discussions were organized by four core faculty: Neil Smelser (Sociology), Martin Trow (Public Policy), Reinhard Bendix (Political Science), and Melvin Webber (City and Regional Planning).

17. Statement on "Public Higher Education: External Environment and Internal Process," signed by Reinhard Bendix, Martin Trow, Neil Smelser, and Mel Webber, no date. Circulated with cover letter to selected individuals at the University of California, Berkeley, in March 1989.

18. Interview with Arthur Hu.

19. Interview with Grace Tsuang.

20. Neoconservative may, in fact, be too liberal an appellation for him. Rohrabacher has been associated with the extreme right of the Republican party on many issues. He voted with Jesse Helms to block funding of NEA and joined the far right in criticism of Bush's 1990 budget.

21. H. Res. 147, 101st Cong., 1st sess., June 1989. See also Edison (1989) and Stewart (1989).

22. Interview with Dana Rohrabacher.

22. Dana Rohrabacher, *Congressional Record*, vol. 135, no. 125, September 26, 1989.

23. Interview with Dana Rohrabacher.

24. Interview with Dana Rohrabacher.

25. Interview with Dana Rohrabacher.

27. Interview with Dana Rohrabacher.

28. This claim is controversial because it assumes that the qualifications of the applicant pools under comparison are similar. The question, of course, is what does it mean to say that two applicant pools are similar? One answer would be that they have relatively similar average GPA and test scores. University officials, when they rejected claims of discrimination, were essentially saying that Asians were not as well qualified—that is, that the pools were not the same.

29. Here, too, the claim is a controversial one. If the enrollment of Asians falls during a certain year, how can we know that it fell because more blacks were let in? Increases in black enrollment may not correspond with Asian enrollment.

30. This does not mean that Asian American students and faculty have not been active participants in the various campus racial political struggles, but, rather, that conceptually the position of Asians has been at odds with the racial politics defined by black and white experiences.

6. The Race for Class

1. Two pages from the Stanford University *Bulletin*, for example, show Joan Baez speaking before a campus antiapartheid rally, snow-covered Half-Dome in Yosemite Park, rolling green hills from the Napa Valley, and the Pacific Ocean accompanied by text: "Stanford is one of the few places where you can dream of going skiing, sunning on the beach, or playing golf, and then do all three on the same weekend."

2. The issue of "fighting words" has received a good deal of media attention. See, for example, Bernstein (1990), Martine and Stent (1991), Foreman (1991), and O'Dowd (1991).

3. Cited by Wiener (1990).

4. Interviews with L. Ling-chi Wang and Henry Der.

5. Interview with L. Ling-chi Wang.

6. Interview with Jerome Karabel.

7. The chancellor's praise for the Karabel report generated a backlash among his critics at the university. A review of the new Karabel plan in the *Berkeleyan* prompted a critical response from Professor Barnett, who argued that university publications ought to give equal time to opposing views. See Holtz (1989).

8. Seven percent declined to state racial identity.

9. Campus leaflet distributed by a coalition of minority students, UCLA, 1990.

10. My discussion here is based on news reports in the *Daily Californian* and discussions with Professor L. Ling-chi Wang. See Robertson (1990); Nissenbaum (1990a,b); and Good (1990).

11. Interview with Gary Curran.

12. Interview with Andy Sun.

13. These sources wished to remain confidential.

14. Interview with Kathy Lewis.

15. Of course, there are some conservatives, such as Arthur Hu, who take an meritocratic extremist position and would like to see admission based exclusively on grades and test scores.

7. The Retreat from Race

1. Williams was referring to the Supreme Court decision in *Bakke*.

2. The proposal, which was approved by the NCAA coaches in January 1992, raised the minimum freshman GPA from 2.0 to 2.5; established an indexing system whereby freshman college athletes with GPAs as low as 2.0 would be eligible for play if their combined SAT score was 900 or higher; required athletes to complete a set number of courses with a minimum GPA through their third and fourth years of college. See Lederman (1991, 1992).

3. The issue of quotas figured prominently in the campaigns of the Republicans Pete Wilson and Jesse Helms.

4. The key cases include: *Wards Cove Packing Co. v. Antonio* (1989), which ruled that employees must suggest alternative business practices that would eliminate discriminatory impact; *City of Richmond v. J. A. Croson Co.* (1989), which ruled against set-asides for minority contractors; *Price-Waterhouse v. Hopkins* (1989), in which race and sex, along with other reasons, were ruled legitimate for denying employee promotions; *Martin v. Wilks* (1989), in which white employees were allowed to challenge court-ordered affirmative action programs years after the programs were established.

5. See also *Albemarle Paper Co. v. Moody* (1975), in which the court ruled that height and weight requirements for prison guards that disqualified about 40 percent of women applicants, but less than 1 percent of male applicants, were not job-related.

6. See, for example, Marx (1963); Katznelson (1981); Wright (1985); Katznelson and Zolberg (1986).

7. For a general discussion of theories of discourse, see Macdonell (1986). For discussions of "critical pedagogy" in education, see Giroux (1992), and for a review and critique of pedagogy theories, see Ellsworth (1989).

8. This vagueness and indeterminancy in the political is, I think, similar to what Cornel West (1992) describes as a "promiscuous formalism" characterizing deconstructionism.

9. Occasionally, the flexibility of the process backfires (Barron and Farber 1991). In 1990 Princeton admitted Alexis Indris-Santana, a track star "two-miler" who claimed to have had no formal education since kindergarten but who scored an incredible 730 on the verbal section of the SAT and 680 on the math. Admissions officials at both Brown and Princeton were impressed enough with Alexis's file to admit him. A Brown University admissions officer put it this way: "There's something wrong with this file. I can't put my finger on it, so I guess we ought to take him." Alexis, spurred by a generous offer of financial aid, decided to attend Princeton. But he turned out to be a fraud. He was not a self-educated orphan raised at the Lazy T ranch in Utah, as he claimed, but rather was raised by his parents in Kansas City where he attended grade school and high school. Alexis, whose real name is James Hogue, was wanted for violating parole in Utah where he had served time in prison for stolen property charges. In the spring of 1991, when he was discovered to be wanted on criminal charges, Hogue was arrested.

10. Interview with Leonard Ramist.

11. John Childs, for example, in "Constructive Disputing: The Ramifications of African American Caucus Groups for Today's Organizations" (forthcoming in *Studies in Law, Politics, and Society*), has suggested that disputes among caucuses might in some instances be viewed as a constructive politics that leads to greater pluralism and tolerance in organizations.

References

AASA. *See* Asian American Students Association.

AATF. *See* Asian American Task Force on University Admissions.

Acebo, Regina. 1989. "Minority Statement of the Student Representative to the Special Committee on Asian American Admissions." Mimeo of testimony given on 13 March.

Adler, Frank. 1991. "Politics, Intellectuals, and the University." *Telos* (86): 103–109.

Adler, Jerry, with Mark Starr, Farai Chideya, Lynda Wright, Pat Wingert, and Linda Haac. 1991. "Taking Offense: Is This the New Enlightenment on Campus or the New McCarthyism?" *Newsweek*, 24 December, 48–54.

Admissions and Enrollment Committee. 1989. "Freshman Admissions at Berkeley: A Policy for the 1990s and Beyond." University of California, Berkeley, 19 May.

Alcoff, Linda. 1988. "Cultural Feminism versus Post-Structuralism: The Identity Crisis in Feminist Theory." *Signs* 13 (3):405–436.

Allen, Walter, Edgar G. Epps, and Nesha Z. Haniff, eds. 1991. *College in Black and White*. Frontiers in Education. Albany: State University of New York Press.

Alleyne, Reginald. 1987. "Everyone Needs Affirmative Action." *Los Angeles Times*, 15 February.

Allis, Sam. 1991. "Kicking the Nerd Syndrome." *Time*, 25 March, 66.

Altbach, Philip G., and Kofi Lomotey, eds. 1991. *The Racial Crisis in American Higher Education*. Albany: State University of New York Press.

American Association of State Colleges and Universities. 1990. *The Lurking Evil: Racial and Ethnic Conflict on the College Campus*. Edited by Robert Hively. Washington, D.C.

American Council on Education. 1990. *Minorities in Higher Education 1989*. Eighth Annual Status Report. Washington, D.C.: American Council on Education, Office of Minorities in Higher Education.

———. 1991. *Minorities in Higher Education 1990*. Ninth Annual Status Report. Washington, D.C.: American Council on Education, Office of Minorities in Higher Education.

Applebome, Peter. 1990. "Subtly and Not, Race Bubbles Up as Issue in North Carolina Contest." *New York Times*, 2 November.

———. 1991. "Black Conservatives: Minority within a Minority." *New York Times*, 13 July.

Aronowitz, Stanley, and Henry Giroux. 1991. *Postmodern Education*. Minneapolis: University of Minnesota Press.

Asian American Students Association. 1983. "Asian American Admission at Brown University." 11 October. Mimeo. 30 pages.

Asian American Task Force on University Admissions. 1985a. *Report*. San Francisco, Calif. June.

———. 1985b. "Comments on UC's Response to Task Force Report." Press release. San Francisco, Calif. 3 pages.

———. 1987. "Task Force Response to the Report by the Auditor General." San Francisco, Calif. 21 October. Mimeo. 5 pages.

———. 1989. "State of Judges Ken Kawaichi and Lillian Sing, Response to the Shack Report." San Francisco, Calif. 1 March. Mimeo. 11 pages.

Assembly Subcommittee on Higher Education. 1988. "Asian American Admissions at the University of California: Excerpts from a Legislative Hearing." Tom Hayden, chair. Sacramento, Calif. 26 January.

Astin, Alexander. 1982. *Minorities in American Higher Education*. San Francisco: Jossey-Bass.

Atlas, James. 1990. *The Book Wars*. Knoxville, Tenn.: Whittle Direct Books.

Au, Jeffrey, K. D. 1986. Letter to Professor Jeffrey Wine, chairman of C-UAFA, Stanford University. 9 April. 3 pages.

———. 1988. "Asian American College Admissions—Legal, Empirical, and Philosophical Questions for the 1980s and Beyond." Pp. 51–57 in *Reflections on Shattered Windows: Promises and Prospects for Asian American Studies*, edited by Gary Y. Okihiro et al. Pullman: Washington State University Press.

Auditor General. 1987. *A Review of First Year Admissions at the University of California, Berkeley*. P-722. Sacramento: State of California.

Bailey, Robert. 1984a. Memo to Watson M. Laetsch, vice chancellor for undergraduate affairs, Regarding Permanent Aliens. University of California, Berkeley. 28 December.

———. 1984b. Memo to B. Thomas Travers, vice chancellor for undergraduate affairs. University of California, Berkeley. 4 January.

———. 1986. Memo to Recruitment/Rentention Task Force. University of California, Berkeley. 7 April.

Barbanel, Josh. 1991. "Feuds Reopen as U.S. Rejects New York City Districts." *New York Times*, 21 July.

Barrett, Stephen. 1989. "Fairness to Asian Americans in Affirmative Action for Other Groups." Unpublished paper.

———. 1990. Letter to William French Smith, UC Regent. 28 June.

Barrett, Wayne. 1991. "Mapmaker, Mapmaker, Make Me a Map: How the Beastly Politics of Redistricting Pits Minorities against One Another." *Village Voice*, 6 August.

Barringer, Felicity. 1991a. "Census Shows Profound Change in Racial Makeup of the Nation." *New York Times,* 11 March.

———. 1991b. "Banning of Women at Military College Is Upheld." *New York Times,* 18 June.

Barron, James, and M. A. Farber. 1991. "Tracing a Devious Path to the Ivy League." *New York Times,* 4 March.

Barthes, Roland. 1972. *Mythologies.* Translated by A. Lavers. London: Cape.

Bay City News Service. 1985. "UC Berkeley Policy Change Cut Asian Admissions, Panel Says." *Oakland Tribune,* 18 June.

Bell, David A. 1985. "The Triumph of Asian Americans." *New Republic,* 15 and 22 July, 24–31.

Berger, Joseph. 1988. "Scholars Attack Campus 'Radicals.'" *New York Times,* 15 November, A22.

Berke, Richard L. 1991. "Partisan Fight Erupts on Rights Bill." *New York Times,* 13 March.

Berkleyan. 1989. "Building a Model for the 21st Century." 8–21 November, 1, 5.

Bernstein, Richard. 1988. "Asian Students Harmed by Precursors' Success." *New York Times,* 10 July, 16.

———. 1990. "The Rising Hegemony of the Politically Correct." *New York Times,* 28 October, E1.

BFSO. *See* Black Faculty and Staff Organization.

Bhabha, Homi K. 1990. "Interrogating Identity: The Post-Colonial Prerogative." Pp. 183–209 in *Anatomy of Racism,* edited by David Theo Goldberg. Minneapolis: University of Minnesota Press.

Biemiller, Lawrence. 1986. "Asian Students Fear Top Colleges Use Quotas." *Chronicle of Higher Education,* 19 November, 1, 34–37.

Bishop, Katherine. 1990. "Asian American Is Named to Head a Major Campus." *New York Times,* 16 February.

Black Faculty and Staff Organization. 1990. Letter to Chancellor Iva Michael Heyman, University of California, Berkeley. 21 February. Mimeo, "The Karabel Report and Historically Underrepresented Minorities: An Analysis," attachment.

Blauner, Robert. 1972. *Racial Oppression in America.* New York: Harper and Row.

———. 1989. *Black Lives, White Lives.* Berkeley: University of California Press.

Bloom, Allan. 1987. *The Closing of the American Mind.* New York: Simon and Schuster.

Bock, Jane. 1981. "The Model Minority in the Meritocracy: Asian Americans in the Harvard/Radcliffe Admissions Process." Senior thesis, Department of Sociology, Harvard University.

Brand, David. 1987. "The New Whiz Kids." *Time,* 31 August, 42–51.

Brooks, Roy L. 1990. *Rethinking the American Race Problem.* Berkeley: University of California Press.

Brown v. Board of Education, Topeka, Kansas, 347 U.S. 483, 74 S. Ct. (1954).

Brownstein, Ronald. 1991. "Beyond Quotas." *Los Angeles Times Magazine*, 28 July.

Bunzel, John. 1988a. "Choosing Freshmen: Who Deserves an Edge?" *Wall Street Journal*, 1 February.

———. 1988b. "UC Dilemma: Admitting Ethnic Diversity While Maintaining Academic Excellence." *Los Angeles Times*, 4 December, 3, 6.

———. 1988c. "Affirmative Action Admissions: How It 'Works' at UC Berkeley." *Public Interest*.

———. 1989. "Affirmative Action Must Not Result in Lower Standards or Discrimination against the Most Competent Students." *Chronicle of Higher Education*, 1 March.

Bunzel, John, and Jeffrey Au. 1987. "Diversity or Discrimination? Asian Americans in College." *Public Interest* (Spring):49–62.

Burress, Charles. 1990. "The Dark Heart of Japan Bashing." *San Francisco Chronicle*, 18 March.

Butterfield, Fox. 1983. "Violent Incidents against Asian-Americans Seen as Part of Racist Pattern." *New York Times*, 31 August, 8.

———. 1986. "Why Asians Are Going to the Head of the Class." *New York Times*, 3 August, 18.

Cacas, Samuel. 1988. "Racism Isn't Just Black and White." *Daily Californian*, 1 September, 4.

Campus Report. 1986. "Annual Report of the Committee on Undergraduate Admissions and Financial Aid." Stanford University.

Carmody, Deirdre. 1988a. "Top Colleges Turn to Waiting Lists." *New York Times*, 8 June, B5.

———. 1988b. "Asians Increasing at U.S. Colleges." *New York Times*, 9 November, 10.

Carter, Stephen L. 1991. *Reflections of an Affirmative Action Baby*. New York: Basic Books.

Celis, William III. 1990. "Responding to Critics, S.A.T. Ponders Change." *New York Times*, 28 October.

Centre for Contemporary Cultural Studies, ed. 1982. *The Empire Strikes Back*. London: Hutchison.

Chan, Sucheng. 1986. *This Bittersweet Soil: The Chinese in California agriculture, 1860–1910*. Berkeley: University of California Press.

Chang, Irene. 1988a. "Heyman Apologizes to Asians." *Daily Californian*, 27 January, 1.

———. 1988b. "Board Created for Coordination of Admissions." *Daily Californian*, 12 February, 1.

———. 1988c. "Gardner Says Admissions Policy Not His Responsibility." *Daily Californian*, 17 February, 1.

———. 1988d. "Heyman Accused of 'Stalling.'" *Daily Californian*, 9 March, 1.

Chao, Susie, and William Fitzsimmons. 1988. "Statement on Asian-American Admissions at Harvard and Radcliffe." 2 pages.

Chapin, Dwight. 1991. "Will Japanese Owners Price Out Local Golfers?" *San Francisco Examiner*, 21 July.

Chen, Ingfei. 1991. "State Students Hit 20-Year Low on Verbal Portion of SAT Exam." *San Francisco Chronicle*, 21 August.

Childs, John Brown. N.d. "Constructive Disputing: The Ramifications of African American Caucus Groups for Today's Organizations." *Studies in Law, Politics, and Society*. Forthcoming.

Chira, Susan. 1990. "U.S. to Look at Admissions at Berkeley Law School." *New York Times*, 7 April.

Christian, Barbara. 1990. "The Race for Theory." Pp. 37–49 in *The Nature and Context of Minority Discourse*, edited by Abdul R. JanMohamed and David Lloyd. New York: Oxford University Press.

Chuang, Philip. 1988a. "Wada Warns of Minority 'Quota.'" *Daily Californian*, 25 May, 1.

———. 1988b. "UC Asian Admissions Probed." *Daily Californian*, 23 November, 1, 6.

———. 1989a. "Asians Say Report Is 'Whitewash.'" *Daily Californian*, 2 March, 1.

———. 1989b. "Heyman Sorry for Unfair Admissions." *Daily Californian*, 7 April, 1.

City of Richmond v. J. A. Croson Co., U.S. 109 S. Ct. 706 (1989).

Civil Rights Commission. 1973. Asian American Public Hearings. San Francisco, Calif. 23 June.

College Board News. 1988. "Asian Americans' Academic Future Can Be Forecast." Fall.

College Entrance Examination Board. 1991. "College-Bound Seniors: 1991 SAT Profile." New York: The College Board.

Colvig, Ray. Letter to the Editor. *Hokubei Mainichi*. 29 February. 2 pages.

COMA (Committee on Minority Affairs). Subcommittee on Asian American Admissions. 1984. "Report to the Corporation Committee on Minority Affairs." Mimeo, 10 pages. Brown University.

Committee on Minority Issues. 1989. "Final Report of the Committee on Minority Issues." Stanford University. March.

Connolly, Mike. 1988. "Affirmative Action Keeps Asians Out." *San Francisco Examiner*, 1 December, A17.

Cooper, Kenneth. 1991. "Survey Plays Down 'PC' Debate." *San Francisco Chronicle*, 29 July.

Curtis, Diane. 1988. "UC Ethnic Policy Becoming Official." *San Francisco Chronicle*, 20 May.

———. 1990a. "UCLA Calls Probe of Alleged Bias 'Politically Inspired.'" *San Francisco Chronicle*, January 19.

———. 1990b. "College Campuses Lack a Value System, Report Says." *San Francisco Chronicle*, April 30.

———. 1990c. "U.S. to Probe UC Berkeley for Bias against White Applicants." *San Francisco Chronicle*, January 18.

Custred, Glynn. 1990. "New Dissension over Affirmative Action." *San Francisco Chronicle*, April 3.

Cutler, Jacqueline. 1989. "Still a Way to Go for Racial Harmony." *San Jose Mercury News*, 5 April, 2b.

Daily Bruin. 1990. "UCLA Should Promote Diversity, Not Dispute It." Editorial. 3 October.

Daily Californian. 1988. "Leadership Vacuum." Editorial. 23 February, 4.

Daniels, Lee. 1988. "Prejudice on Campuses Is Feared to Be Rising." *New York Times*, 31 October.

de Groot, Brent. 1990. "Why We Need Affirmative Action Now More Than Ever." *Daily Californian*, 24 April.

de Lauretis, Teresa, ed. 1986. "Feminist Studies/Critical Studies: Issues, Terms, and Contexts." Pp. 1–19 in *Feminist Studies/Critical Studies* Bloomington: Indiana University Press.

DePalma, Anthony. 1990. "Colleges Express Great Confusion on Minority Aid." *New York Times*, 20 December.

———. 1991. "Battling Bias, Campuses Face Free Speech Fight." *New York Times*, 20 February.

DeWitt, Karen. 1990a. "U.S. Expands Inquiry of College Bias." *New York Times*, 3 October.

———. 1990b. "Harvard Cleared in Inquiry on Bias." *New York Times*, 7 October.

———. 1991a. "Nominee Criticizes Scholarship Move." *New York Times*, 7 February.

———. 1991b. "Minority Scholarships Get Tentative Approval." *New York Times*, 21 March.

Dickey, Glenn. 1991. "True Student-Athletes Prove a Point." *San Francisco Chronicle*, 1 April.

Dinh, Thy. 1990. "Young Refutes Report's Findings." *Daily Bruin*, 2 October, 1.

Diversity Project. 1989. "An Interim Report to the Chancellor." Institute for the Study of Social Change, Berkeley. June.

Dowd, Maureen. 1990. "Trying to Head Off His Own Veto, Bush Holds Meeting on Rights Bill." *New York Times*, 15 May.

———. 1991. "Bush Sees Threat to Flow of Ideas on U.S. Campuses." *New York Times*, 5 May.

D'Souza, Dinesh. 1991a. "To Free the Universities." Editorial. *Wall Street Journal*, 10 May.

———. 1991b. *Illiberal Education*. New York: Free Press.

East/West. 1986. "UC Admissions Lack Credibility and Accountability." Editorial. 11 December.

———. 1987. "Asian Task Force Meets with UC President Gardner." 19 March, 1.

———. 1988a. "Heyman Apologizes for Handling of Asian Discrimination Charges at UC Berkeley." 28 January, 1–3.

———. 1988b. "UC Chancellor Must Take Charge and Restore Public Confidence." Editorial. 18 February.

———. 1988c. "Will UC Berkeley Appoint an Asian American to Its Administration?" Editorial. 26 May, 3.

Eaton, William J. 1988. "Aide Sees Hints of Colleges' Asian Bias." *Los Angeles Times*, 1 December, 3, 32.

Edison, Andrew. 1989. "College Entry Bias Alleged." *San Francisco Examiner*. 9 June.

Edsall, Thomas Byrne, and Mary D. Edsall. 1991a. "Race." *The Atlantic*, May, 53–86.

———. 1991b. *Chain Reaction: The Impact of Race, Rights, and Taxes on American Politics*. New York: W. W. Norton.

Eisenberg, Ira. 1990. "Fighting Words: Race and Free Speech at the University of California." *San Francisco Examiner*, 9 September.

Ellison, Ralph. 1952. *Invisible Man*. New York: Random House.

Ellsworth, Elizabeth. 1989. "Why Doesn't This Feel Empowering? Working through the Repressive Myths of Critical Pedagogy." *Harvard Educational Review* 59 (August):297–324.

Eskanazi, Gerald. 1991. "Athletes' Advantages Cited in Graduations." *New York Times*, 26 March.

Evans, David. 1988. "Racism Resurges When Black History Isn't Learned." *Sacramento Bee*, 7 December.

Ezorsky, Gertude. 1991. *Racism and Justice*. Ithaca: Cornell University Press.

Fanon, Frantz. 1967. *Black Skin, White Masks*. New York: Grove Press.

Fanucchi, Kenneth J. 1985. "Reasons Sought for Drop in UCLA Asian Enrollment." *Los Angeles Times*, 7 July.

Farnsworth, Clyde. 1989. "5,000 March to Protest Court Action on Rights." *New York Times*, 27 August.

Fetter, Jean H. 1991. "Undergraduate Admissions: Statistical Updates." Presentation to Board of Trustees, Stanford University. 14 June. Mimeo. 26 pages.

Fiske, Edward B. 1982. "Fewer Blacks Enter Universities: Recession and Aid Cuts Are Cited." *New York Times*, 28 November, 1.

———. 1987. "Enrollment of Minorities in College Stagnating." *New York Times*, 19 April, 1, 24.

Foreman, Amanda. 1991. "High Noon at the PC Corral." Letter to the editor. *New York Times*, 20 March.

Fortune. 1986. "America's Super Minority." 24 November, 148–161.

Frank, Austin. 1985. Letter to Whom It May Concern, re: Tables in the Task Force Report. Office of Student Research. 21 pages. Attachment to "Memo to Media," press release, Office of Public Information, University of California, Berkeley, 1985.

Gans, Herbert. 1979. "Symbolic Ethnicity: The Future of Ethnic Groups and Cultures in America." *Ethnic and Racial Studies* 2 (January):1–18.

Gardner, David. 1988. Letter to Henry Der, Asian American Task Force. 16 February.

Garrison, Jayne. 1985. "Task Force Says UC Denies Asian Enrollment." *San Francisco Examiner*, 19 June.

Gates, Henry Louis. 1986. "Introduction." *Race, Writing, and Difference*. Chicago: University of Chicago Press.

Gibbs, Nancy. 1990. "Bigots in the Ivory Tower." *Time*, 7 May.

Gibney, James. 1988. "The Berkeley Squeeze." *New Republic*, 11 April, 15–16.

Gilliam, Dorothy. 1987. "A New Restrictive Racial Quota." *Washington Post*, 5 February.

Gilroy, Paul. 1982. "Steppin' Out of Babylon—Race, Class, and Autonomy." Pp. 276–319 in *The Empire Strikes Back*, edited by the Centre for Contemporary Cultural Studies. London: Hutchison.

Giroux, Henry. 1992. "Resisting Difference: Cultural Studies and the Discourse of Critical Pedagogy." In *Cultural Studies*, edited by Lawrence Grossberg, Cary Nelson, and Paula Treichler. New York: Routledge.

Gitell, Seth. 1988. "Federal Probers Check Harvard for Asian Quota." *Boston Globe*, 18 November, 21, 26.

Glazer, Nathan. 1988. "Canon Fodder." *New Republic*, 22 August, 19–21.

Glenn, Evelyn Nakano. 1986. *Issei, Nisei, War Bride: Three Generations of Japanese American Women in Domestic Service*. Phildelphia: Temple University Press.

Goldberg, David Theo. 1990a. "Introduction." In *Anatomy of Racism*, edited by David Theo Goldberg. Minneapolis: University of Minnesota Press.

———. 1990b. "The Social Formation of Racist Discourse." Pp. 295–318 in *Anatomy of Racism*, edited by David Theo Goldberg. Minneapolis: University of Minnesota Press.

Gonzalez, David. 1990. "Koreans See a Gain from Boycott: Unity." *New York Times*, 25 September.

Good, Joshua B. 1990. "Diversity Coalition Stages Campus Protest." *Daily Californian*. 22 March.

Goode, Stephen. 1989. "On the Outs Over Who Gets In." *Insight*, 19 October.

Gordon, Larry. 1988. "UC Berkeley Apologizes for Handling of Bias Charges." *Los Angeles Times*, 27 January, 1.

———. 1990. "Anti-Asian Bias Found in UCLA Program." *Los Angeles Times*, 2 October, B1.

Gossett, Thomas. 1965. *Race: The History of an Idea*. New York: Schocken.

Graubard, Stephen G. 1988. "Why Do Asian Pupils Win Those Prizes?" *New York Times*, 29 January.

Greenhouse, Linda. 1991. "Court, 6–3, Applies Voting Rights Act to Judicial Races." *New York Times*, 21 June, 1.

Griggs v. Duke Power Co., 401 U.S. 424, 85 S. Ct. 849 (1971).

Gust, Kelly. 1986. "Asians Say Bias in Education Troubles Them." *Tribune* (Oakland, Calif.), 11 May, A1, D9.

Habermas, Jürgen. 1984. *Theory of Communicative Action*. Boston: Beacon Press.

Hacker, Andrew. 1989. "Affirmative Action: The New Look." *New York Review of Books* 30 (15):63–68.

Hall, Stuart, Chas Critcher, Tony Jefferson, John Clarke, and Brian Roberts. 1978. *Policing the Crisis*. New York: Holmes and Meier.

Halpert, David. 1989. "University Entry Bias Sought."-*Press-Telegram* (Long Beach, Calif.), 9 June, 1.

Harris, Marvin. 1968. *Rise of Anthropological Theory: A History of Theories of Culture*. New York: Crowell.

Harris, Michael. 1988. "Perfect Grades Not Enough for UC Berkeley." *San Francisco Chronicle*, February 19.

Harris, Ron. 1991. "Experts Say the War on Drugs Has Turned into a War on Blacks." *San Francisco Chronicle*, 24 April.

Hassan, Thomas E. 1986–87. "Asian American Admissions: Debating Discrimination." *College Board Review* (142):19– 46.

Hayashi, Patrick. 1988. Letter to Professor William Shack. 7 April.

———. 1990. Letter to the affiliated faculty of Afro-American Studies, University of California, Berkeley. 14 March.

Hazelrigg, Lawrence. 1986. "Is There a Choice between 'Constructionism' and 'Objectivity'?" *Social Problems* 33 (October-December):1–13.

Hechinger, Fred. 1987. "The Trouble with Secret Quotas." *New York Times*, 10 February.

Heller, Scott. 1989. "Colleges Becoming Havens of 'Political Correctness,' Some Scholars Say." *Chronicle of Higher Education*, 21 November, 1.

Heyman, Ira Michael. 1990a. Letter to William French Smith, UC Regent. 9 May.

———. 1990b. "'Ethnic Diversity' at UC Berkeley." Editorial. *San Francisco Chronicle*, 16 June.

Hibino, Thomas. 1990. Letter to President Derek Bok, Harvard University. 4 October.

Hickey, Shannon. 1986. "Admissionsgate! UC Berkeley Discriminates against Qualified Asians." *East/West*, 11 December, 1–9.

———. 1987. "Legislators Call for Investigation of UC Admission Policies." *East/West*, 19 March.

Himmelfarb, Gertrude. 1988. "Stanford and Duke Undercut Classical Values." Letter to the editor. *New York Times*, 5 May, 31.

Ho, David, and Margaret M. Chin. 1983. "Admissions Impossible." *Bridge* 8 (Summer):7–51.

Hoachlander, Gareth E., and Cynthia L. Brown. 1989. "Asians in Higher Education: Conflicts over Admissions." *Thought and Action* 5 (2):5–20.

Holmes, Steven A. 1991a. "Battle Lines Form on New Rights Bill." *New York Times*, 8 February.

———. 1991b. "Mulling the Idea of Affirmative Action for Poor Whites." *New York Times*, 18 August, E3.

Holtz, Debra Levi. 1989. "UC Administration Paper Assailed." *San Francisco Chronicle*, 25 December.

Hsia, Jayjia. 1988. *Asian Americans in Higher Education and at Work*. Hillsdale, N.J.: Lawrence Erlbaum Associates.

Hsia, Jayjia, and Marsha Hirano-Nakanishi. 1989. "The Demographics of Diversity." *Change* (November-December):20–27.

Hsu, Evelyn. 1985. "Asian Americans Talk of UC Berkeley 'Bias.' " *San Francisco Chronicle*, 18 June, 6.

Hsu, Spencer. 1988. "Ed. Dept. Reviews Harvard Admissions." *Harvard Crimson*, 16 November, 1.

Hu, Arthur. 1989a. "Time to Rethink Admissions Quotas for Minority." *Asian Week*, 10 February.

———. 1989b. "Hu's on First?" *Asian Week*, 28 April.

———. 1989c. "Asian Americans: Model Minority or Double Minority?" *Amerasia* 15 (1):243–257.

———. 1989d. Letter to Gary Curran, Office of the Assistant Secretary for Civil Rights, U.S. Department of Education. 22 May.

———. 1989e. "Part I: The End of Asian Quotas?" *Asian Week*, 2 June.

———. 1989f. "Part II: Affirmative Action after Asian Quotas." *Asian Week*, 23 June.

———. 1990. "Mailbag on UC." Editorial. *Asian Week*, 7 August.

Ichioka, Yuji. 1988. *Issei: The World of the First Generation—Japanese Immigrants, 1885–1924*. New York: Free Press.

Innerst, Carol. 1988. "Asian Americans Top List of Students Taking Most Rigorous Studies." *Washington Times*, 5 May.

Ipson, Steve, and Mary Tjoa. 1987. "Prof Doubts Credibility of Faculty Asian Panel." *Daily Californian*, 12 October.

Irving, Carl. 1989. "UC Berkeley's Face Changing: Whites Losing Out to Affirmative Action." *San Francisco Examiner*, 20 August, 1, A15.

———. 1990. "UC-Berkeley Uses Race Quotas, Critic Says." *San Francisco Examiner*, 14 February.

Iverem, Esther. 1987. "The Delicate Balancers of Affirmative Action." *New York Times*, 26 June, 42.

Jacobs, Joanne. 1988. "Why Immigrant Kids Excel." *Philadelphia Inquirer*, 10 May.

Jaschik, Scott. 1988. "350 Asian American Leaders Create Statewide Lobbying Group to Influence the Politics of Higher Education in California." *Chronicle of Higher Education*, 9 March, 21, 24.

———. 1989a. "Conservative Lawmaker Attracts Attention and Ire with Crusade for Asian American Students." *Chronicle of Higher Education*, 15 November A28–A33.

———. 1989b. "Education Dept. Mislays Complaints against Colleges by Asian-Americans." *Chronicle of Higher Education*, 6 December, A17, A20.

———. 1990. "U.S. Finds Harvard Did Not Exclude Asian Americans." *Chronicle of Higher Education*, 17 October, 1, 26.

———. 1991. "Doubts Are Raised about U.S. Inquiry on Harvard Policies." *Chronicle of Higher Education*, 6 February.

Johnson, Julie. 1989. "Wider Door at Top Colleges Sought by Asian-Americans." *New York Times*, 9 September, 1, 8.

Johnson, Kirk. 1990. "At Wesleyan, a Day to Reflect on Racial Tension." *New York Times*, 8 May, 8.

Karabel, Jerome. 1984. "Status-Group Struggle, Organizational Interests, and the Limits of Institutional Autonomy." *Theory and Society* 13:1–40.

Karabel, Jerome, and David Karen. 1989. "Go to Harvard; Give Your Kid a Break." *New York Times*, 8 December.

Karen, David. 1985. "Who Gets in to Harvard: Selection and Exclusion at an Elite College." Ph.D. dissertation, Dept. of Sociology, Harvard University.

———. 1990. "Toward a Political-Organizational Model of Gatekeeping: The Case of Elite Colleges." *Sociology of Education* 63 (October):227–240.

Katznelson, Ira. 1981. *City Trenches*. Chicago: University of Chicago Press.

Katznelson, Ira, and Aristide Zolberg, eds. 1986. *Working-Class Formation: Nineteenth-Century Patterns in Western Europe and the United States*. Princeton: Princeton University Press.

Kaufman, Wendy. 1987. "Affirmative Action and Asian Americans." *Morning Edition*. National Public Radio. 26 October.

Kazmin, Amy Louise. 1987. "State Looks at Enrollment of Asians at UC." *Daily Californian*, 16 March, 1.

———. 1988. "Attorney General Sparks Ethnic Feuds, Prof Says." *Daily Californian*, 6 December, 1.

Kilborn, Peter. 1991. "U.S. Managers Claim Job Bias by the Japanese." *New York Times*, 3 June, 1, 9.

Kilson, Martin, and Clement Cottingham. 1991. "Thinking about Race Relations." *Dissent* (Fall):520–530.

Kimball, Roger. 1990. *Tenured Radicals*. New York: Harper and Row.

Kolb, Ron. 1988. "Admissions: A Stretch for the Fairest Process." *UC Focus* 2 (February).

Kur, Bob. 1989. "Report on University Admissions for Asian Americans and Other Groups." NBC Nightly News. New York, July 26.

Lederman, Douglas. 1991. "Emboldened Presidents' Commission Urges NCAA to Toughen Its Academic Requirements for Athletes." *Chronicle of Higher Education*, 3 July, A25.

———. 1992. "Easy Passage Expected for Proposals to Raise NCAA's Academic Standards." *Chronicle of Higher Education*. 8 January.

Levine, Art, and I. Pazner. 1988. "On Campus, Stereotypes Persist." *U.S. News and World Report*, March 28.

Lewis, Neil. 1990. "President's Veto of Rights Measure Survives by One Vote." *New York Times*, 25 October.

Lindsey, Robert. 1986. "Asian Americans Press to Gain Political Power." *New York Times*, 10 November, 6.

———. 1987. "Colleges Accused of Bias to Stem Asians' Gains." *New York Times*. 19 January.

Los Angeles Times. 1989. "Racism Still Plagues Campus Life." Editorial. 10 April, II:4.

Lum, Grande. 1988. "Memo May Have Prodded UC Chancellor's Apology." *East/West*, 4 February, 1–2.

Lye, Colleen. 1986. "Is There a 'Ceiling' under the Table?" *Berkeley Graduate* 1, no. 3 (November).

Lynn Committee. 1987. Draft Report of the Subcommittee on Asian-American Admissions of the Committee on Admissions and Enrollment, "Issues Relating to the Admission of Asian-Americans to UC Berkeley."

Lyons, Judith. 1988. "Chang Voted President at UC Berkeley." *Asian Week*, 22 April.

McBee, Susanna, George White, Joseph L. Galloway, Sarah Peterson, Pat Lynch, and Michael Bosc. 1984. "Asian Americans: Are They Making the Grade?" *U.S. News and World Report*, 2 April, 41–47.

Macdonell, Diane. 1986. *Theories of Discourse*. New York: Basil Blackwell.

McGrath, Ellie. 1983. "Confucian Work Ethic." *Time*, 28 March, 52.

The Madison Plan: One Year Later. 1989. Madison: Office of the Chancellor.

Manzagol, Michael. 1986. "Asian Enrollment Figures Subject of Federal Inquiry." *Daily Californian*, 31 October, 1.

Marrett, Cora. 1980. "The Precarious Position of the Black Middle Class." *Contemporary Sociology* 9 (January):16–19.

Marriot, Michael. 1990a. "Intense College Recruiting Drives Lift Black Enrollment to a Record." *New York Times*, 15 April.

———. 1990b. "Colleges Basing Aid on Race Risk Loss of Federal Funds." *New York Times*, 12 December, 1, 9.

———. 1991a. "White Accuses Georgetown Law School of Bias in Admitting Blacks." *New York Times*, 15 April.

———. 1991b. "Storm at Georgetown Law on Admissions." *New York Times*, 17 April.

Martine, Judith, and Gunther Stent. 1991. "Say the Right Thing—Or Else." Letter to the editor. *New York Times*, 20 March.

Marx, Karl. 1963. *The Eighteenth Brumaire of Louis Bonaparte*. New York: International Publishers.

Mathews, Jay. 1985. "Asian American Students Creating New Mainstream." *Washington Post*, 14 November, 1, A6.

———. 1990. "Bias against Asians Found in Admission to UCLA." *Washington Post*, 2 October, A5.

Mathews, Linda. 1987. "When Being Best Isn't Good Enough." *Los Angeles Times Magazine*, 19 July, 22–28.

Metro Broadcasting, Inc. v. Federal Communications Commission, S. Ct. 89–453 (1990).

Mills, Nicolaus. 1990. "The Endless Autumn." *The Nation*, 16 April, 529–531.

Molotsky, Irvin. 1988. "Harvard and UCLA Face Inquiries on Quotas." *New York Times*, 20 November, 35.

Mooney, Carolyn J. 1988. "Conservative Scholars Call for a Movement to 'Reclaim' Academy." *Chronicle of Higher Education*, 23 November, A1, A11.

Moore, Michael. 1987. "Pride and Prejudice." *Image Magazine*, 15 November, 14–34.

Moore, Thomas H. 1989. "Some Top Colleges Admit More Asian Americans But Deny That the Increase Is Due to Pressure." *Chronicle of Higher Education*, 28 June, A21–A22.

Morganthau, Tom, with Marcus Mabby, Laura Genao, and Frank Washington. 1991. "Race on Campus: Failing the Test?" *Newsweek*, 6 May, 26–27.

Morrison, Gary. 1990. Memo to Ira Michael Heyman, chancellor, University of California, Berkeley. 2 January.

Murray, Charles. 1984. *Losing Ground*. New York: Basic Books.

Muwakkil, Salim. 1991. "Race, Class, and Candor." *In These Times*, 22 May, 12–22.

Nakanishi, Don T. 1988. "Asian Americans and Selective Admissions." *Journal of College Admissions* 118 (Winter):17–26.

———. 1989. "A Quota on Excellence? The Asian American Admissions Debate." *Change* (November/December):39–47.

Nakano, Erich. 1990. "Are Asians against Affirmative Action?" *Daily Californian*, 22 March, 4.

Nakao, Annie. 1987. "Thorny Debate at UC: Too Many Brainy Asians?" *San Francisco Examiner*, 3 May.

National Center for Education Statistics. 1986. *Digest of Educational Statistics*. Office of Educational Research and Development. Washington, D.C.: U.S. Department of Education.

———. 1989. *Digest of Education Statistics*. Washington, D.C.: Office of Education.

———. 1990. *Faculty in Higher Education Institutions, 1988*. NCES 90-365. Washington, D.C.: U.S. Department of Education, Office of Educational Research and Improvement.

New York Times. 1981a. "Harvard Law Review's Ethnic Screening Criticized." 24 February, 12.

———. 1981b. "Harvard Letter by Bok Urges Racial Understanding." 27 February, A11.

———. 1982. "Harvard Students Call for Affirmative Action." 26 November, 17.

———. 1984. "U.S. Panel Urging Congress to Alter Civil Rights Policy." 29 March, 20.

———. 1986. "Affirmative Actions." Editorial. 5 August, 22.

———. 1988. "When Racism Goes to College." Editorial. 10 June.

———. 1991a. "Devastating Signal to Minority Students." Editorial. 14 January.

———. 1991b. "Student at Brown Is Expelled under a Rule Barring 'Hate Speech.'" 12 February.

———. 1991c. "Vermont U. Students Occupy Offices over Ethnic Demands." 28 April.

————. 1991d. "Rights Chief Sees Race as Factor in Election." 1 May.

Newsweek. 1971. "Outwhiting the Whites." 21 June, 24–25.

————. 1982. "Asian-Americans: A 'Model Minority.'" 6 December, 39–51.

Nissenbaum, Dion. 1990a. "Heyman Agrees to Protestors Demands, Talks Continue Today." *Daily Californian.* 23 March.

————. 1990b. *Diversity Demonstrators Plan Actions This Week.*" *Daily Californian,* 2 April.

Njeri, Itabari. 1989. "Intercultural Etiquette." *Los Angeles Times.* 2 April, 1, 16.

O'Dowd, Maureen. 1991. "Bush Sees Threat to Flow of Ideas on U.S. Campuses." *New York Times,* 5 May.

Official Register. 1988. *Harvard and Radcliffe: Official Register of Harvard University.* Cambridge: Office of the University Publisher.

Okihiro, Gary Y. 1991. *Cane Fires: The Anti-Japanese Movement in Hawaii, 1865–1945.* Philadelphia: Temple University Press.

Omi, Michael, and Howard Winant. 1986. *Racial Formation in the United States.* New York: Methuen.

Osajima, Keith. 1988. "Asian American as the Model Minority: An Analysis of the Popular Press Image in the 1960s and 1980s." Pp. 165–174 in *Reflections on Shattered Windows: Promises and Prospects for Asian American Studies,* edited by Gary Y. Okihiro, Shirley Hune, Arthur A. Hansen, and John M. Liu. Pullman: Washington State University Press.

Ossias, Geoff, and Jennifer Packer. 1990. "Report Examines UCLA Admissions." *Daily Californian,* 2 October, 1.

Palomino, John E. 1990. Letter to Chancellor Charles Young, UCLA. 1 October.

Pan, David. 1990. "Ivory Tower and Red Tape: Reply to Adler." *Telos* (86):109–117.

Pan, Suzanne. 1989. "Hu's Views Are His Own." *Asian Week,* 2 June, 2.

Papillon, Kimberly, and Amy Louise Kazmin. 1987. "Report Shows Lower Asian Admittance Rate." *Daily Californian,* 8 October.

Paradise, United States v., 480 U.S. 149, 107 S. Ct. 1053 (1987).

Pear, Robert, 1983. "Reagan Reported Planning to Name Four to Rights Panel." *New York Times,* 22 May, 1, 25.

————. 1985. "U.S. and San Diego Win End to Quotas." *New York Times,* 9 May, 12.

————. 1990. "Courts Are Undoing Efforts to Aid Minority Contractors." *New York Times,* 16 July.

————. 1991. "U.S. Bars New York District Plan, Finding Hispanic Voters Are Hurt." *New York Times,* 20 July.

Petersen, William. 1966. "Success Story: Japanese American Style." *New York Times,* 9 January, V1–V20.

Pettigrew, Thomas. 1979. "The Changing But Not Declining Significance of Race." *Michigan Law Review* 77 (January–March):917–924.

————. 1990. *Tom Bradley's Campaign for Governor: The Dilemma of Race and Political Strategies.* Washington, D.C.: Joint Center for Political Studies.

Philp, Tom. 1986. "Stanford Studies Possible Asian Bias." *San Jose Mercury News*, 12 November, 2B.

Phung, Quan. 1990. "Asian-American Finalist Drops Out." *Stanford Daily*, 6 February, 1.

Piccone, Paul. 1991. "Artificial Negativity as a Bureaucratic Tool? Reply to Roe." *Telos* (86):127–140.

Pickell, David. 1988. "The 'Temporary 400': An Exercise in Damage Control." *Berkeley Graduate* 2 (April):6.

Pinkney, Alphonso. 1984. *The Myth of Black Progress*. New York: Cambridge University Press.

Poster, Mark, ed. 1985. *Jean Baudrillard: Selected Writings*. 1985. Stanford: Stanford University Press.

Puddington, Arch. 1979. "Race or Class." *New Oxford Review* (June):21–22.

Quindlen, Anna. 1987. "The Drive to Excel." *New York Times Magazine*, 2 February, 32–39.

Ramirez, Anthony. 1986. "America's Super Minority." *Fortune*, 24 November, 148–161.

Ramist, Leonard. 1976. "A Review of Admissions Testing Program Ethnic Group Data." Educational Testing Service. Unpublished paper.

Raspberry, William. 1987. "When White Guilt Won't Matter Anymore." *Washington Post*, 4 November.

———. 1990. "Asian Americans—Too Successful?" *Washington Post*, 10 February.

Regents of the University of California v. Bakke, 438 U.S. 265 (1978).

Regents of the University of California. 1987. Minutes of the Meeting of the Board of Regents. Riverside. 20 November.

———. 1988. "University of California Policy on Undergraduate Admissions." Mimeo. 20 May. 1 page.

Reichmann, Deb. 1989. "Colleges Tackle Increase in Racism on Campuses." *Los Angeles Times*, 30 April.

Reinhold, Robert. 1991. "California Is Torn by Political Wars over Seven New Seats." *New York Times*, 3 March.

Reynolds, William B. 1988. "Discrimination against Asian Americans in Higher Education: Evidence, Causes, and Cures." Department of Justice. Mimeo. 17 pages.

Rhoden, William C. 1991. "Educators to Examine Special-Admit Athletes." *New York Times*, 3 May.

Rieder, Jonathan. 1985. *Canarsie: The Jews and Italians of Brooklyn against Liberalism*. Cambridge: Harvard University Press.

Roberts, Jerry. 1990. "Wilson Spurns Quotas to Woo Conservatives." *San Francisco Chronicle*, 21 September.

Robertson, Scott. 1990. "Students Mixed over New Policy." *Daily Californian*, 16 January.

Rodamor, William. 1990. "Diversity and Its Discontents." *California Monthly*, June.

Rodriguez, Richard. 1982. *Hunger of Memory*. New York: Bantam.

Roe, Emery M. 1991. "Artificial Negativity and Affirmative Action in Universities." *Telos* (86):117–127.

Rohter, Larry. 1991. "With a Smile, Calling a Floridian a 'Cracker' May Be a Hate Crime." *New York Times*, 22 August, A15.

Rosenthal, Andrew. 1990. "White House Retreats on Ruling That Curbs Minority Scholarships." *New York Times*, 18 December, 1.

Rothenberg, Randall. 1990. "U.S. Ads Increasingly Attack Japanese and Their Culture." *New York Times*, 11 July.

Salholz, Eloise. 1987. "Do Colleges Set Asian Quotas?" *Newsweek*, 9 February, 60.

San Diego Union. 1986. "UC Fee Formula Was Born of Student Fear of Huge Hikes." 21 December, C6–C8.

San Francisco Chronicle. 1990. "Bush Officials Keeping Most of Minority Ban." 19 December, 1.

Sarich, Vincent. 1990a. "The Institutionalization of Racism at the University of California, Berkeley." Letter to William French Smith and memo. Berkeley, 4 April. 7 pages.

———. 1990b. "The Cost of UC's Admission Policies." *San Francisco Chronicle*, 16 June.

Scheer, Roderick A. 1990. "Many Boycott Class." *Harvard Crimson*, 18 April, 1, 9.

Schreiner, Tim. 1985. "Asians Raise U.S. Standards." *San Francisco Chronicle*, 10 October, 4.

Scott-Blair, Michael. 1986. "Ethnic Background Results in Added Pressure to Do Well." *San Diego Union*, 28 December, A10.

Seligman, Daniel. 1989. "Quotas on Campus: The New Phase." *Fortune*, 30 January.

Shack, William. 1989. "Report of the Special Committee on Asian American Admissions." Berkeley. February.

Shogan, Robert. 1990. "Bennett Scores Affirmative Action Plans." *Los Angeles Times*, 20 November.

Sing, Lillian, and Ken Kawaichi. 1987a. Letter to Bud Travers. 6 March. 4 pages.

———. 1987b. Letter to Professor Scott Lynn. 10 October. 2 pages.

———. 1988a. Letter to Chancellor Heyman. 4 March. 3 pages.

———. 1988b. Letter to Frank Clark, chairman of the UC Regents. 15 June. 4 pages.

Sleeper, Jim. 1990. *Closest of Strangers: Liberalism and the Politics of Race in New York*. New York: W. W. Norton.

Smith, John L. 1988. "UC Chancellor Apologizes to Asians." *Tribune* (Oakland, Calif.), 27 January, 1.

Smith, Page. 1990. *Killing the Spirit*. New York: Penguin Books.

Smith, Lynn, and Bill Billiter. 1985. "Asian Americans: Emphasis on Education Paying Off." *Los Angeles Times* (Orange County edition), 19 December, 1–3, 35.

Sowell, Thomas. 1984. *Civil Rights: Rhetoric or Reality?* New York: William Morrow.

———. 1989. "The New Racism on Campus." *Fortune*, 13 February.

———. 1990a. "Quotas against Asians." *New Dimensions* 4 (December):42–43.

———. 1990b. *Preferential Policies: An International Perspective.* New York: William Morrow.

Spector, Malcolm, and John I. Kitsuse. 1987. *Constructing Social Problems.* New York: Aldine de Gruyter.

Stanford Observer. 1986. "Fetter Initiates Steps to Eliminate Unconscious Discrimination." 9 November.

Steele, Shelby. 1989. "The Recoloring of Campus Life." *Harper's Magazine*, February, 47–55.

———. 1990. *The Content of Our Character.* New York: St. Martin's.

Stevenson, Richard W. 1991. "California Shows Hispanic Increase." *New York Times*, 26 February.

Stewart, Robert W. 1989. "Rohrabacher Seeks Anti-Asian College Admissions Probe." *Los Angeles Times.* 9 June.

Stone, Keith. 1991. "Fear at the Market: Korean-Black Tensions Fester in LA." *San Francisco Examiner*, 21 April.

Sue Stanley, and Jennifer Abe. 1988. *Predictors of Academic Achievement among Asian American and White Students.* College Board Report no. 88-11. New York: College Entrance Examination Board.

Sunoo, Brenda Paik. 1984. "Educators Ask 'Are Asian Americans Making the Grade in Education?'" *East-West*, 20 June, 4.

Suro, Robert. 1991. "When Minorities Start Becoming Majorities." *New York Times*, 23 June.

Synott, M. G. 1979. *The Half-Opened Door: Discrimination in Admissions at Harvard, Yale, and Princeton, 1900–1970.* Westport, Conn.: Greenwood.

Takagi, Dana. 1990. "From Discrimination to Affirmative Action: Facts in the Asian American Admissions Controversy." *Social Problems* 37 (November):578–592.

Takagi, Paul. 1973. "The Myth of 'Assimilation in American Life.'" *Amerasia* 2 (Fall):149–157.

Takaki, Ronald. 1984. "Have Asian Americans Made It?" *San Francisco Examiner*, 10 January, B3.

———. 1988. "An Educated and Culturally Literate Person Must Study America's Multicultural Reality." *Chronicle of Higher Education*, 8 March.

———. 1989. *Strangers from a Different Shore.* Boston: Little, Brown.

Taylor, John. 1991. "Are You Politically Correct?" *New York*, 21 January, 32–40.

Taylor, Stuart. 1985. "Justices Urged to Bar Racial Preference Plan." *New York Times*, 7 November, A23.

———. 1986a. "Breaking New Ground on Affirmative Action." *New York Times*, 21 May, 28.

———. 1986b. "High Court Bars a Layoff Method Favoring Blacks." *New York Times*, 20 May, 1, 20.

Tifft, Susan. 1988. "Welcome to Madison Avenue U." *Time Magazine*, 19 December.

———. 1989. "Bigots in the Ivory Tower." *Time Magazine*, 23 January.

Today Show. 1988. "Asian Americans Subjected to Discrimination on College Campuses?" NBC Television Network, 28 December.

Toner, Robin. 1990. "Issue of Job Quotas Sure to Affect Debate on Civil Rights in the 90s." *New York Times*, 10 December.

Toth, Jennifer. 1991. "College Affirmative Action: How Serious Is the Backlash?" *Los Angeles Times*, 16 May.

Travers, B. Thomas. 1985. *Letter to the Honorable Ken Kawaichi and the Honorable Lillian Sing*. 26 July. 8 pages.

———. 1987. Letter to Asian community members. 23 January. 14 pages.

Tribune (Oakland, Calif.). 1986. "UC Chief Wants a Better Ethnic Mix." 12 December.

Trinh, Minh-ha T. 1989. *Woman, Native, Other*. Bloomington: Indiana University Press.

Trudeau, Gary. 1989. *Read My Lips, Make My Day, Eat Quiche and Die!* Kansas City: Andrews and McMeel, Universal Press Syndicate.

Tsuang, Grace. 1989. "Assuring Equal Access of Asian Americans to Highly Selective Universities." *Yale Law Journal* 98:659–678.

Turner, Wallace. 1981. "Rapid Rise in Students of Asian Origin Causing Problems at Berkeley Campus." *New York Times*, 6 April, A16.

U.S. Bureau of the Census. *Census of Population, 1960*. PC(1)1C. Washington, D.C.: Government Printing Office.

———. *Census of Population, 1970*. PC(2)1G. Washington, D.C.: Government Printing Office.

———. *Census of Population, 1970*. PC(2)1B. Washington, D.C.: Government Printing Office.

———. *Census of Population, 1980*. PC80-2-1-E. Washington, D.C.: Government Printing Office.

———. "Race of the Population by States: 1980." PC80-S1-3. Washington, D.C.: Government Printing Office.

U.S. Department of Education. Office of Civil Rights, Region I. 1990. Statement of Findings (Harvard University). Compliance Review #01-88-6009. October.

U.S. Senate. Committee on Labor and Human Resources. 1988. *Hearings*. 89-540. 100th Congress, 2nd sess. Washington, D.C.: Government Printing Office.

U.S. News and World Report. 1966. "Success Story of One Minority Group in U.S." 26 December, 73–76.

Vieira, Norman. 1990. *Constitutional Civil Rights*. St. Paul, Minn.: West Publishing.

Vobejda, Barbara. 1988. "Harvard, UCLA Admissions Policies Probed." *Washington Post*, 18 November.

Wallace, Michelle. 1990. *Invisibility Blues: From Pop to Theory*. London: Verso.

———. 1991. "Beyond Assimilation." *Village Voice*, 17 September, 42–43.

Walsh, Joan. 1990. "School Colors." *San Francisco Chronicle*. 4 Feburary, 11–13.

Wang, L. Ling-chi. N.d. Comments on Travers Memo. Mineo. 3 pages.

———. 1986. Letter to David Gardner, president, University of California. 16 December.

———. 1987a. Letter to Professor Scott Lynn, chair, Special Committee on Admissions. 20 July. 6 pages.

———. 1987b. "Meritocracy and Diversity in Higher Education." Paper presented at Brown University. 26 pages. 19 November.

———. 1988a. "Meritocracy and Diversity in Higher Education." *Urban Review* 20 (3):189–210.

———. 1988b. Written statement. 3 February. 2 pages.

———. 1989a. Letter to interested parties. 1 March.

———. 1989b. "Asian Admissions Report Fails to Address the Issue of Bias." 6 March. 6 pages.

Wards Cove Packing Co. v. Antonio, 109 S. Ct. 2115 (1989).

Washington Post. 1988. "The Specter of Quotas." Editorial. 17 December.

Waters, Mary. 1990. *Ethnic Options*. Berkeley: University of California Press.

Wattenberg, Ben. 1987. "Chu, Wu, Hor, and Harvard." *Washington Times*, 3 September.

Weiss, Samuel. 1991. "Southern College Group Seeking Tougher Supervision of Athletics." *New York Times*, 19 May.

Wellman, David. 1977. *Portraits of White Racism*. Cambridge: Cambridge University Press.

Werner, Donald. 1988. "College Admissions: Shaky Ethics." Opinion piece. *New York Times*, 4 June.

West, Cornel. 1992. "The Postmodern Crisis of the Black Intellectual." Pp. 689–705 in *Cultural Studies*, edited by Lawrence Grossberg, Cary Nelson, and Paula Treichler. New York: Routledge.

White House. 1988. "Remarks by the President at the Signing Ceremony for Asian Pacific Heritage Week." Press release. Office of the Press Secretary, Washington, D.C., 3 May.

Wiener, Jon. 1990. "Racial Hatred Rocks Campuses." *Utne Reader*, May/June, 62–68.

Wilkerson, Isabel. 1991. "A Tale of Two Proms, One Black, One White." *San Francisco Chronicle*, 19 May.

Wilkerson, Margaret, William Banks, Charles Henry, Percy Hintzen, Jacques Depelchin, William Lawson, Julianne Malveaux, Grace Massey, Pedro Noguera, A. Stanford Robinson, Roy T. Thomas, and Opa P. Adisa. 1990. Letter to Patrick S. Hayashi, vice chancellor of admissions, UC Berkeley. 23 February.

Wilkins, Roger. 1991. "Bush's Quota Con." *Mother Jones*, March/April, 22–23.

Will, George. 1989. "Prejudice against Excellence." *Washington Post*, 16 April, B7.

Williams, Lena. 1986. "Officials Voice Growing Concern over Racial Incidents on U.S. Campuses." *New York Times*, 15 December.

Williams, Denise, Diane McDonald, Lucy Howard, Margaret Mittelbach, and Cynthia Kyle. 1984. "A Formula for Success." *Newsweek*, 23 April, 76–78.

Willie, Charles. 1978. "The Inclining Significance of Race." *Society* 15 (July/August):10–15.

Wilson, William J. 1978. *The Declining Significance of Race*. Chicago: Univeristy of Chicago.

———. 1987. *The Truly Disadvantaged*. Chicago: University of Chicago Press.

Winant, Howard. 1990. "Postmodern Racial Politics." *Socialist Review* 90 (1): 121–147.

Winerip, Michael. 1985. "Asian-Americans Question Ivy League's Entry Policies." *New York Times*, 30 May, 1.

Woo, Elaine. 1988. "UCLA Denies Any Policy of Limiting Asian Admissions." *Los Angeles Times*, 19 November, 1, 4.

Woolgar, Steve, and Dorothy Pawluch. 1985. "Ontological Gerrymandering: The Anatomy of Social Problems Explanations." *Social Problems* 33:214–227.

Woolridge, Veronica. 1989. "Race Relations on Campus." *New York Times*, 5 April.

Wright, Erik Olin. 1985. *Classes*. London: Verso.

Wu, Jeffrey. 1990. "250 Rally in the Rain." *Harvard Crimson*, 18 April, 1, 7.

Yardley, Jonathan. 1988. "The Ivory Tower Doesn't Rise above Bigotry." *San Jose Mercury News*, 4 June, 13C.

Zlatos, Bill. 1988. "Asian Prejudice Charge Hits CMU." *Pittsburgh Press*, 1 December, B1, B4.

Zweigenhaft, Richard L., and G. William Domhoff. 1991. *Blacks in the White Establishment*. New Haven: Yale University Press.

Index